Contents

Introduction

This book has been written especially to cover the content and skill of the OCR GCSE Religious Studies specifications B 1931 (full course) and 1031 (short course) Philosophy and Ethics. However, it is also suitable for use with some of the specifications of other awarding bodies.

The entire content of the course for each of the ten units and each of the four religions available is covered by the text.

In order to make the text more accessible for students, the strict specification order is not necessarily followed within each Topic. Teachers should also note that the sub-headings within the topics, although following those of the specification, have also been simplified.

Where it is helpful for all students to have general background information about a Topic, this is provided in an introductory spread, before the religion-specific content.

A number of conventions have been adopted in this text. All spellings conform to the SCAA Glossary of Religious Terms 1994. The sacred texts used for quotations are those used by OCR in examination papers:

Holy Bible New International Version, International Bible Society, Colorado, 0-340-56782-1

The Stone Edition Tanach, Mesorah Publications, 0-88906-269-5

The Meaning of the Holy Qur'an, Ali, Amana Publications, 0951595755-8

Hindu Scriptures, Zaehner, Everyman, 1-85715-064-3

The transliteration of Arabic words in the text is based on the SCAA Glossary 1994 and 'A Popular Dictionary of Islam', I R Netton, Curzon Press, London, 1992, 0 7007 0233 4. The Arabic letters 'ayn and hamza are transliterated throughout as ' and ' respectively.

In the Jewish scriptures, G-d's name is spelt with four consonants YHWH (this is called the **Tetragrammaton** or 'four letters'), but Jewish teaching says that the name is so holy that only the High Priest knew how to pronounce it and that he only spoke it once a year, alone, in the Holy of Holies in the Temple at Jerusalem. When they see these four letters Jews usually say the name **Adonai** instead, this means Lord. Many Jews will not write the word which is a translation of this name and instead put G-d. In some parts of the **Tenakh** the name HASHEM is also used for G-d.

In Islam Muslims use the words '**Salla-llahu alaihi wa sallam**' – peace and blessings of Allah upon him, every time the Prophet Muhammad ﷺ is mentioned. Similar respect is accorded to the other Prophets. The Arabic colophon ﷺ in the text represents these words.

UNIT 1

The Nature of God

Christianity

Christian beliefs about the nature of God

Christians are **monotheists**. This means that they believe there is only one God. According to Christianity, and many other religions too, God is unlike anything else that exists. This means that it can be very difficult to describe God, because everyday language is always about ordinary things but God is not ordinary. God is often described as 'holy', which means special, separate and different.

Christians believe:
- God is eternal, beyond time and space.
- God is not limited by having a physical body, and is everywhere at all times.
- God is the creator of the world and everything in it, and has a purpose for the world.
- God is perfectly good and perfectly loving.
- God is interested in how people behave, and wants them to treat each other properly.
- God is all-powerful (**omnipotent**) and all-knowing (**omniscient**).
- God will judge each individual.

Sometimes it can be difficult for people to understand how God can be the creator of the universe and at the same time be interested in the lives of individual believers. One of the ways that Christians try to express their understanding of what God is like is called the **doctrine of the Trinity**. This belief tries to express how God can be understood in three different ways: as God the Father, as God the Son, and as God the Holy Spirit. This does not mean that there are three different gods; for example, a girl could be Sarah the daughter, Sarah the best friend and Sarah the swimmer, while being the same person all the time. The doctrine of the Trinity shows how God's relationship with humanity works in different ways.

God the Father
Calling God 'Father' is a way of showing belief that God created everything. It is also a way of showing a close and loving relationship, where the father cares about his children and they can rely on him. Some Christians also talk about God as 'Mother', to show that God is not limited to being either male or female.

God the Son
Christians believe that Jesus of Nazareth was the Son of God. They believe that God chose to come to earth as a man, to teach people the right way to live, to show them what life will be like when God reigns (the **kingdom of God**, or **kingdom of heaven**), and to sacrifice himself so that people could be forgiven for doing wrong. They believe that after Jesus was crucified, he rose from the dead (the **resurrection**) and showed that God has power over death.

God the Holy Spirit
Christians believe that after Jesus rose from the dead and went back into heaven (the **ascension**), God sent the Holy Spirit to live on in the world in the lives of Christians, giving them courage, comforting them, inspiring them and guiding them in their decisions. In Christian art, the Holy Spirit is often shown in the form of a dove, a symbol of peace and hope.

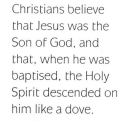

Christians believe that Jesus was the Son of God, and that, when he was baptised, the Holy Spirit descended on him like a dove.

Why do Christians believe in God?

Christians give many reasons for believing in God, and often one believer might have several different reasons. They might say:

- The universe cannot just have come into existence by accident; there must be a Creator who started everything. Nothing happens without a reason, and God is the only possible reason for the existence of the universe.
- Everything in the world is so beautifully designed for its purpose that there must be a God who planned it all.
- We all have a sense of right and wrong, and we feel guilty when we do wrong even if we know no-one will find out. There must be a God who gives people consciences.
- People can have a personal experience of God, perhaps as an answer to prayer, or a healing, or a strong feeling that God is present with them. They might have had a conversion experience, perhaps as a result of listening to other Christians or from reading the Bible.
- Some people are brought up in Christian families, and Christianity is a part of their lives they have never been without.

Many people who have no religious belief would argue that these are not good reasons for belief in God. They might say that the universe could have happened by accident, just as the result of a 'Big Bang', and there does not need to have been any God to start it off. Or they might say that

things in the world which seem to have been designed are the result of evolution, not God. Some people say that our consciences are just the result of the way we were brought up, so that we have a sense of right and wrong because of our parents, not because of God. They might say that coming from a Christian family shows that Christianity is part of someone's customs, but does not show it is true; and they might say that a personal religious experience could be mistaken.

No-one can prove that God exists; but no-one can prove that there is no God, either. It is something that has to be a personal decision, based on faith.

Discussion

Do you think that Christianity provides convincing reasons for belief in God? Explain why, or why not.

Activity

1 Make a list of the characteristics of God, according to Christianity.

2 Explain what is meant by the doctrine of the Trinity. Include a brief description of what Christians mean by each of: God the Father, God the Son, and God the Holy Spirit.

The authority of the Bible for Christians

The Bible is the holy book of Christianity. It is made up of two collections of books: the Old Testament, and the New Testament.

The **Old Testament** has the same content as the Jewish scriptures. It contains 39 books of stories, poems, laws, history, myths, prophecy and songs, all of which show the relationship between God and his people over many hundreds of years.

The **New Testament** contains 27 books. There are four **gospels** which tell the story of the life, teaching, death and resurrection of Jesus, and also other books containing history, letters of advice to new Christians, and poetic description of the future end of the world. For many Christians, although the Old Testament is important and sacred, the New Testament is even more special because it contains the story of Jesus and gives a new understanding of God.

When Christians say that the Bible has authority for them, they mean that they believe that it comes from God and they try to understand its teachings and put them into practice in their daily lives. They read about people who are praised in the Bible, and they try to behave in the same way themselves, following the examples set in the stories. They look to the Bible for teaching about moral issues, to help them decide what to do if they are having difficulty making decisions.

Christians have different opinions about how the Bible should be interpreted. Some believe that it comes directly from God, and that every word in it is perfect and should not be challenged. They believe that the stories in the Bible all really happened exactly as described. If scientists or historians suggest that the Bible is wrong, then they should not be believed, because God does not make mistakes.

Other Christians believe that there are many different kinds of truth to be found in the Bible, but some passages are not meant to be taken literally. They say that some of the stories are myths, which give important and true messages, but they do not necessarily describe real events. They also say that although God was responsible for the writing of the Bible, the human authors also had a part to play, writing in their own words and using their own ideas and experiences to help them.

All Christians believe that the Bible is very special and more important than any other book. The Bible is read in church services on Sundays, and at important occasions such as weddings and funerals, and many Christians read the Bible on their own at home or in small groups with other Christians. The Bible is used for help and advice, and to settle disagreements. Because Christians believe that the Bible is so important, it is often used in this country in courts of law, when people promise to tell the truth and use the Bible to show that they really mean it.

God in the world

Christians believe that God did not just start off the world and then go away. According to Christianity, God has had a relationship with humanity ever since the first people were created, and this relationship continues today.

Many Christians believe that God acts in the world through miracles. They believe that God occasionally changes the rules of nature so that people can have a glimpse of God's nature and reach a better understanding. Some people believe that they have been miraculously healed, even from illnesses that are usually incurable. Others believe that they have been saved in times of danger, or that they have been sent a special sign from God. In the Bible, there are many stories of Jesus performing miracles. For example, in Luke's gospel there is the story of a blind beggar, who was given back his sight:

> 'What do you want me to do for you?' 'Lord, I want to see,' he replied. Jesus said to him, 'Receive your sight; your faith has healed you.' Immediately he received his sight and followed Jesus, praising God. When all the people saw it, they also praised God.
>
> *(Luke 18:41–43)*

Christians believe that the Holy Spirit continues to work miracles. Lourdes is a place of pilgrimage for Roman Catholics, because it is believed to be the site of a miraculous vision of the Virgin Mary. It is visited by Christians who go there to pray together and who often hope that their faith will bring them miraculous healings.

Christians believe that we do not have to wonder what God is like, because God came into the world and showed us. Many people have found it difficult to understand how a person could be completely human, and also God, at the same time, and there have been many different attempts to explain this idea; but most Christians accept that it is a mystery. They say that because God came into the world, it demonstrates that God cares enough about people to want to teach them things, and to share in their happiness and their suffering.

Discussion

Do you think that miracles happen today? If someone told you that he or she had experienced a miracle, would you believe it? Explain why or why not.

Activity

1 Explain what Christians mean when they say that the Bible has authority.

2 Describe how Christians might use the Bible in their daily lives.

3 What do Christians mean when they call something a miracle? Give examples of events which might be described as miraculous.

Christians believe that God sometimes works through miracles. Some visit Lourdes, a centre of Christian pilgrimage, in the hope of receiving miraculous cures.

In Christianity, the most important way that God showed his involvement with the world was when he came to the earth as Jesus Christ. The writer of John's gospel expresses it like this:

> The Word became flesh and made his dwelling among us. We have seen his glory, the glory of the One and Only, who came from the Father, full of grace and truth.
>
> *(John 1:14)*

Hinduism

Hindu beliefs about the nature of God

Hinduism is a religion of variety. There are many different beliefs about the nature of God, and some Hindus do not believe in God at all. Others believe that there is only one God, while others believe that there are many different gods and goddesses, and they will have their own particular favourite.

The gods and goddesses, or **deities**, all have their own special characteristics.

Shiva, for example, is often called the 'lord of the dance'; he dances in a circle of flame, representing the endless circle of life, and is the creator and the destroyer.

Ganesha is a god shown with an elephant's head; he is the 'remover of obstacles' and a god of good fortune, with a particular concern for young people and for education.

Lakshmi is a goddess of beauty and of prosperity, a particular favourite with people who own businesses.

Rama and **Sita** are the heroes of an epic tale called the **Ramayana**, and worshipped because of their devotion to one another and their faithfulness to God.

However, although most Hindus believe in many gods, this is not the whole truth. Many Hindus also believe that behind it all, there is only one God, who is the **Supreme Reality**; all the different deities are different ways of understanding this same God, in different aspects. This one God is called **Brahman**. In some ways the belief could be compared with other religions, where God is sometimes worshipped as creator at harvest time, sometimes as a judge, sometimes as a king, sometimes as a friend, but in the end it is all the same God. Hindus might say that people cannot understand God all at once, because it is too big an idea for the human mind, and worshipping different deities is a way of looking at God from different angles in the search for better understanding.

Brahman is traditionally divided into three main parts (the **trimurti**): the gods Brahma, Shiva and Vishnu. They represent the ways in which the universe is created, preserved and destroyed. Brahma is the creator, often shown with four faces to illustrate the creation of the four 'corners' of the world. Shiva is the destroyer, who dances a dance of destruction and terror. Vishnu preserves the order of the universe, and comes to earth in human form to set things straight in times of trouble. Shiva and Vishnu each have large numbers of worshippers, but Brahma is less popular.

Most Hindus believe that God exists in everything, and contains all things: creation and destruction, male and female, good and evil, movement and stillness. God is also present in every person, as the eternal spirit called **Atman**.

Ganesha is one of the deities of Hinduism, always shown with an elephant's head.

Why do Hindus believe in God?

Hindus who believe in God give many different reasons for their beliefs.

- Some Hindus refer to their own personal religious experience. Hindus pray and meditate as part of their worship, and some believe that they have met with God in this way.
- Hindus might say that the existence of the universe, and the way everything depends on everything else, shows that ultimately, everything is part of the same reality, which is God.
- Many Hindus have their beliefs because of tradition; this is part of their culture, and the way they have been taught by their parents.

Some religions try hard to convince others of the existence of God, and produce arguments to support their beliefs. Hinduism is not like this. It includes many different ways of understanding the world, and is more concerned with tolerance than with trying to change the minds of other people.

Hindu sacred writings

Hinduism has many sacred writings, written in the holy language of **Sanskrit**. The oldest and most important are called the **Vedas**. These are known as **sruti**, which means 'that which is heard'. Other texts, which are less important, are called **smriti**, 'that which is remembered', because they contain human wisdom rather than the eternal wisdom of the Vedas. According to Hindu belief, the Vedas were not composed by any human being, but were heard by wise people called **rishis** and have been repeated ever since. The Vedas did not begin as written books, but as spoken words passed on from one generation to the next, and they were only put into writing many hundreds of years later.

Most Hindus have not read the Vedas for themselves, but they are still familiar with passages from it because they have heard the words repeated during worship and at sacred ceremonies.

The Vedas contain hymns, myths, songs, chants and prayers. They tell stories of the gods, and raise questions which people have been asking since the beginning; how did the world come into existence? Can people gain immortality? What is wisdom, and where can it be found?

The **Upanishads** are also very important for Hindus. The name 'Upanishad' means 'sitting at the feet of the teacher', because the Upanishads provide a written record of the discussions between religious teachers (**gurus**) and their students.

The **Bhagavad Gita** is another sacred text which is very much loved by Hindus. It is part of a long story known as the **Mahabharata**. In the Bhagavad Gita, Krishna, who is really God in human form, tells a warrior called Arjuna about the importance of doing his duty and of showing devotion to God.

Hindu sacred writings tell many stories and give many different teachings. Although they are very much respected by Hindus, they are not read and studied each week in the same way as the holy books from many other religions. The important ideas are usually taught by word of mouth, as was originally intended, and are repeated during worship so that 'that which is heard' and 'that which is remembered' can go on being heard and remembered by future generations.

Discussion

What do you think might be the advantages and disadvantages of passing on religious ideas and stories by word of mouth, rather than by writing them down?

Activity

1 Explain what Hindus mean when they say that they worship one God with many different aspects.

2 Why are the Vedas believed to be more important than other kinds of Hindu literature?

3 Describe how Hindu sacred texts are usually used.

Avatars

Hindus believe that sometimes a god will appear on the earth, in the form of a person or sometimes another animal. These appearances are known as **avatars**. According to the teachings of the Bhagavad Gita, avatars appear at times of danger, when people are forgetting the sacred law of **dharma** (often translated as moral duty, or eternal truth) and are turning towards evil.

The most important of the avatars in Hindu mythology are appearances of the god Vishnu. He is believed to have come to the earth nine times so far, and Hindus are still expecting his tenth avatar.

1 The first avatar was in the form of a fish, when Vishnu appeared to save the great teacher and ancestor of humanity, called Manu, from a great flood. There was the danger that his holy books would be lost.

2 Vishnu appeared as a giant tortoise, when the gods lost sacred objects, including their holy drink **amrit**, and were in danger of losing their immortality. The tortoise helped the gods to retrieve the amrit from the bottom of the sea, by using his curved shell to support a mountain of dry land.

3 The earth was in danger from being sent to the bottom of the ocean by a demon, but Vishnu appeared in the form of a boar and was able to keep it afloat by using his tusks.

4 Vishnu appeared as half lion, half man, in order to overcome another evil demon. The demon had found out a magical secret so that he could not be killed, but Vishnu destroyed him by tearing him to pieces.

5 The fifth avatar was Vishnu in the form of a dwarf. He came to save the world from a demon, who told him he could have only as much land as he could cover in three steps. Vishnu miraculously became a giant and, with his three steps, covered the entire earth and saved it, stamping the evil demon into the underworld as he went.

6 The social structure of Hinduism was threatened when the warrior class, the Kshatriyas, threatened to overthrow the Brahmins. Vishnu became 'Rama with the axe' and kept Hindu society organised in the way it was meant to be.

7 The seventh avatar of Vishnu is one of the most popular characters in Hinduism. He was called Rama, and came to earth when it was under threat from an evil demon. He came to set an example of honourable conduct, and to demonstrate how to live according to dharma. The story is told in the Hindu epic tale the **Ramayana**.

Rama, as an avatar of Vishnu, defeated the many-headed demon Ravanna.

Rama, prince of Ayodha, was heir to the throne, but was sent into exile by a jealous stepmother who wanted the throne to go to her own son. Rama's faithful wife, Sita, and his loyal younger brother Lakshmana went to live in exile as forest-dwellers for 14 years. During their time in the forest, when Rama and Lakshmana were off hunting, Sita was approached by a demon who had disguised himself as a beggar. She took pity on him, but when she went closer to see what she could do to help, she was kidnapped, and taken away and held prisoner by the many-headed demon Ravanna. Rama and Lakshmana had many adventures while searching for Sita, in which they overcame evil and demonstrated the right way to live. Eventually Rama and Lakshmana were helped by Hanuman, the monkey god, to find Sita and rescue her, and they destroyed the evil Ravanna.

Rama and Sita are popular deities for Hindu worship. They act as role models, showing the ideal husband and wife who work faithfully to protect each other.

8 The eighth avatar of Vishnu was Krishna, who, like Rama, is also a very popular deity and is worshipped in many Hindu homes. He is nearly always shown as young, blue in colour to show that he is a god, and playing on his flute. There are many stories connected with the childhood of Krishna, some told by the great Hindu poet Surdas, where Krishna is described as a mischievous boy, always up to tricks but with miraculous powers. As he grew up, he was a great favourite with the young women called **gopis** who looked after the cows and goats; they all adored him, but the most devoted was Radha. Radha and the other gopis are often used to symbolise the love between God and his worshippers. Krishna is particularly popular, because love for a young child and love between men and women are relationships that everyone can relate to.

Krishna is also worshipped as the great teacher of the Bhagavad Gita, appearing on the battlefield in a war between rivalling families, to teach the way to live according to Hindu dharma. Krishna came to earth as an avatar because of the disputes between these different families, to teach the need for duty and devotion to God.

9 The ninth avatar, according to Hinduism, was Siddharta Gautama the Buddha, the founder of Buddhism. He came to earth at a time when Hinduism was becoming corrupted by too much emphasis on ritual, and too much greed for social position. The Buddha taught about the importance of not clinging to possessions, and about the need for harmlessness (**ahimsa**).

Hindus believe that the tenth avatar of Vishnu has not yet come. When there is another need for Vishnu to fight evil, he will come again in the form of Kalki, carrying a flashing sword and riding a white horse.

According to Hinduism, God does not just come to the earth from time to time, but influences people's lives every day. Hindus will pray to different deities and ask for their help; for example, they might pray to Lord Ganesha and ask him to help their children at school, or they might pray to the goddess Lakshmi if they needed help with money problems. They believe that God will help them if they worship with devotion.

Krishna is a very popular Hindu deity, often shown playing a flute.

Discussion

If you asked Hindus whether they believed in one God, or many gods, what do you think they would say?

Activity

1 Explain what is meant by an avatar.

2 Describe the special characteristics of Rama and of Krishna, and say why they are popular gods in Hindu worship.

Muslim beliefs about the nature of Allah

Muslims are **monotheists**. This means that they believe there is only one God – Allah. According to Islam, Allah is unlike anything else that exists and no attempt is made to describe him.

Muslims believe:
- Allah is eternal, beyond time and space.
- Allah is not limited by having a physical body, and is everywhere at all times.
- Allah is the creator of the world and everything in it, and has a purpose for the world.
- Allah is perfectly good and perfectly loving.
- Allah is interested in how people behave, and wants them to treat each other properly.
- Allah is all-powerful (omnipotent) and all-knowing (omniscient).
- Allah will judge each individual.

Muslim life is an expression of **Islam** (submission) to the will of Allah and is lived according to the words of the **Qur'an** and following the teaching and example of Muhammad ﷺ.

The importance of Allah to Muslim life is stressed in the first **Surah** of the Qur'an:

> In the name of Allah, Most Gracious, Most Merciful. Praise be to Allah, the Cherisher and Sustainer of the Worlds.

At the centre of Muslim belief in Allah is the **Shahadah** and the Qur'an.

The Shahadah is the first pillar of Islam and the central statement of belief. It states the importance of Allah:

> *La ilaha illal lahu Muhammad Dur rasulul lah*
>
> There is no god but Allah, Muhammad is the messenger of Allah.

This importance is stressed in **salah**, daily prayers.

The **adhan**, or call to prayer, has the following statements:

Allah is the Greatest (x 4)
I bear witness that there is no god but Allah (x 2)
I bear witness that Muhammad is Allah's messenger (x 2)
Rush to prayer (x 2)
Rush to success (x 2)
Allah is the Greatest (x 2)
There is no god but Allah

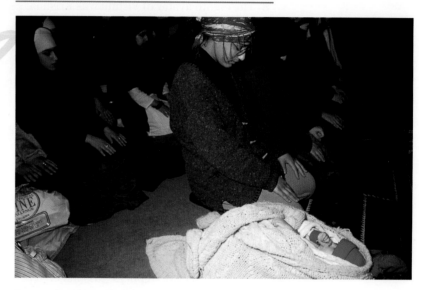

Prayer five times a day is an essential part of Muslim life

A statement of the seven basic beliefs of Islam is contained in **Al-Imanul Mufassal**:

> I believe in Allah, in His angels, in His books, in His messengers, in the Last Day and in the fact that everything good or bad is decided by Allah, the Almighty, and in the Life after Death.

Tawhid – the 'oneness' – of Allah is clearly expressed in the Qur'an and is the most important aspect of Islamic belief:

> Say: He is Allah, the One and Only; Allah, the Eternal, Absolute; He begetteth not, nor is He begotten; and there is none like unto Him.
>
> *(Surah 112:1–4)*

Muslims say that they must let Tawhid grow in their heart, and shape and control the whole of their lives. By following Tawhid Muslims become contented, trusting in Allah and dedicate their lives to seeking his pleasure.

From the Qur'an and the **Hadith**, Muslims have collected the 99 'most beautiful names' of God, and these are often used in meditation.

Tradition says that the hundredth name is a secret, known only to the camel. Muhammad ﷺ taught that:

> There are ninety-nine names that are Allah's alone. Whoever learns, understands and enumerates them enters Paradise and achieves eternal salvation.

These principles of Muslim belief can all be found in the last sermon which Muhammad ﷺ preached on Mount Arafat at the end of the **Hajj**:

> O people, listen to my words carefully, for I know not whether I would meet you again on such an occasion.

> O people, just as you regard this month, this day, this city as sacred, so regard the lip and property of every Muslim as a sacred trust. Remember that you will indeed appear before Allah and answer for your actions…

> O people, listen carefully! All the believers are brothers…

> O people, none is higher than the other unless he is higher in obedience to Allah. No Arab is superior to a non-Arab except in piety.

> O people, reflect on my words. I leave behind me two things, the Qur'an and my example, and if you follow these, you will not fail.

> Listen to me carefully! Worship Allah and offer Salah, observe Saum in the month of Ramadan and pay Zakah…

> O people, no prophet or messenger will come after me and no new faith will emerge.

> All those who listen to me shall pass on my words to others, and those to others again.
>
> *(Hadith)*

Why do Muslims believe in Allah?

Muslims believe in Allah because of the evidence of his goodness which they see in their daily lives and in creation and also because of his revelation of the Qur'an to Muhammad ﷺ.

In their daily lives, Muslims see the influence of Allah through their belief in **Al-Qadr**: belief that Allah has laid down a pre-determined course for the world and knows the destiny of every living creature. However, this does not mean that people do not have free will. Allah made humans his **khalifahs**, or agents, on earth. People are not forced to obey Allah's will and may choose to disobey him but he knows what decisions people will make. Humans are judged on these decisions at **Akirah**, the day of judgement.

Allah communicates with humanity by **Risalah** – the Prophets. According to Muhammad ﷺ there are 124,000 prophets but only 25 are mentioned in the Qur'an. Many of these prophets are the same people as are found in the Jewish and Christian scriptures, showing part of the common origins of these three religions.

Muhammad ﷺ was the last prophet and received the final revelation from Allah. He is sometimes called the 'Seal of the Prophets'.

Discussion

Do you think that Islam provides convincing reasons for belief in Allah? Explain why, or why not.

Activity

1 Make a list of the characteristics of Allah.

2 Explain what is meant by Muhammad ﷺ being the Seal of the Prophets.

Muslim sacred writings

The Qur'an is the holy book of Islam but other books are mentioned in it as being revealed by God: Zabur Psalms of David, Tawrat Torah of Moses, Injil Gospels of the New Testament, Suhuf-i-Ibrahim Scrolls of Abraham. Islam teaches that only the Qur'an still exists in its original form and that these other revealed books have been changed from the true words of God.

The Qur'an is, in some ways, very different from the holy books of Judaism and Christianity.

Muslims say that the Qur'an was revealed to Muhammad ﷺ by the angel Jibril and is the actual words of Allah.

In 611 CE, Muhammad ﷺ, then aged 40, was meditating in a cave. Jibril appeared to him and ordered him to read. Muhammad ﷺ said that he could not read. This happened three times and eventually the angel said:

> Proclaim! (or read) in the name of thy Lord and Cherisher, Who created – created man, out of a (mere) clot of congealed blood. Proclaim! And thy Lord is Most Bountiful – He Who has taught (the use of) the Pen – taught man that which he knew not.
>
> *(Surah 96:1–5)*

Muhammad ﷺ recited these words and then the angel said, 'O Muhammad, you are the messenger of Allah and I am Jibril', and left.

Muhammad ﷺ continued to receive visits from Jibril over the next 23 years. Finally, just before his death, he received the final verse:

> This day have I perfected your religion for your benefit, completed My favour upon you, and have chosen for you Islam as your religion.
>
> *(Surah 5:3)*

Because Muhammad ﷺ could not read or write, he memorised the Qur'an as he heard it and then dictated it to his secretary, Zaid Bin Thabit. It was not compiled as one book until after his death.

The cave on Mount Nur where Jibril spoke to Muhammad ﷺ.

Every copy of the Qur'an records these words of Allah completely unchanged from the manner in which they were received by Muhammad ﷺ. For this reason, versions of the Qur'an in languages other than Arabic are not called translations because Muslims say that it is not possible successfully to translate God's words into any other language without changing them.

The Qur'an is not written in chronological order, the order Muslims believe Muhammad ﷺ received it from Allah. Surah 1 is the shortest and is then followed by the longest Surah. The Surahs then grow progressively shorter until the last which is 114.

No form of critical study of the Qur'an is undertaken because it is the word of Allah. Because every word is seen as a direct revelation there is no idea of discussing who wrote it and why. Islam does not consider these ideas as they would be irrelevant and disrespectful.

The Qur'an is seen as unchanging, unchangeable and untranslatable **Iman** (faith), and is regarded as the complete and final book of guidance from Allah for the whole of humanity forever.

In this way the Qur'an and the teachings of Islam are regarded as absolute truth. It can be said that Muslims do not therefore have to believe because they actually know these teachings to be true.

Allah in the world

Miracles do not play a particularly important part in Islam. Because Muhammad ﷺ was a prophet and in no way was seen as a god, there is no reason why he should have performed miracles.

Allah, of course, can perform miracles and the revelation of the Qur'an to Muhammad ﷺ is often viewed as a living miracle.

It can be seen that, in order to protect the message of the Qur'an and the religion of Islam, there are many instances in the life of Muhammad ﷺ when Allah intervened.

One story relates to Muhammad's ﷺ birth. On the night that he was born a great star appeared in the sky. His grandfather Abd al-Muttalib prayed for six days to decide on a name for the child. On the seventh day both he and Muhammad's ﷺ mother dreamt that he should be called Muhammad ﷺ the 'Praised One'.

The most important miraculous event in the life of the Prophet was **Al-Mi'raj** – the Ascent. Muslims believe that Muhammad ﷺ was woken by Jibril who took him to Jerusalem, riding on an animal with wings, called Buraq. In Jerusalem Muhammad ﷺ met the prophets Adam, Ibrahim, Musa, 'Isa and Harun and he then travelled through the heavens until he came into the presence of Allah.

By choosing Muhammad ﷺ as his messenger and by revealing the Qur'an to him, Allah ensured the protection and preservation of Islam. It is this revelation which can be viewed as the greatest intervention of Allah in the world.

Discussion

Do you think that an event like the revelation of the Qur'an could still happen today? Give reasons to support your answer.

Activity

1 Explain what Muslims mean when they say that Qur'an is revealed.

2 Describe how Muslims might use the Qur'an in their daily lives.

Jewish beliefs about the nature of G-d

In the Jewish scriptures, G-d's name is spelt with four consonants YHWH (this is called the **Tetragrammaton** or 'four letters'), but Jewish teaching says that the name is so holy that only the High Priest knew how to pronounce it and that he only spoke it once a year, alone, in the Holy of Holies, in the Temple at Jerusalem. When they see these four letters Jews usually say the name **Adonai** instead, this means Lord. Many Jews will not write the word which is a translation of this name and instead put G-d. In some parts of the **Tenakh** the name **HASHEM** is also used for G-d.

Jews are **monotheists**. This means that they believe there is only one G-d. G-d is unlike anything else that exists, and this means that it can be very difficult to describe G-d, because everyday language is always about ordinary things but G-d is not ordinary. G-d is often described as '**holy**', which means special, separate and different.

Jews believe:
- G-d is eternal, beyond time and space.
- G-d is not limited by having a physical body, and is everywhere at all times.
- G-d is the creator of the world and everything in it, and has a purpose for the world.
- G-d is perfectly good and perfectly loving.
- G-d is interested in how people behave, and wants them to treat each other properly.
- G-d is all-powerful (omnipotent) and all-knowing (omniscient).
- G-d judges each individual.

The Jewish picture of G-d is found in the Tenakh, the Jewish scriptures, and in particular in the **Torah**, the five books of Moses.

The Torah is the most sacred of the Jewish scriptures.

Genesis, the first book of the Jewish Scriptures, opens with a description of G-d creating the world:

> In the beginning of G-d's creating the heavens and the earth – when the earth was astonishingly empty, with darkness upon the surface of the deep, and the Divine Presence hovered upon the surface of the waters – G-d said, 'Let there be light,' and there was light.
>
> *(Genesis 1:1–2)*

Later, G-d speaks to Moses through a bush which is burning and Moses asks G-d's name:

HASHEM answered Moses, 'I SHALL BE AS I SHALL BE.'

(Exodus 3:14)

This is the first time that the name of G-d is given in the Tenakh but it is not very clear.

The Jewish scriptures say that Moses spoke to G-d:

As Moses would arrive at the Tent, the pillar of cloud would descend and stand at the entrance of the Tent, and He would speak with Moses... HASHEM would speak to Moses face to face, as a man would speak with his fellow.

(Exodus 33:9, 11)

but later, when Moses was receiving the Ten Commandments, he asked to see G-d:

He said, 'I will make all My goodness pass before you, and I shall call out with the Name, HASHEM before you...' He said, 'You will not be able to see My face, for no human can see My face and live.' HASHEM said, 'Behold! there is a place near Me; you may stand on the rock. When My glory passes by, I shall place you in a cleft of the rock; I shall shield you with My hand until I have passed. Then I shall remove My hand and you will see My back, but My face may not be seen.'

(Exodus 33:19–23)

Throughout the scriptures there are times when G-d appears to the Jews, but only in the Garden of Eden is there a suggestion of G-d in a human form:

So G-d created Man in His image, in the image of G-d He created him; male and female He created them.

(Genesis 1:27)

They heard the sound of HASHEM G-d manifesting itself in the garden toward the evening.

(Genesis 3:8)

For the rest of the Tenakh G-d is sometimes a pillar of cloud or flame, and sometimes just a voice, as when he spoke to the prophet Elijah:

[The word of G-d] then said, 'Go out [of the cave] and stand on the mountain before HASHEM.' And behold, HASHEM was passing, and a great, powerful wind, smashing mountains and breaking rocks, went before Hashem. 'HASHEM is not in the wind' [Elijah was told]. After the wind came an earthquake. 'HASHEM is not in the earthquake.' After the earthquake came a fire. 'HASHEM is not in the fire.' After the fire came a still, thin sound.

(1 Kings 19:11–12)

On other occasions G-d is shown as a powerful king:

...I saw the Lord sitting upon a high and lofty throne, and its legs filled the Temple. Seraphim were standing above, at His service. Each one had six wings... And one would call to another and say,

'Holy, holy, holy is HASHEM, Master of Legions; the whole world is filled with His glory.'

The doorposts moved many cubits at the sound of the calling, and the Temple became filled with smoke.

(Isaiah 6:1–4)

Discussion

Do you think that Judaism provides convincing reasons for belief in God? Explain why, or why not.

Activity

1 Make a list of the particular characteristics of the Jewish G-d.

2 Explain what is special about the name of G-d for Jews.

Reasons Jews give in support of their belief in G-d

For Jews the truth lies in their Holy Scriptures, the Torah and in their special relationship with G-d. Above everything else, Jews believe that there is only one G-d and this is stated in one of the central Jewish prayers – the **Shema**.

The centre of Jewish belief is contained in the Shema:

> Hear, O Israel: HASHEM is our G-d, HASHEM is the One and Only. You shall love HASHEM, your G-d, with all your heart, with all your soul, and with all your resources. And these matters that I command you today shall be upon your heart. You shall teach them thoroughly to your children and you shall speak of them while you sit in your home, while you walk on the way, when you retire and when you arise. Bind them as a sign upon your arm and let them be ornaments between your eyes. And write them on the doorposts of your house and upon your gates.
>
> *(Deuteronomy 6:4–9)*

This statement of belief in one G-d is at the centre of Jewish life.

Judaism teaches that Abraham entered into a special relationship with G-d called a **covenant**. This was an agreement between them that Abraham and his family would worship this one G-d and no others, and that G-d would look after his family and descendants forever.

(Genesis 22:17–18)

This covenant relationship is broken again and again by the Jews in the Bible, but G-d always forgives them when they repent and so the relationship still continues.

The authority for Jews of the Torah and Talmud

The Torah is of great importance to Jews. It contains five books which, in English, are called Genesis, Exodus, Leviticus, Numbers and Deuteronomy.

The Torah (Law) is the first part of the Tenakh. The other two parts are the **Ketuvim** (Writings) which contains 11 books and the **Nevi'im** (Prophets) which has 16 books. Although people often say that the Jewish scriptures are the same as the Old Testament of the Christian Bible, the books appear in a different order.

Jewish tradition teaches that the five books of the Torah were all written by Moses who was inspired by G-d – so they are revealed. Jews do not necessarily claim that every word in the Torah is literally true and some of it may, perhaps, be allegorical (picture language). For example, the story of Creation and of Adam and Eve may not be historical fact, but it does contain essential truths about G-d and about human nature. If it is accepted that these books were all written by Moses, there are still some difficult questions to answer. It may be possible that G-d told Moses about the creation of the world and the events which took place before he was born, but many Progressive Jews have found it difficult to accept such things as Moses actually writing the account of his own death at the end of Deuteronomy.

The Torah is treated with great respect by all Jews. It is handwritten by a scribe on large pages made of animal skin and is placed on large rollers. These **scrolls** are decorated with covers and hung with bells and other decorations. When they are not in use the scrolls are kept in a cupboard in

Both the tefillin, used for prayer and the mezuzah on the doorposts of Jewish homes contain a scroll on which is written the words of the Shema (see page 40).

A silver pointer called a yad is used to follow the text so that it is not touched by hand.

the synagogue called the **Aron Hakodesh** (the ark). When they are being read they are not touched by hand but a **yad** (pointer) is used so that the reader can follow the text.

Whilst Orthodox Jews believe that the Torah must be accepted as the word of G-d and therefore the teachings cannot be altered, Progressive Jews argue that it must be interpreted to suit the times in which it is being read. There are places in the Torah where the text is sometimes unclear and difficult to understand but tradition has long since provided an explanation of these. Where there are difficulties in interpreting the text the **Talmud**, or 'Oral Torah', is used.

Jews believe that the Oral Torah was given to Moses at the same time as G-d gave him the Written Torah and that it is intended to be used to interpret the written text. The Talmud is a collection of the teachings of many generations of rabbis arguing and discussing the texts and offering explanations as to exactly what is meant. Sometimes part of the text of the Torah may appear unintelligible but can be understood if one word is changed. The written word is referred to as the **k'tiv** (written) whilst the word used in its place is the **keri** (read). The respect given to the Torah and the **mitzvot** (laws) which it contains show its great importance to Jews as a document that contains the truth about G-d and about their relationship with him.

The Bible of course contains the Ten Commandments (Exodus 20:1–17) but these are only ten of the 613 mitzvot and by living these out in their daily lives, Jews demonstrate their belief in G-d and the covenant relationship. They also live in preparation for the coming of the Messiah which is promised in the Bible and which they are waiting for.

Belief in G-d intervening in the world through miracles and through the words of the prophets

There are many stories of miracles in the Torah, in particular the accounts of Moses and his stick which turned into a snake, the plagues of Egypt, the parting of the Red Sea, and the food which the Israelites were given by G-d in the desert. To believe in these as actual facts means accepting that G-d will intervene and break the physical laws of nature in order to help humanity. While there is no reason why an omnipotent G-d cannot do this, it seems unlikely that G-d would create something as complex as the universe, and then decide to break its rules. Perhaps it does not matter whether people accept these miracles as actually true or as an attempt to understand G-d, in either case we can say that G-d was teaching the people and looking after them.

Throughout the Tenakh there are prophets chosen by G-d who warn the people of what might happen if they ignore G-d's teachings and do not follow the laws which they have been given. Many of these prophets are found in the Nevi'im. These include: Isaiah, Jeremiah, Ezekiel, Hosea, Joel, Amos, Obadiah, Jonah, Micah, Nahum, Habbakuk and Zepahaniah.

Some of these prophesied punishment for breaking G-d's Law whilst others saw a time of peace which would come when all G-d's laws were obeyed.

Discussion

Do you think that miracles happen today? If someone told you that he or she had experienced a miracle, would you believe it? Explain why or why not.

Activity

1 Explain what Jews mean when they say that the Torah is revealed.

2 Describe how Jews might use the Torah in their daily lives.

3 Explain the importance of the prophets for Jews today.

Practice GCSE questions

Christianity

(a) Describe what Christians believe about the nature of God. (8 marks)

(b) Explain how a Christian might show respect for the Bible in his or her daily life. (7 marks)

(c) 'There is no evidence that God exists.' Do you agree? Give reasons to support your answer, and show that you have thought about different points of view. You must refer to Christianity in your answer. (5 marks)

Hinduism

(a) Describe what Hindus believe about the nature of God. (8 marks)

(b) Explain how a Hindu might show respect for the Vedas in his or her daily life. (7 marks)

(c) 'There is no evidence that God exists.' Do you agree? Give reasons to support your answer, and show that you have thought about different points of view. You must refer to Hinduism in your answer. (5 marks)

Islam

(a) Describe what Muslims believe about the nature of Allah. (8 marks)

(b) Explain how a Muslim might show respect for the Qur'an in his or her daily life. (7 marks)

(c) 'There is no evidence that God exists.' Do you agree? Give reasons to support your answer, and show that you have thought about different points of view. You must refer to Islam in your answer. (5 marks)

Judaism

(a) Describe what Jews believe about the nature of G-d. (8 marks)

(b) Explain how a Jew might show respect for the Torah in his or her daily life. (7 marks)

(c) 'There is no evidence that God exists.' Do you agree? Give reasons to support your answer, and show that you have thought about different points of view. You must refer to Judaism in your answer. (5 marks)

Tips

For all four questions

In part (a), you are asked to describe religious beliefs. You do not need to give your own opinion of the beliefs, because you are being tested just on your knowledge. You should try and allow yourself about ten to fifteen minutes to answer this part of the question. Try and give as much detail as you can remember, and try to use the correct terms for the beliefs. For example, if you were writing about Judaism, you might be able to use the word 'monotheism', and if you were writing about Christianity, you could use the word 'Trinity'.

In part (b), you are being tested on your understanding. You should allow about ten minutes for this part of the question. Try and think about how the holy books might be important for the religious believer; for example, they might use words from the holy books in their prayers, or try to follow the commands as they go about their everyday lives, or use the books as a source of information. For high marks, try to think of several different ideas, and explain what you mean as clearly as you can.

In part (c), you are being tested on your evaluation. This means that you need to show that you realise people might have different opinions. You should explain what a religious believer might say in answer to this question, and also show what someone of a different belief, or no belief, might say. Perhaps a religious believer would say that the design of the world is evidence for the existence of God; and perhaps a non-believer (atheist) might say that this is because of evolution, not God. You also need to give your own view, and try to back it up with a reason.

UNIT 2

The Nature of Belief

✝ Christianity

The architecture of the church

There are many different styles of church building. Some are enormous, beautifully decorated cathedrals, which dominate the landscape, some are traditional parish churches, and others are small, simple chapels. Usually, churches from the Roman Catholic and Anglican traditions are built in the shape of a cross, to symbolise the crucifixion and resurrection of Jesus. Many churches have a steeple, tower or spire, pointing upwards to show that Christianity is not only about this world but is directed beyond it towards God. This feature makes the church building immediately recognisable, even from a distance.

Near the door where people come in is the **font**, which holds water for baptisms, showing that baptism is the point at which people enter the Christian faith. Not all churches have the font near the door; some prefer to have them nearer the centre of the building, so that services of baptism take place right in the middle of the congregation. In Roman Catholic churches there is also a **stoup** near the door; this is a smaller water container for people to use to make the sign of the cross as they enter the building. At the east wall of the church, in the direction of Jerusalem, is the **altar** where Holy Communion is celebrated. At the front, facing the congregation, is a **lectern**, which is a stand on which the Bible rests when it is being read aloud. The lectern is often carved in the shape of an eagle, to represent the word of God being taken across the world. The **pulpit** is a raised platform where the person who is giving the sermon stands, so that he or she can be seen and heard clearly by the congregation. In Roman Catholic and Anglican churches, the altar is the most important feature to emphasise the sacrifice of Christ, but in other traditions such as the Methodist church, the pulpit is given greater prominence to show the importance of preaching Christianity.

Christian worship

Christians worship on their own (private worship) and also with other people (communal or corporate worship). Both kinds of worship are important for Christians. Private worship helps them to develop their own, personal relationship with God, where they can focus on things that are important in their own lives. Communal or corporate worship reminds them that they are part of a group of believers, all working together and sharing the same beliefs and traditions.

Many church buildings are designed in the shape of a cross, as a symbol of important Christian beliefs.

Private worship

Many Christians set aside a special time of the day for private worship. They might read a passage from the Bible, perhaps with the help of another book which explains the passage and gives them some questions to think about. They will probably also pray silently, about anything which is of particular concern to them, such as a friend who is ill, or something they have done wrong, or money worries, or an important event that is coming up, or something they have heard about in the news. Christians often feel that private worship gives them time to establish a personal relationship with God.

Communal worship

Most Christians belong to a church in their neighbourhood, and go to church on Sundays to worship with other people. Different kinds of Christian Church have different ways of worshipping, but most services include:

- **Hymns**, which are sung together. These are usually prayers set to music, and they are a way of helping Christians to worship together, so that they feel a sense of unity with other worshippers who are also praising God by singing the same hymn. Traditional tunes can help believers to remember that they are part of a long tradition; but some churches prefer to use more modern music, with guitars and drums, to create a lively atmosphere and to remind people Christianity is relevant for today.
- **Bible reading**, where a passage from the Bible is read aloud for everyone to hear and think about. Many churches follow a pattern for Bible reading, according to the time of year.
- **A sermon**, which is a talk given by the priest, minister or vicar. It is often about the Bible passages which were read, explaining what they might mean and showing the congregation how they might use the message of the story in their own lives.
- **Prayers**, where believers can talk to God, sometimes silently, sometimes by listening to the words of someone else who is leading the prayer, or sometimes by saying the same words together. The most famous prayer in Christianity is known as the Lord's Prayer, which is usually said aloud by everyone together. It comes from the New Testament, and Christians believe that the words of this prayer come from Jesus himself when he was teaching his followers how to pray:

> This, then, is how you should pray:
> 'Our Father in heaven,
>   hallowed be your name,
> your kingdom come,
> your will be done
>   on earth as it is in heaven.
> Give us today our daily bread.
> Forgive us our debts,
>   as we also have forgiven our debtors.
> And lead us not into temptation,
> but deliver us from the evil one.'
> *(Matthew 6:9–13)*

Another popular prayer for Christians is called the Grace, which is often said as a blessing at the end of church services, or at the end of other Christian meetings such as Bible study groups:

> Now may the grace of our Lord Jesus Christ, and the love of God, and the fellowship of the Holy Spirit, be with us all, now and evermore. Amen.

Church services also have times of silence, where worshippers can offer their own thoughts and prayers.

Many church services include **Holy Communion**, or **Mass**, or the **Eucharist**, where believers share bread and wine which has been blessed as the body and blood of Christ. In some Christian traditions this is given greater prominence than others.

Discussion

What do you think are the advantages and disadvantages of worshipping publicly, with a lot of other people?

Activity

Describe the main features of a service of worship in a Christian church.

The use of food and fasting as a response to God

In Christianity, unlike some other religions, there are no religious food laws telling believers what they must and must not eat. It seems likely that Jesus ate meat, like other Jews, and there are stories in the New Testament which tell of Jesus performing miracles providing fish for hungry crowds and enabling fishermen to make great catches:

> When he had finished speaking, he said to Simon, 'Put out into deep water, and let down the nets for a catch.'
>
> Simon answered, 'Master, we've worked hard all night and haven't caught anything. But because you say so, I will let down the nets.'
>
> When they had done so, they caught such a large number of fish that their nets began to break. So they signalled to their partners in the other boat to come and help them, and they came and filled both boats so full that they began to sink.
>
> *(Luke 5:4–6)*

Some Christians are vegetarians, but most are not, and those who choose not to eat meat usually do it for reasons that have little to do with religion. Christians, then, do not avoid certain foods or prepare them in any particular way as a part of their religion, and when Christians visit non-Christian countries there is not usually any problem about what may or may not be eaten. In the Acts of the Apostles, the story of the vision of Peter shows how Christians were given permission to eat all kinds of creatures (Acts 10:9–16).

Some foods, however, are used symbolically in Christianity, as part of Christian worship. In the Eucharist, also known as Mass, Holy Communion or the **Lord's Supper**, bread and wine are used as ways of showing Jesus' continued presence in the world. The minister, or vicar, or priest, blesses bread and wine as the body and blood of Christ, and this is shared with the congregation. They remember the Last Supper that Jesus shared with his disciples before he was crucified, and when they share the bread and wine they feel united with one another as believers.

> The Lord Jesus, on the night he was betrayed, took bread, and when he had given thanks, he broke it and said, 'This is my body, which is for you; do this in remembrance of me.' In the same way, after supper he took the cup, saying, 'This cup is the new covenant in my blood; do this, whenever you drink it, in remembrance of me.'
>
> *(1 Corinthians 11:23–25)*

Sharing bread and wine is an important part of Christian worship.

Other foods, too, are traditionally eaten on Christian festivals, such as hot cross buns on Good Friday or mince pies at Christmas, but these are customs and not things that Christians are expected to do for religious reasons.

Fasting

Fasting is a time of going without food, and sometimes drink as well. Some people believe that times of fasting help religious faith, because fasting encourages self-discipline, and it is a constant reminder of human dependence on God and the need to be less selfish. Fasting does not have a very important place in the lives of most Christians, but some people choose to give up luxuries during Lent (the 40 days before Easter) to remind themselves of the suffering of Jesus and as a way of concentrating on the things they have done wrong. Monks and nuns often eat a very simple diet, as a way of showing that they have given their lives to God.

The use of music and art in Christian worship

Art and music have always played an important part in Christian worship, although Christians from different traditions have different ideas about the ways in which they are best used. In some churches, such as the Orthodox, the Roman Catholic and the Anglican, art is used in many different ways. The churches are often richly decorated, with paintings, carvings, needlework, stained glass and statues, all showing different aspects of Christian belief, different Christian symbols and different stories from the Bible. Many worshippers find this very helpful; they can look around the church building and be made aware that they are in a special place of worship, where the best is offered to God, and where they are reminded everywhere they look of different aspects of the Christian faith. Other Christians, however, have different views, and feel that too much decoration is a distraction, rather than a help, for people who are trying to concentrate their minds on God. The Religious Society of Friends, usually known as the Quakers, use art and music very little. They meet in simple rooms and often worship in silence.

In Christianity, music is often seen as a way of giving God the best that humanity has to offer, and some of the most beautiful music in Western culture was written for use in Christian worship. Hymns are used by nearly every kind of Christian Church, as a way of uniting the worshippers and of praising God.

Organ music is traditionally used as an accompaniment to hymns, and if a church is large enough it might have a choir to lead the singing. Some churches use the organ almost all the time, while other churches have a more informal style, and singing might be accompanied by guitars and drums for more simple or modern songs.

Symbols in Christianity

The most famous and important symbol in Christianity is the cross:

This is a reminder of the death of Jesus on a cross, which Christians believe brought the opportunity for forgiveness from sin and everlasting life with God.

Another Christian symbol is the Chi-Rho:

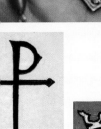

This is made from two Greek letters, which are the first two letters of the word 'Christ'.

Alpha and Omega are also Greek letters, at the beginning and end of the alphabet, used to represent God as the beginning and end of all things.

The fish symbol is often used by Christians for badges and car stickers. In the earliest days of Christianity, when Christians were persecuted and killed, this symbol was used as a secret code message by which one Christian could recognise another. The initial letters, in Greek, of the words 'Jesus Christ, Son of God, Saviour' spell out the word for 'fish'.

Discussion

Why do you think that Christianity uses symbols, rather than just words?

Activity

1 Explain what Christians mean by the Eucharist, and describe its importance for Christianity.

2 Why do some Christians like to have richly decorated churches, while others prefer plain and simple church buildings?

3 Draw and explain some of the different symbols used in Christianity.

ॐ Hinduism

Hindu worship in the home

Although many Hindus visit mandirs, most Hindu worship takes place in the home, within the family. Nearly every Hindu home has its own shrine for worshipping God. In many houses, this is a corner of a room, or a special shelf, set aside for holy pictures and objects, but Hindus who can afford to will keep aside a whole room especially for worship. Little shrines are found everywhere in Hindu societies, in restaurants, on the dashboards of taxis and lorries, in shops and by the roadside. Whether the shrine is large or small, it will be treated as a special, holy place.

The household shrine has a statue or picture, known as a **murti**, of the deity which is particularly important for the family. Other deities might be represented as well, alongside the family favourite. These deities are always treated with great respect, because they are believed to contain the presence of God, and it is usually the job of the woman of the house to make sure that the proper rituals are followed. Each day, in the morning and in the evening, special acts of worship (known as **puja**) are carried out.

Before puja begins, the worshipper has a bath or shower and dresses in clean clothes, as a sign of respect and as a way of showing pure intentions. Then, special prayers from the Vedas are said, and a bell is rung to focus attention on the worship and to bring the presence of God to life in the statues or pictures in the shrine. The murti is washed with clarified butter, yoghurt, sugar and water, as an offering, and then cleaned with clear water and dressed in fresh clothes. The murti is brushed with coloured powders and is offered fresh flowers and sweet-smelling incense. Sometimes the worshipper meditates in silence, or chants a prayer: the most popular is called the **Gayatri mantra**. Then the **arti** ceremony is performed. A special lamp with five wicks is lit and moved in a circle around the deity; the worshipper passes both hands over the flame and then over his or her head. This shows that the worshipper is sharing something of the presence and light of God with the murti. It is a sign of blessing, and a way of asking for 'enlightenment', or wisdom of understanding.

Hindus believe that the value of the offering to the murtis is not important. What matters is the attitude of the worshipper. In the Bhagavad Gita, one of the most popular Hindu holy books, the god Krishna taught that any offering, even a leaf, was acceptable if it was made because of love for God.

The arti ceremony is an important part of Hindu worship in the home and in the mandir.

Prayer and meditation

Hindus believe that devotion to God (**bhakti**) is one of the most important ways in which salvation can be achieved. Prayer is used as an expression of love for God, and as a way of asking for God's guidance in daily life.

Meditation also plays an important part in the lives of many Hindus. Some Hindus meditate by repeating the name of God over and over again; others try to empty their minds of everyday concerns and aim to focus on becoming detached from worldly concerns such as money, food and personal comfort, trying instead to reach a greater sense of union with the Supreme Reality. In a form of Hinduism known as **yoga**, meditation is a central part of religious life, and some Hindu holy men give up their homes, jobs and families in order to spend their time meditating.

The architecture of the mandir

A Hindu temple is known as a **mandir**. Hindus do not usually meet in the mandir as a congregation, except on very special occasions and festivals. The mandir is used instead for private worship and for small groups, who will sometimes take time out of the day to stop at the mandir and offer worship. Some Hindus visit the mandir every day, as part of their routine, but others go very rarely, preferring instead to worship at home. In India, there are mandirs in every town and village, and people call in for a few moments of quiet time before continuing with their jobs for the day.

The most important and holy part of a mandir is the place where the murtis, or images of the deities, are kept. This is called the **garbha-griha** and is in the most central part of the building, the inner shrine or **vimana**. Over the garbha-griha is the tallest part of the mandir, which might be a tower, or a spire, or a dome. This shows the importance of the deities, and symbolises the movement of the mind from ignorance to enlightenment. Many Hindus show respect for the deities by walking clockwise around them, and so there is enough space allowed as a passage for worshippers to do this.

When Hindus visit the mandir, they take off their shoes, as a sign of respect and in order to keep the temple clean. Most mandirs therefore have a porch or hall where shoes can be kept during worship. As they enter the building, they will pass smaller shrines which house the vehicles (vahana) or consorts of the deities in the garbha-griha. For example, if the mandir is dedicated to Rama, it might have Hanuman, the monkey god, in an entrance shrine, or if it is dedicated to Shiva, there might be a murti of Nandi the bull.

The space in front of the garbha-griha is called the **mandapa**, where worshippers can gather to look at the murtis and make their offerings. Most Hindu mandirs have at least one priest, who takes the offerings from the worshippers and presents them to the murtis.

Discussion

Why do you think that worship in the home is usually considered to be the responsibility of the woman?

Activity

1 Explain the main features of a Hindu mandir.

2 Describe what Hindus do when they practise puja in the home.

Worship in the mandir

Worship in the mandir usually has three main features:

Bhajan – the singing of sacred songs, using words from famous Hindu poets such as Surdas and Tulsidas.

Havan – the sacrifice of sacred fire to the deities. Fire represents the Vedic god Agni, and is also the way in which sacrifices are consumed, and so using flames in worship is an ancient way for Hindus to show a meeting between the worshipper and god. The priest uses ghee (clarified butter) and wood to light a small symbolic fire in front of the murtis.

Arti – the five flames of the arti lamp are waved in front of the murti and then shared around the people present, who pass their hands over the flame and then over their heads in the same way as they do when worshipping at home.

Food and fasting

Hindus are committed to the principle of **ahimsa** (non-violence), and because of this, most Hindus are vegetarian. Meat-eating is considered by many to be impure, or spiritually polluting, and is avoided, especially by members of the Brahmin (priestly) caste of Hindus. Hindus believe that all life is sacred, and so it is wrong to take life, whether human or animal. There are also practical reasons for vegetarianism, especially in India; meat is more expensive to buy, and more difficult to keep fresh in a hot climate. The vast majority of Hindus avoid all meat and meat products, including fish and eggs, and instead eat a diet of spiced vegetables, lentils, rice and bread. Different parts of India have their own traditional dishes.

Some Hindus do eat meat, but beef is prohibited, because the cow has a special status in Hinduism as a sacred animal. The bull is associated with the god Shiva, and the cow with the god Krishna. The cow is believed to symbolise life itself, because it is involved in so many different aspects of daily life in India; as a source of milk and milk products (especially the ghee, or clarified butter, which is used as an offering to the gods), as labour in the fields pulling ploughs and carts, and as a source of fuel when dried cow manure is used to make fires. For these reasons, cows are treated with great respect, and to harm a cow or to eat beef would be considered wrong by Hindus. It would result in bad karma, and bring misfortune.

Fasting is an important part of the religious life of many Hindus. Going without food on holy days is seen as a good discipline, because it concentrates the mind on God and encourages the worshipper not to be too attached to pleasures such as good food, but to realise that ultimate truth is more important. Going without any kind of food is something which is done only by those who are fit and healthy, and only on special occasions. More often, Hindus will undertake a partial fast, where they only eat certain sorts of food and go without others. Some people, especially women, fast for one day each week as a religious discipline, and as a way of asking God to protect their husbands.

The use of music and art in Hindu worship

Music is used in worship when sacred songs are sung (**bhajan**), and is sometimes accompanied with instruments such as drums or small finger cymbals. Dance is a popular way of telling religious stories; for example, the Bharata-natyam tradition of Indian dance uses singers, drums and a dancer to tell stories of the gods, such as the childhood of Krishna, in a way that captures the imagination, especially for children or for those unable to read. The costumes and elaborate hand and eye movements of Hindu dancers all contribute to a tradition which goes back for hundreds of years.

Art has always been an important part of Hinduism. Sculptures and carvings representing the deities are an important feature of every Hindu home and temple. Paintings and batiks also feature prominently in Hindu homes, depicting the deities or episodes from the stories of the Ramayana or Bhagavad Gita. In India, many of the mandirs are completely covered with carvings, often in frieze designs. **Murtis** are usually beautifully made from a variety of materials, and their presence in the home and the mandir gives Hindus an object on which to focus their prayers and worship.

Sometimes, Hindu art is used in traditional ways at special occasions. At weddings, the hands and feet of the bride are decorated with henna to make patterns known as **mehndi**. At the festival of Divali, patterns called **rangoli** are drawn on the pavements in coloured chalks, or with sprinkled powders, to welcome in the new year.

Symbols in Hinduism

The most important symbol in Hinduism is the sacred sound **AUM**, sometimes spelt **Om**. It is found everywhere in Hinduism in the temples and in shrines in the home, and at weddings and on greetings cards. It is made of three sounds, A, U and M, and when it is spoken and heard, it has different levels of symbolism. It can represent:

- the three great deities, Brahma, Shiva and Vishnu
- the three worlds of earth, atmosphere and heaven
- the cycle of birth, death and eternity
- three of the most ancient and important Hindu texts – Samaveda, Yajurveda and Rigveda.

The Aum sound is believed to be eternal, and chanting it during meditation is believed to bring the worshipper closer to God and to ultimate reality.

The **swastika** is also an important Hindu symbol, although it has become much less popular in the West since the Second World War gave it a different and much more sinister meaning. The swastika is an ancient symbol, representing prosperity

and good fortune, and is used by Hindus at times of celebration, such as weddings and Divali.

Discussion

Do you think that meat-eating is a form of violence? Are there some animals that you would eat, but others that you never would? Give reasons for your answer.

Activity

1 Explain why many Hindus are vegetarian, and why they avoid beef in particular.

2 Draw the Aum symbol and the swastika, and explain what each represents.

Islam

Muslim worship

In Islam, there are many ways in which spirituality and worship are demonstrated.

'Islam' means submission to the will of Allah and it is by living according to this will that Muslims can demonstrate their belief.

At the centre of Islamic life and belief are the Five Pillars:

● **Shahadah** – the declaration of faith which states

> There is no god except Allah, Muhammad is the Messenger of Allah.

● **Salah** – five compulsory daily prayers for communicating with, and worshipping Allah. These are performed under specific conditions, in the manner taught by the Prophet Muhammad ﷺ and are said in Arabic.

The prayers are said at fixed times and can be performed alone or with other people. The five set times during which these can be said are:

Fajr – from dawn until just before sunset

Zuhr – after mid-day until afternoon

'Asr – from late afternoon until just before sunset

Maghrib – after sunset until daylight ends

'Isha' – night until midnight or dawn

Before prayer Muslims must clean themselves by performing wudu. In order, people wash their hands, mouth, nose, face, arms, head, ears and feet.

Now they are ready to repeat the set prayers.

● **Zakah** – this is literally 'the purification of wealth by the payment of an annual welfare due'. Muslims pay 2½ % of their savings each year. Zakah began in al-Madinah to care for the widows and orphans. Wealth is a gift from Allah and should be shared. The remainder of a person's wealth is kept pure and people are kept free from greed and selfishness. As well as this, Muslims are urged to make additional voluntary payments called **Sadaqah**.

When praying all Muslims follow a particular set of prayers and prayer positions as taught by Muhammad ﷺ.

- **Hajj** – the annual pilgrimage to Makkah, which each Muslim must carry out at least once in a lifetime if he or she has the health and wealth. A Muslim man who has completed Hajj is called Hajji, and a woman, Hajjah. The pilgrimage is made during Dhul Hijjah, the twelfth month.
- **Sawm** – fasting from just before dawn until sunset during the month of **Ramadan**, the ninth month. Muslims must abstain from all food and drink (including water) as well as smoking and sexual relations.

The fulfilment of these five duties is the duty of every Muslim as a demonstration of their obedience to God's wishes.

These five actions are all **ibadah** – these are acts of worship which are performed with the intention to obey Allah.

One of the major demonstrations of Islamic spirituality lies in Shari'ah. This is living according to Muslim law. In countries where the government is Muslim, the whole of the legal system is based on Shari'ah. Shari'ah itself is formed from the teachings and instruction found in the Qur'an and Sunnah.

All Muslim worship takes place in Arabic. This was the language of Muhammad ﷺ and the Qur'an was received and written in Arabic. All prayer is said in Arabic and Muslims have a duty to learn Arabic in order that they can understand worship and also read the Qur'an. Unlike most other sacred writings, the Qur'an is not translated into other languages. It is permitted to make a version of it in non-Arabic languages but it is believed that these cannot be accurate and that to understand Islam and Allah's will it is necessary to learn to understand it in Arabic.

Discussion

Do you think it is an advantage or a disadvantage for a religion to have strict rules to follow?

Activity

1 What do you consider to be the most important aspects of Muslim worship.

2 Explain what is meant by 'ibadah'.

The mosque

The masjid (place of prostration) or mosque, is the central place of worship for Muslims. Muslim men gather there for **Salat-ul-Jumu'ah**, midday prayer on Fridays, and listen to the **Khutbah** or speech given by the Imam.

In the Qur'an rules are given about the mosque:

> The mosques of Allah shall be visited and maintained by such as believe in Allah and the Last Day, establish regular prayers, and practise regular charity, and fear none (at all) except Allah. It is they who are expected to be on true guidance.
>
> (Surah 9:18)

In fact, the whole world can be thought of as a mosque because it is all God's creation. A mosque belongs to Allah and cannot be owned by any individual or organisation. In the same way a mosque cannot be sold, mortgaged or rented.

Many mosques are very beautiful buildings. The design may vary from place to place but there are certain features that all mosques must have.

The main open space in the mosque is the prayer hall. One wall must face the **Ka'bah** in **Makkah** and a **mihrab** or niche in the wall shows Muslims the direction in which they must face when they pray. In addition there is a platform or **minbar** on which the Imam stands to give the Khutbah. There will be a separate area for women to pray and this is behind a curtain or screen so that they will not distract the men.

Most mosques have at least one **minaret** from which the **Adhan** or call to prayer is made. A dome represents the heavens and God's creation. Finally, there will be facilities with running water so that people can perform wudu.

Mosques are usually very simple buildings and yet they may be highly decorated. There are no pictures, statues or photographs showing living beings because this would be against Muslim teaching. However, the walls may be decorated with verses from the Qur'an, the name and attributes of Allah and the name of Muhammad ﷺ in Arabic calligraphy.

Although the mosque is the centre of the Muslim community, most daily worship takes place in the home where prayers may be said and where people can study the Qur'an. Because Muslims have to pray five times a day, many of these prayers will be said in their place of work or whilst travelling. The important aspect of prayer is that it is said, it does not matter where provided that the place is clean and the Muslim can pray towards Makkah.

No music is used in Muslim worship. In fact many Muslims would say that no music is permitted within Islam.

The Qur'an says that:

> But there are, among men, those who purchase idle tales, without knowledge (or meaning), to mislead (men) from the Path of Allah and throw ridicule (on the Path): for such there will be a humiliating penalty.
>
> *(Surah 31:6)*

Music is seen as one of these 'idle diversions'. Also, the Prophet Muhammad ﷺ warned that:

> there will be (at some future time) people from my Ummah (nation) who will seek to make lawful… the use of musical instruments.
>
> *(Sahih Al-Bukhari)*

Tawhid and shirk

Tawhid and **shirk** are two very important ideas in Muslim belief and are closely related to each other.

Tawhid is the belief in the Oneness of Allah – absolute monotheism. This idea was a significant part of the message of Muhammad ﷺ. It is found particularly in the later, Makkan surahs. Allah is not only the creator but also the sustainer of the universe and he rules and controls everything.

Muslims have to place Allah first in their lives. If, for example, Muslims were to live in order simply to make money this would be shirk. Shirk is the sin of believing in anything other than Allah or of associating anything with Allah as equal to him and is the most serious sin possible.

It is for this reason that images, pictures or statues are forbidden in Islam. To make an image of a living person or creature is shirk because Allah is the sole creator.

Food and fasting

For the whole of the month of Ramadan, all adult Muslims are required to fast during the hours of daylight. Daylight is when a white thread and a black thread can be distinguished from each other.

> Until the white thread of dawn appear to you distinct from its black thread
>
> *(Surah 2:187)*.

During the fast Muslims should not eat, drink, smoke or have any activity. People are allowed to clean their teeth and accidental swallowing does not count.

If someone deliberately breaks their fast without a good reason they have to provide a meal for 60 people or, alternatively, fast for a further 60 days. Children under the age of puberty, women during menstruation, pregnancy or breastfeeding, the old, the sick, travellers and soldiers are exempt. However, apart from the elderly and children, all the others should make up the missing days as soon as possible.

Allah sees everything and knows what is in people's hearts so there is no point in trying to cheat.

At the end of each day Muslims say:

> 'O God! For your sake we have fasted and now we break the fast with food you have given us.'

Each day, Muhammad ﷺ broke his fast with some dates or a drink and most Muslims follow this tradition by eating something that is light. Later the whole family joins together for a big meal. However, Muslims are not supposed to eat too much at this meal because this would go against the whole idea of the fast.

Discussion

Consider whether music might help people in worship or whether it might distract them.

Activity

Describe the main features of a service of worship in a mosque.

Jewish worship

Jews are born into Judaism. Everyone who has a Jewish mother is a Jew and should follow G-d's will as an expression of their spirituality. This will is contained in the Ten Commandments and is stated in the Shema:

> Hear, O Israel: HASHEM is our G-d, HASHEM, the One and Only. You shall love HASHEM, your G-d, with all your heart, with all your soul and with all your resources. Let these matters that I command you today be upon your heart. Teach them thoroughly to your children and speak of them while you sit in your home, while you walk on the way, when you retire and when you arise. Bind them as a sign upon your arm and let them be tefillin between your eyes. And write them on the doorposts of your house and upon your gates.

This if the first of the three paragraphs of the Shema. These paragraphs are found in the Torah in Deuteronomy 6:5–9, Deuteronomy 11:13–21 and Numbers 15:37–41.

Jews believe in G-d as being omnipresent (everywhere), omnipotent (all powerful) and omniscient (all-knowing). These beliefs are found in the teachings of the Tenakh such as in Isaiah 6:1-4.

Jews also restate this belief when they say the Kaddish (see page 80).

Spirituality is expressed in every aspect of Jewish life as they follow the 613 mitzvot or commandments which are found in the Torah. These give rules for many parts of life including clothing, food, sexual relations, and prayer and worship.

Many Jewish ceremonies are based in the home and the family but at the centre of Jewish life and worship in Israel was the Temple in Jerusalem. This temple was first built by King Solomon and then rebuilt by Herod the Great.

Here people offered daily sacrifices according to the rules in the Torah and, at first, the Ark of the Covenant, containing the tablets of stone on which Moses had written the Ten Commandments was kept here.

Many attempts were made by other nations to take the Temple and there are stories of the Jews fighting to keep it. It was finally destroyed by the armies of the Roman Empire in 70 CE and has not been rebuilt. As the House of G-d it had provided a focus for Jews where prayer and worship could be centralised. Following its destruction worship turned to the home and to the synagogues that are found in each Jewish community all over the world. No sacrifices can be performed in a synagogue but they contain the Sefer Torah copies of the scrolls of the Torah.

Jews should pray at least three times a day. The three set times for prayer are:

Shacharit – dawn

Minchah – afternoon

Maariv – evening.

Worship in the synagogue

Jews also go to the **synagogue** to pray and to hear the Torah read. Services are held every day, with the most important time being **Shabbat,** when services are held on Friday evenings and on Saturday mornings.

The synagogue is usually a plain building. The main room, or sanctuary, is an area of seats. The Aron Hakodesh, the ark which contains the scrolls, is usually sited on the wall of the synagogue which faces towards Jerusalem. The scrolls are covered by a door or a curtain and often have richly decorated mantles or covers as well as rimmonim (bells) and a breastplate which represents the breastplate worn by the High Priest in the Temple.

There are no statues, pictures or photographs in the sanctuary because of the commandment:

You shall not make yourself a carved image nor any likeness of that which is in the heavens above or on the earth below or in the waters beneath the earth. You shall not prostrate yourself to them nor worship them; for I am HASHEM, your G-d – a jealous G-d.
(Exodus 20:4–5)

There may be a seven-branched candlestick called a **menorah** which represents the candlestick described as being in the Temple, and there will be a **bimah** or platform from which the Torah is read. Orthodox synagogues have a gallery for the women or a partition which they sit behind. This is to prevent the men being distracted from their prayers by the presence of women. In Progressive synagogues men and women will sit together.

The worship in a synagogue is lead by a **chazan** who will sing much of the service. In Orthodox services, although there is probably an organ, the singing is always unaccompanied on Shabbat because playing musical instruments is considered to be work and no form of work is permitted on Shabbat, except in very special circumstances. In Progressive synagogues the organ may be used.

Hebrew is the ancient language of the Jews and the Torah is always read in Hebrew. In Progressive synagogues some of the prayers during the service may be in English but Orthodox Jews have all services and prayers in Hebrew.

Jews believe that the Torah is the word of G-d and that it should be written and read in the original language. However, the scriptures are available in many languages for people to study and so that those who cannot read Hebrew can still understand them.

Discussion

Consider whether music might help people in worship or whether it might distract them.

Activity

Describe the main features of a service of worship in a synagogue.

Worship in the home

Although the synagogue is important to Jews the main place for worship remains in the home and within the family. Here the many food laws have to be carried out. On Friday evenings a special meal is prepared and two candles are lit to welcome Shabbat into the house. At the end of Shabbat the service of **Havdalah** is performed as the new week begins. Also worship within the home reminds people of the importance of the family in Jewish life.

Jewish culture is very rich and has been influenced by the places Jews live. Judaism is an ancient religion and since the destruction of the Temple Jews have lived all over the world in the Diaspora. Therefore, Jewish spirituality is expressed in many ways through music, art and the architecture and design of synagogues. The design of the synagogue, echoing that of the Temple in Jerusalem, will also be influenced by the culture of the country in which the Jews live. Many synagogues are modern with modern designs but, in order to obey the Ten Commandments, still there will be no presentation of living beings.

Instead there may be sacred texts used as decoration, and symbols such as the **Magen David** – the Star of David.

In the home there are traditional Jewish objects such as Shabbat candlesticks, a special plate and knife for the **challah** and a cloth (**decke**) to cover it; a havdalah spice box; a seder plate (for Pesach) and a **Hanukiah**, the seven-branched candlestick used at **Hanukah**. Also, on every doorpost except the bathroom, is a **mezuzah**.

Prayer

Prayer is a very important aspect of Judaism. If Jews are at home or at work during the prayer times, they will stop their activity and pray wherever they are. Although there are regular set prayers for the times of day, including the Shema which is always said on getting up and on going to bed, Jews are also encouraged to use informal spontaneous prayers.

Synagogue services consist almost entirely of readings from the Torah and Haftarah and prayers taken from the Tenakh. Throughout the service G-d is praised.

Food and fasting

After the Creation of the world, G-d said:

> Let us make Man in Our image, after Our likeness. They shall rule over the fish of the sea, the birds of the sky, and over the animal, the whole earth, and every creeping thing that creeps upon the earth.
>
> *(Genesis 1:26)*

> God said, 'Behold, I have given all herbage yielding seed that is on the surface of the entire earth, and every tree that has seed-yielding fruit; it shall be yours for food'.
>
> *(Genesis 1:29)*

At this point it seems that people were not meant to eat animals, but, after the flood, G-d told Noah:

> Every moving thing that lives shall be food for you; like the green herbage I have given you everything. But flesh; with its soul its blood you shall not eat.
>
> *(Genesis 9:3–4)*

So it seems that at this time G-d intended people to eat all kinds of meat provided that there was no blood in it.

Later, when the Israelites were in the desert after they had escaped from Egypt, they were given much stricter rules to follow. These can be found in the book of Leviticus (Leviticus 11:1–10, 13–23, 41–42).

HASHEM spoke to Moses and to Aaron, saying to them. Speak to the Children of Israel, saying: These are the creatures that you may eat from among all the animals that are upon the earth. Everything among the animals that has a split hoof, which is completely separated into double hooves, and that brings up its cud – that one you may eat. …

This may you eat from everything that is in the water: everything that has fins and scales in the water, in the seas, and in the streams, those may you eat.

There is a list of birds which are forbidden, probably because they live off carrion. Most insects are forbidden as are reptiles.

As well as these rules, Jews are not permitted to eat the sciatic nerve of an animal:

Therefore the Children of Israel are not to eat the displaced sinew on the hip-socket to this day, because he struck Jacob's hip-socket on the displaced sinew.

(Genesis 32:32)

they are not allowed to mix dairy products and meat in the same meal:

You shall not cook a kid in its mother's milk.

(Deuteronomy 14:21b)

and, finally, they should not eat meat and fish together (Shulchan Arukh: Yoreh Deah 87:3).

The food that Jews are able to eat is called **kosher** (permitted), food which they can not eat is **terefah** (forbidden). All meat must be slaughtered by a method known as **schechitah**: a blessing is said over the animal and then it is killed by a single cut across the throat with a sharp knife, it is then hung upside down for the blood to drain out.

This method of killing animals has concerned some people who believe that the so-called 'humane' method, where the animal is stunned before being killed is kinder.

The food laws and their strict observance are central to Jewish life and are a very important aspect of Jewish worship both in the home and beyond.

There are several days in the year when Jews fast but most important is **Yom Kippur**. Every year, in preparation for Yom Kippur, the Day of Atonement, Jews apologise to everyone whom they might have upset or hurt during the year and they also apologise to G-d for everything they have done wrong during the year. They do not make an individual apology but instead they apologise on behalf of everyone, listing all the sins which the Jewish people may have committed.

On Yom Kippur Jews fast for 25 hours in order that they can show obedience to G-d's wishes and also concentrate on prayer.

Discussion

Do you think it is easier to worship in a very plain building, or in one which is highly decorated?

Activity

1 Why do food laws play such an important part in Jewish life?

2 Explain the significance to Jews of Yom Kippur.

43

Practice GCSE questions

Christianity

(a) Describe Christian attitudes towards the use of music and art in worship. (8 marks)

(b) Explain how the architecture of a church helps Christians to worship. (7 marks)

(c) 'God can be worshipped anywhere, so there is no need for churches.'
Do you agree? Give reasons to support your answer, and show that you have thought about different points of view. You must refer to Christianity in your answer. (5 marks)

Hinduism

(a) Describe Hindu attitudes towards the use of music and art in worship. (8 marks)

(b) Explain how the architecture of a mandir helps Hindus to worship. (7 marks)

(c) 'God can be worshipped anywhere, so there is no need for mandirs.'
Do you agree? Give reasons to support your answer, and show that you have thought about different points of view. You must refer to Hinduism in your answer. (5 marks)

Islam

(a) Describe Muslim attitudes towards the use of music and art in worship. (8 marks)

(b) Explain how the architecture of a mosque helps Muslims to worship. (7 marks)

(c) 'God can be worshipped anywhere, so there is no need for mosques.'
Do you agree? Give reasons to support your answer, and show that you have thought about different points of view. You must refer to Islam in your answer. (5 marks)

Judaism

(a) Describe Jewish attitudes towards the use of music and art in worship. (8 marks)

(b) Explain how the architecture of a synagogue helps Jews to worship. (7 marks)

(c) 'G-d can be worshipped anywhere, so there is no need for synagogues.'
Do you agree? Give reasons to support your answer, and show that you have thought about different points of view. You must refer to Judaism in your answer. (5 marks)

Tips

For all four questions

In part (a), you are asked to describe religious attitudes to the use of art and music in worship. The religion you are studying might use music and art a great deal, in which case you might be able to give some examples of how and when they are used. Perhaps you have been studying a religion that does not agree with using music or art in worship, and if so, you need to explain the reasons and say how members of the religion express their beliefs in other ways.

In part (b), you need to be able to describe the architecture of the place of worship for the religion you have been studying. You should not draw in the examination; you have to answer using prose, so you need to use sentences to describe the building. A good answer would explain the different features, and show the ways in which they help the worshipper to think about God, rather than just concentrating on a description.

For part (c), you are being tested on your evaluative skills. You need to show that you recognise that people might have different ideas and opinions. Think about how a religious believer would respond to the statement, and explain the reasons that they might give. Explain your own view. Imagine someone disagreeing, and explain what they might say and the reasons that they might give to support their opinion. Perhaps they might think that religious buildings are a waste of money that should be given to the poor. Perhaps they might think that religious buildings give believers somewhere where they can worship without any distractions.

UNIT 3

Religion and Science

Introduction

Scientific theories about the origins of the world

Since the holy scriptures of the different world religions were written, scientists have come to understand a lot more about the way in which the universe probably began, and the origins of life on earth. Can ancient myths and stories from religion say anything useful about the origins of the world, or has it all been disproved by the scientists? People used to believe that the earth was the centre of the universe, and that the sun, moon and stars were just lights in the sky made to light up the earth. They believed that the whole world existed just so that people could live in it. Now we know that our world is just one tiny planet among many, and that our galaxy is just one of many millions. We know that there are many other life forms apart from our own. Can people still believe that there is something special about human life?

The origins of the universe

Study of the origins of the universe is called **cosmology**. Scientists believe that the universe is much older than people first imagined – about 18 billion years old. Some people have suggested that even this enormous age is not correct; they argue that the universe has always existed, and that there was never a 'beginning' at all. But this view is not widely accepted, because there is quite a lot of evidence to suggest that there was a point at which the universe came into being.

Most scientists believe that the universe was made by a massive explosion, known as the **Big Bang**, which sent matter and gases flying out in all directions. All of the galaxies in the universe were formed, and they are still moving away from each other rapidly as the universe expands. As the gases cooled, they formed the stars and the planets, including the earth. This is not just an imagined idea that people have had, but is supported by evidence; for example, background radiation has been discovered which seems to have been left over from the Big Bang itself. It can be detected with powerful telescopes.

The origins of humanity

The theory of **evolution** is widely accepted by scientists as a way of explaining how humanity came into existence. It was made famous in the nineteenth century by the work of Charles Darwin, who travelled the world on a ship called *The Beagle* in order to study plant and animal life from different countries. His studies led him to the conclusion that the different species in the world had not always existed in the way that we see them today. They had developed gradually, adapting to fit the environment. When conditions change, such as the climate becoming warmer or colder, the members of the species which are best able to cope with the change survive and reproduce and the others die out. The next generations have slightly different characteristics, and so the different species gradually change. The process where the strongest animals and plants survive and the weaker ones die out (become extinct) is known as **natural**

Our planet is just one among many millions, and not the centre of the universe at all.

selection. Darwin published his ideas in a book called *On the Origin of Species*.

Darwin's ideas meant that human beings must have evolved too. At some point in the past, humans did not exist in the form that we know today. People, according to Darwin's theories, share some of their ancestors with apes. They are not an especially important species set above others, but are animals that happen to have adapted well to the modern environment. Also, at one time, there must have been no people at all, so perhaps the world was not made just for the benefit of humanity. Perhaps the religious stories which say that people were made when the world was made can be questioned.

When Darwin's ideas were first published, many people were shocked by them, and refused to accept that they could share ancestors with apes. Cartoons appeared in the newspapers making fun of Darwin. But

as time passed and Darwin's theories were supported by fossil evidence of extinct creatures such as dinosaurs, gradually the theory of evolution became much more widely accepted.

Does everything happen by chance?

Religious believers often say that there is a purpose to the existence of the universe. They argue that each of us is here in the world for a reason, and that the world itself was also made as part of a big plan. But scientific theories often seem to suggest the opposite. They seem to say that we are here just by chance. There is no reason for it, and no plan; it might not have happened this way, but by chance, it did.

Science and religion in conflict

Some people think that, because scientists and religious believers often have very different ideas about the origins of the world, this must mean that science and religion can never agree. Perhaps people have to choose whether to follow scientific ideas, or whether to have religious beliefs instead; perhaps one day scientists will come up with enough evidence to disprove religion. Possibly religious believers will one day be proved right, and the scientists will have firm evidence that there is a God after all. But there are many people who combine a religious faith with a career in science. They think that the more we find out about the world, the more we can learn about God. Maybe it is possible to combine the two different ways of thinking, and to see science and religion as compatible.

Discussion

Is there any need for religious ideas to help in understanding the existence of the universe, now that scientists have explained so much?

When Darwin first introduced his theory of evolution, people refused to believe it and made fun of him.

Christianity

Christian ideas about the origins of the world and of humanity

The Bible gives its own story about how the world was made, and this is different from the views held by most scientists. The book of Genesis, which introduces the Bible, teaches that the universe was made by God, and that God made it all out of nothing.

> In the beginning God created the heavens and the earth. Now the earth was formless and empty, darkness was over the surface of the deep, and the Spirit of God was hovering over the waters. And God said, 'Let there be light,' and there was light.
>
> *(Genesis 1:1–3)*

Genesis describes, in two stories, how God made the world for people to live in. God planned it all, and then made it exactly according to plan, putting everything in its place. Nothing happened by chance or by accident. It was all made because that was what God intended. Everything in the world exists for a reason, and God has a purpose for it.

According to the teachings of Genesis, all of the different species were there from the beginning:

> And God said, 'Let the land produce living creatures according to their kinds: livestock, creatures that move along the ground, and wild animals, each according to its kind.' And it was so. God made the wild animals according to their kinds, the livestock according to their kinds, and all the creatures that move along the ground according to their kinds. And God saw that it was good.
>
> *(Genesis 1:24–25)*

In Genesis, God made men and women as a special creation and gave them pride of place. They were made in the image

of God, and given the Garden of Eden in which to live. Everything was perfect until Adam and Eve disobeyed God.

God made all the different animals, and presented them to the first man so that he could choose names for them, showing that from the very beginning, people had control over the animals:

> Now the LORD God had formed out of the ground all the beasts of the field and all the birds of the air. He brought them to the man to see what he would name them; and whatever the man called each living creature, that was its name.
>
> *(Genesis 2:19)*

This teaching has presented difficulties for some Christians, who realise that the story in the book of Genesis contradicts scientific ideas about evolution, because it says that all the different species were there from the start, rather than evolving gradually. It also contradicts scientific theories about how the universe began, because it does not mention any explosion

The book of Genesis teaches that people were present on the earth right from the beginning.

or expanding universe. It gives the impression that the Earth existed in the way we know it today, right from the start, rather than gradually cooling over millions of years.

Many modern Christians believe that the scientists are probably right, and that the universe began with a Big Bang. They also believe that people evolved gradually, rather than being created in the beginning as a completed species. These Christians believe that the creation stories in the Bible are a poetic way of describing important truths, but that they tell the truth using myth – stories which contain important truths, but do not necessarily describe exactly what happened historically. The events in the Bible are not always meant to be taken literally. The Bible accounts are perhaps rather like a hymn, praising God for creation rather than giving accurate details about how everything began.

Some Christians, however, believe that the Biblical accounts are literally true. The Bible, they believe, comes from God, and God does not make mistakes. If God says that this is how the world began, then it is true, whatever the scientists might think. These Christians believe that interpreting Genesis as a myth is dangerous, because people might then interpret a lot of other important events as myth too, such as the Virgin Birth or the resurrection of Jesus, and say that they did not really happen.

Christian views about people and animals

According to Christianity, people are different from the rest of the animal world, because unlike animals, they have souls. In Genesis, when God makes the other animals, they are made just as the plants are made; but when Adam is created, he is special. Humanity is made 'in the image of God':

> So God created man
> in his own image,
> in the image of God
> he created him;
> male and female
> he created them.
>
> *(Genesis 1:27)*

In Genesis, people are seen to be a special creation, different from everything else in the world. It is not clear what it means to be made 'in the image of God'. Perhaps it means that the writers of Genesis thought that people actually looked like God; or perhaps they meant that humans share something of the nature of God. When Adam is created, God gives him something extra, which the animals do not have, and this is symbolised as the 'breath of God'.

> the LORD God formed the man from the dust of the ground and breathed into his nostrils the breath of life, and the man became a living being.
>
> *(Genesis 2:7)*

Christians believe that people, unlike animals, have a soul, something which does not die when the body dies, but can live on after death. For this reason, people are different from other animals, in Christian belief. Their lives are sacred, and they have special rights and duties which other animals do not share.

Discussion

Do you think it is possible for modern people to believe the story of Adam and Eve? If the story is not literally true, does that mean the whole Bible is wrong?

Activity

1 What do you think people might mean when they say that Genesis is a 'myth'?

2 Explain why Christians might disagree about the theory of evolution.

Christian ideas about stewardship

Christians, like Jews, believe that people were put on the earth to act as 'stewards'. A steward is someone who takes responsibility for the welfare of others, for example at a festival a steward might show people where to park their cars or where to find lost children. In the Bible, people were given this kind of care-taking role as soon as they were created:

> Then God said, 'Let us make humankind in our image, according to our likeness; and let them have dominion over the fish of the sea, and over the birds of the air, and over the cattle, and over all the wild animals of the earth, and over every creeping thing that creeps upon the earth.'
>
> *(Genesis 1:26)*

Christians believe that this means they should take responsibility for the earth and the other species in it. They should care for it, protect it, and preserve it for future generations. They should recognise that the world belongs to God, and that they are looking after it for God; it does not belong to them. The writer of Psalm 24 reminds people that God the King is the creator of the world:

> The earth is the Lord's, and all that is in it, The world, and those who live in it.
>
> *(Psalm 24:1)*

Christianity also teaches that people should not take and use more than is necessary. They should not be greedy, and judge their success in life by the amount that they consume, but should concentrate instead on God and on caring for the poor. It is wrong, according to Christianity, to be too concerned about having possessions and wearing the most fashionable clothes:

> He said to his disciples, 'Therefore I tell you, do not worry about your life, what you will eat, or about your body, what you will wear. For life is more than food, and the body more than clothing.'
>
> *(Luke 12:22–23)*

Although the Bible contains many teachings warning people about greed, people in rich countries still consume far more than they really need, and are using up the world's natural resources a lot more quickly than they can be replaced.

Christian responses to environmental issues

Christians have not always been concerned about environmental issues. Some people, in fact, blame Christianity for giving people the impression that they have the right to do whatever they want with the world, because of the Biblical teaching that people should rule over the other species. In general, the Church has not encouraged people to be more aware of environmental issues, and the organisations that have done the most to help protect the environment have not been Christian.

Christianity teaches that people are responsible for the world and all the creatures in it. Although they are allowed to rule over the animals, they should also protect them when necessary.

But recently, Christians have become very much more aware that the environment faces serious problems. Large areas of rainforest have been destroyed, the seas have been fished too intensively, poisonous waste has been carelessly dumped and many species have been lost forever because of human actions. Many Christians believe that they have a duty, as stewards of the earth, to take better care of the world around them. Sometimes, this involves joining campaigns and protests, such as those organised by Greenpeace or the Worldwide Fund for Nature.

Christians can also take more care in their everyday lives to avoid causing unnecessary damage to the environment. For example, they might make an effort to recycle things rather than just throw them away. They might try to reduce the amount of pollution produced by cars, by cycling to work or by using public transport. They might try to find out the environmental policies of different candidates whenever there are elections, so that they can use their votes in ways that support care for the environment.

Discussion

Some people say that Christians are partly to blame for problems with the environment, because they encourage the view that humans are supposed to rule over other animals and plants. Do you think this view is fair?

Activity

1 Explain what a 'steward' does, and why Christians believe that people are the 'stewards' of the earth.

2 Find out more about the problems facing the environment today – you might visit the web-sites of Friends of the Earth or Greenpeace. Make a list of some of the ways in which Christians could help to conserve the environment.

ॐ Hinduism

Hindu ideas about the origins of the world and humanity

Hinduism teaches that the origins of the world are mysterious. In a hymn called the Nasadiya Sukta, the writer looks in wonder at how the world came to be. He or she assumes that there must have been a time where there was absolutely nothing:

> There was neither non-existence nor existence then; there was neither the realm of space nor the sky which is beyond.
>
> What stirred? Where? In whose protection? Was there water, bottomlessly deep?
>
> *(Nasadiya Sukta)*

Many questions are raised, but the writer does not give an answer, beyond saying that only God knows what happened; or perhaps even God himself does not know:

> Whence this creation has arisen – perhaps it formed itself, or perhaps it did not – the one who looks down on it, in the highest heaven, only he knows – or perhaps he does not know.
>
> *(Nasadiya Sukta)*

This ancient hymn expresses feelings of awe and wonder. It does not try to give any suggestions of what might have happened. But other passages in Hindu literature give other ideas.

In a hymn known as the Purusha Sukta the creation of the world is explained in a myth in which a great 'cosmic man' is sacrificed in order to make the world. It is seen as the first sacrifice, and it sets the pattern for Hindus to make symbolic sacrifices to the gods every day in their homes as well as in the temples. Sacrifice is seen as 'the other side of the coin' to creation, so that when sacrifices are made, the gods continue to create and sustain the world, and then it continues in its existence. In the Purusha Sukta, different parts of the 'cosmic man', known as Purusha, make different elements of the universe:

> His mouth became the Brahmin; his arms were made into the Warrior, his thighs the People, and from his feet the Servants were born. The moon was born from his mind; from his eye the sun was born. Indra and Agni came from his mouth, and from his vital breath the Wind was born.
>
> *(Purusha Sukta 12, 13)*

The Nasadiya Sukta does not give an answer to questions of how the world came into being; it says that it is a mystery that we will probably never understand.

According to this hymn, the different social classes or **varnas** were formed. It suggests that people existed from the beginning of time, not as primitive Neanderthals or any other early form of humanity, but in the same form as we know people today, complete with different social groups. In the hymn, the other species were all created separately in the beginning as well, and there is no suggestion of any form of evolution.

Hindus also teach that the whole of nature works in a cycle. Everything is subject to change; things come into being, grow, change, fade away and die, and then other things come into being again and the whole cycle repeats itself. The theory of evolution fits in quite well with this belief, because both views understand the world in terms of change, rather than as a complete and finished object. Scientific theories about the universe expanding and contracting also fit well with an Eastern view of everything coming into and out of existence.

The religious beliefs of Hindus do not clash with the theories of science in the way that many other beliefs do. This is because, in Hinduism, there is no absolute set of beliefs which everyone has to have. People have all different kinds of understandings of God, and are still Hindus; some Hindus believe that ultimately, there is no God at all. Because there are no rules about what must be believed, it does not present a difficulty for Hindus when scientists come up with theories that are different from the Hindu myths. Hinduism does not insist that its followers take the sacred writings literally, and therefore if people are inclined to think that the theories of modern science are right, there is no problem.

The Hindu writings themselves do not agree about the origins of the world. Some say that the world was made by God; others say that the gods were created after the world was formed; some say that the world is eternal and has always existed, so there was no creation at all. The central message of Hindu teaching about the origins of the world is that it is a mystery, beyond human understanding, and a question that will never be completely answered.

Discussion

Do you think we will ever understand exactly how the world began?

Activity

1 How far do you think Hindu views of the origins of the world are compatible with the views of science?

2 Why do you think that religions often use myths to explain how the world began, instead of just giving facts?

Hindu views about people and animals

Hindus believe that all living things, whether they are people, animals or plants, all come from the same source, and are all united and related to one another because of their relationship with God. Many Hindus believe that it is not only possible to be reborn as another human being, but that someone could be born into the animal kingdom too. Therefore, there is a chance that any animal might be a relation reborn; it could be an ancestor. Perhaps, in past lives, a boy and his dog used to be brothers. Because of this link between all living creatures, many Hindus are vegetarian, partly because killing another creature for food brings the danger of killing a relative, and partly because meat is seen to be unclean.

Animals are also closely associated with many of the Hindu deities. The animals are 'vehicles' (vahana) of the gods; for example, the peacock is the vehicle of the goddess Saraswati, and the tortoise is associated with the elephant-headed god Ganesha.

Hindus believe that humans are higher than animals in the natural order of things, in just the same way as a priest is superior to a shoemaker; but this does not give humans the right to treat animals with any kind of cruelty. The concept of **ahimsa** (harmlessness) is central to Hinduism, and it includes not harming animals.

Hindu responses to environmental issues

In India, many people live in poverty, and environmental issues which are important in the West are not particularly relevant. For example, the use of too much packaging in supermarkets is not a concern in India, where most of the food is grown at home or bought from the market, and when there is often not much to buy. Recycling is a way of life for poorer people, and nothing is allowed to go to waste if a use can be found for it. Those who are very poor sometimes search rubbish dumps, in the hope of finding something useful that someone else has thrown away. Ideas such as car-sharing and energy-efficient light bulbs are not appropriate in India except for a few. Many homes do not have cars or electricity, and so for most people there is no opportunity to be wasteful with fuel even if they wanted to.

Instead, the environmental issues which are of most concern to Hindus in India are to do with basic hygiene. People are encouraged not to pollute water sources, because of the rapid spread of diseases such as cholera and typhoid. The need for householders to dispose of their rubbish carefully is emphasised, in order to keep the streets clean and discourage vermin.

For Hindus, there are two main reasons for wanting to protect the environment:

● The whole world is an aspect of God, and therefore care for the world is a way of showing respect to God.

Peacocks are protected animals in India, because of their association with the goddess Saraswati.

- Because Hindus believe in rebirth, the future of the planet is of immediate concern to them, as they will be living in it themselves when they are reborn.

Hindus in India are concerned about environmental issues such as the conservation of forests and tree-planting, to try and protect wildlife and also to provide a moisture-trap for areas where drought is a problem. Some Hindus have become involved in projects that use natural sources of energy, such as hydro-electric power, where the force of moving water can be changed into energy to provide electricity to homes. However, the situation is not always simple. Sometimes, in order to provide electricity, dams need to be built to channel the water, and these dams mean that some villages have to be flooded to make way for them and the people have to move elsewhere. This is not an easy choice to make, when people have owned a small patch of land for several generations.

People in richer countries are more responsible for the causes of environmental problems then people in poorer countries such as India. It is the richer countries that produce the oil that is sometimes spilt into the sea, and the chemical waste which is difficult to dispose of safely. The richer countries are the ones which consume most of the world's resources. However, it is often people in poor areas who suffer the consequences of this bad treatment of the environment. If there is climate change, droughts and floods can destroy everything they own. If the seas are polluted or over-fished, the poor people who depend on fishing for their survival are the first to suffer. The worst industrial accident in world history happened in India. In 1984, an American-owned chemical factory in Bhopal leaked a deadly poisonous gas, and thousands of people were killed outright. Many more died slow and painful deaths over the years that followed, or were blinded or suffered other serious injuries. This event led to the chemical industry producing much stricter rules about safety and the protection of the environment.

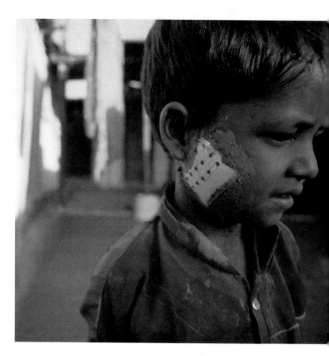

The leaking of poisonous gas from a Union Carbide factory in Bhopal in 1984 was an environmental disaster which affected the lives of thousands of Hindus.

Discussion

Do you think animals should have the same rights as humans? Should we treat some animals (e.g. dogs) better than we treat others (e.g. head lice)? Give reasons for your answers.

Activity

1 Explain why Hindus usually show respect for animals.

2 What are the main environmental issues for most Hindus? Why are these different from the issues that affect people in more developed countries?

Islam

Muslim ideas about the origins of the world and of humanity

The Qur'an contains an account of creation which says that:

> Your Guardian-Lord is Allah, Who created the heavens and the earth in six Days, then He established Himself on the Throne (of authority): He draweth the night as a veil o'er the day, each seeking the other in rapid succession: He created the sun, the moon, and the stars, (all) governed by laws under His Command…
>
> It is He Who sendeth the Winds like heralds of glad tidings, going before His Mercy: when they have carried the heavy-laden clouds, We drive them to a land that is dead, make rain to descend thereon, and produce every kind of harvest therewith…
>
> From the land that is clean and good, by the Will of its Cherisher, springs up Produce, (rich) after its kind…
>
> *(Surah 7:53–58)*

The Qur'an does not give an order of creation, but it says that Allah created everything. The word which is translated here as 'days' is ayyam which means 'long periods' or 'ages'. It would seem then that the Qur'an is simply saying that Allah created the universe over a long period of time.

The creation of humans is also explained:

> I have created Jinns and men, that they may serve Me. No Sustenance do I require of them, nor do I require that they should feed Me. For Allah is He Who gives (all) Sustenance – Lord of Power – Steadfast (forever).
>
> *(Surah 51:56–57)*

The **Jinn** are spirits usually described as being made of fire. They are neither good nor evil. Allah also made **Mala'ikah** who are angels and messengers of Allah. They have no free-will and no physical bodies although they can take on human shape.

Islam has always been very closely linked to science, and modern theories of cosmology and evolution do not create any problem for Muslims. They believe that the Qur'an is the Word of Allah and true, they also believe that Allah is in charge of the world and controls it, but this does not mean that science cannot explain what is not said in the Qur'an.

However, the Qur'an does contain some details that are surprising considering that it was written down long before many scientific discoveries were made:

> Do not the unbelievers see that the heavens and earth were joined together (as one unit of Creation), before We clove them asunder? We made from water every living thing? Will they not then believe?… It is He Who created the Night and the Day, and the sun and the moon: all (the celestial bodies) swim along, each in its rounded course.
>
> *(Surah 21:30, 33)*

This seems to be saying already that life began in what scientists now call the 'primordial soup', as well as showing understanding of the fact that the sun and moon are in particular and separate orbits. Muslims explain this by saying that as such scientific discoveries had not been made at this time, it was God's wish to explain these things through the revelation of the Qur'an.

The Qur'an also explains the passage of water and its role in the growth of life:

> Seest thou not that Allah sends down rain from the sky, and leads it through springs in the earth? Then He causes to grow, therewith, produce of various colours: then it withers; thou wilt see it grow yellow; then He makes it dry up and crumble away.
>
> *(Surah 39:21)*

There is also knowledge that bodies can carry out physical changes on substances:

> And verily in cattle (too) will ye find an instructive Sign. From what is within their bodies, between excretions and blood, We produce, for your drink, milk, pure and agreeable to those who drink it.
>
> *(Surah 16:66)*

Because the Qur'an contains these explanations of life, scientific discoveries are welcomed and accepted as they are seen as further explanations of the wonder of Allah's creation. Neither arguments about cosmology or evolution create any real problem for Muslims, instead they demonstrate humanity's gradual understanding of what was already revealed.

Discussion

'Scientific theories about the origins of life are bound to be more reliable than those in ancient sacred texts.' Consider this statement and different points of view about it.

Activity

Explain why modern theories of evolution might be acceptable to Muslims.

Muslim ideas about the place of humanity in the world

It is clear from the teachings of Islam that Allah is seen as the creator of the world and that humans are only here as 'vice-regents' or 'trustees' – they are to look after the world and rule it as Allah wished but they do not own it. Their task is not to destroy the world but to safeguard it for God and for future generations.

> So set thou thy face steadily and truly to the Faith: (establish) Allah's handiwork according to the pattern on which He has made mankind: no change (let there be) in the work (wrought) by Allah.
>
> *(Surah 30:30)*

> Allah is He Who raised the heavens without any pillars that ye can see; then He established Himself on the Throne (of Authority); He has subjected the sun and the moon (to his Law)! Each one runs (its course) for a term appointed. He doth regulate all affairs, explaining the Signs in detail, that ye may believe with certainty in the meeting with your Lord. And it is He Who spread out the earth, and set thereon mountains standing firm, and (flowing) rivers: and fruit of every kind He made in pairs, two and two: He draweth the Night as a veil o'er the Day. Behold, verily in these things there are Signs for those who consider!
>
> *(Surah 13:2–3)*

> Say: 'Shall I seek for (my) Cherisher other than Allah, when He is the Cherisher of all things (that exist)?' Every soul draws the meed of its acts on none but itself: no bearer of burdens can bear the burden of another. Your goal in the end is towards Allah: He will tell you the truth of the things wherein ye disputed. It is He Who hath made you (His) agents, inheritors of the earth…
>
> *(Surah 6:164–165)*

Both Judaism and Christianity have calendars that are based on the regular cycle of seasons through spring, summer, autumn and winter. Many of the festivals of these two religions are tied in to seasonal changes and began in the customs and celebrations of earlier religions. Islam, however, has a religious year which, at 354 days, is shorter than the Western calendar year of usually 365 days. The calendar is based on a 30 year cycle of 360 lunar months which vary between 29 and 30 days. By doing this Islam, unlike some other religions, avoided any link to earlier pagan feasts and so the Muslim religious festivals fall at a different time from year to year.

Therefore, there is no 'harvest festival' in Islam but this does not mean that Muslims are not constantly giving thanks to Allah for his Creation and for their food.

> The Earth is green and beautiful, and Allah has appointed you his stewards over it.

> The whole earth has been created a place of worship, pure and clean.

> Whoever plants a tree and diligently looks after it until it matures and bears fruit is rewarded.

> If a Muslim plants a tree or sows a field and humans and beasts and birds eat from it, all of it is love on his part.
>
> *(Hadith)*

Islam believes that humanity has a responsibility to look after animals:

> And take not life – which Allah has made sacred – except for just cause.
>
> *(Surah 17:33)*

The Prophet taught that animals must be treated well, they must not be branded or beaten. He told a story of a prostitute who, on a hot day, took water from a well to give to a dog. For this one act of kindness, he said, Allah forgave her all her sins.

Islam has always been known for its scientific knowledge and discoveries.

Muslim medicine traditionally concentrated on the use of drugs and herbs rather than on surgery. Ibn Sina, who died in 1037 CE described how epidemics spread and al-Razi (d. 925 CE) was the first scientist to distinguish between smallpox and measles. Remembering also that many traditional Muslim countries are dry and arid with large areas of desert, it is not surprising therefore that Islam has shown itself particularly concerned with plant life and the environment.

How might the arid region in which the religion of Islam began have shaped Muslim ideas about the environment?

The Qur'an is clear on the responsibility of humanity:

> It is He Who hath made You (His) agents, inheritors of the earth.
>
> *(Surah 6:165)*

At the World Wide Fund for Nature International at Assisi in 1986, the Muslim representative, Dr Abdullah Omar Nasseef, stressed the human responsibility to look after the earth:

> The central concept of Islam is tawheed or the Unity of God. Allah is Unity; and His Unity is also reflected in the unity of mankind, and the unity of man and nature. His trustees are responsible for maintaining the unity of His creation, the integrity of the Earth, its flora and fauna, its wildlife and natural environment. Unity cannot be had by discord, by setting one need against another or letting one end predominate over another; it is maintained by balance and harmony. There Muslims say that Islam is the middle path and we will be answerable for how we have walked this path, how we have maintained balance and harmony in the whole of creation around us.

> So unity, trusteeship and accountability, that is tawheed, khalifa and akhrah, the three central concepts of Islam, are also the pillars of the environmental ethics of Islam. They constitute the basic values taught by the Qur'an. It is these values which led Muhammad ﷺ, the Prophet of Islam, to say: 'Whoever plants a tree and diligently looks after it until it matures and bears fruit is rewarded'.

Islam sees the benefit and well-being of all humanity as being a human responsibility in looking after the world which God has created for us to live in and believes that every effort must be made to be 'green' and to slow down and halt destructive trends.

Discussion

Consider the responsibilities of being given control over the earth.

Activity

1 Explain why Muslims usually show respect for animals.

2 What are the main environmental issues for Muslims?

Judaism

Jewish ideas about the origins of the world and of humanity

A concern for the whole of the living world is at the centre of Jewish belief. The Tenakh, or Jewish scriptures, begins with G-d's creation of the world:

> In the beginning of G-d's creating the heavens and the earth – when the earth was astonishingly empty, with darkness upon the surface of the deep, and the Divine Presence hovered upon the surface of the waters – G-d said, 'Let there be light,' and there was light. G-d saw that the light was good, and G-d separated between the light and the darkness. G-d called to the light: 'Day,' and to the darkness He called: 'Night'. And there was evening, and there was morning, one day.
>
> *(Genesis 1:1–5)*

The account of creation in the Jewish scriptures is found in the book of Genesis which is the first book of the Torah. The Torah is sometimes called the Five Books of Moses: Genesis, Exodus, Leviticus, Numbers and Deuteronomy.

Jewish belief is that these books were written down by Moses but were revealed to him by G-d. This means that they are considered to be the 'Word of G-d'. If this is the case, then one would expect the stories in them to be true.

Of course, one of the difficulties with accepting that they are all true is that in some places there are two or more accounts of an event and the versions appear to disagree with one another. Some Jews would say that this is because we do not understand them properly and would then offer an explanation. Progressive Jews, on the other hand, say that the reason for these differences is that the accounts were written by different people and at different times and only later put together in the Torah. They do not say that the Torah is not the Word of G-d but they

accept that it was written down by more than one human being and not simply revealed to Moses.

One of these questions appears in the account of the creation of human beings.

In the first chapter of Genesis it says:

> So G-d created Man in His image, in the image of G-d he created Him; male and female He created them.
>
> *(Genesis 1:27)*

while the version in chapter two is:

> And HASHEM G-d formed the man of dust from the ground, and He blew into his nostrils the soul of life; and the man became a living being.

Jews believe the Torah is the word of G-d.

So HASHEM G-d cast a deep sleep upon the man and he slept; and He took one his sides and He filled in flesh in its place. Then HASHEM G-d fashioned the side that He had taken from the man into a woman, and He brought her to the man. And the man said, 'This time it is bone of my bones and flesh of my flesh. This shall be called Woman, for from man was she taken.'

(Genesis 2:7, 21–23)

Some people have said that these are just two versions of the same event. Others say that it shows that there are two different groups of people writing who have different attitudes towards the relationship between men and women. The first account (which some scholars believed was written much later than the second one) shows G-d creating man and woman at the same time and so they appear equal. In the second account man is created first and woman only exists as part of him: this has led some people to argue that G-d intended women to be under the authority of men and that men are more important in G-d's eyes.

A belief that the Torah is all the work of Moses has caused problems for some Jews and it can also cause difficulties in accepting modern scientific explanations of creation and evolution. Some people believe that it is true as scientific fact which means they cannot accept modern scientific discoveries, however, most people would now see it as an attempt at understanding the existence of life and an explanation of the work of G-d as Creator, Sustainer and Provider to his creation.

This view of G-d looking after the world is expressed in the Book of Psalms in the Jewish Scriptures:

HASHEM, our Master, how mighty is Your Name throughout the earth, [You] Who places Your majesty on the heavens. Out of the mouths of babes and sucklings You have established strength, because of Your enemies, to silence foe and avenger. When I behold Your heavens, the work of Your fingers, the moon and the stars that You have set in place, [I think,] 'What is frail man that You should remember him, and the son of mortal man that You should be mindful of him?' Yet, You have made him but slightly less than the angels, and crowned him with soul and splendor. You give him dominion over Your handiwork, You placed everything under his feet: sheep and cattle, all of them, even the beasts of the field; the birds of the sky and the fish of the sea; for [man] even traverses the lanes of the sea. HASHEM, our Master, how mighty is Your Name throughout the earth!

(Psalm 8: 2–10)

Discussion

What difference does it make whether the Torah is the word of G-d or writings by people who were inspired?

Activity

1 What do you think people might mean when they say that Genesis is a 'myth'?

2 Explain why Jews might disagree about the theory of evolution.

Jewish ideas about the place of humanity in the world

The relationship between people and animals

The Jewish scriptures do not have very much to say about animal rights. Animals are seen as very valuable and they were offered as sacrifices to G-d in the Temple in Jerusalem.

However, it is clear that the early Jews were concerned about their animals. G-d gave Adam control over all the animals:

> And G-d said, 'Let us make Man in our Own image, after Our likeness. They shall rule over the fish of the sea, the birds of the sky, and over the animal, the whole earth, and every creeping thing that creeps upon the earth.' So G-d created Man in His image, in the image of G-d He created him; male and female He created them. G-d blessed them and G-d said to them, 'Be fruitful and multiply, fill the earth and subdue it; and rule over the fish of the sea, the bird in the sky, and every living thing that moves on the earth.'
> *(Genesis 1:26–28)*

and:

> Now, HASHEM G-d had formed out of the ground every beast of the field and every bird of the sky, and brought them to the man to see what he would call each one; and whatever the man called each living creature, that remained its name. And the man assigned names to all the cattle and to the birds of the sky and to every beast of the field.
> *(Genesis 2:19–20)*

Knowing the name of a person or animal was believed to give you special power over them.

It is here that humanity's stewardship of the planet begins. This stewardship of the world is seen both as a gift and an obligation.

That animals are to be shown respect is shown in several passages:

> You shall not muzzle an ox in its threshing.
> *(Deuteronomy 25:4)*

> The righteous one knows [the needs of] his animal's soul.
> *(Proverbs 12:10)*

Animals are also mentioned in the Ten Commandments:

> Safeguard the Sabbath day to sanctify it, as HASHEM, your G-d, has commanded you. Six days shall you labour and accomplish all your work; but the seventh day is Sabbath to HASHEM, your G-d, you shall not do any work – you, your son, your daughter, your slave, your maidservant, your ox, your donkey, and your every animal, and your convert within your gates, in order that your slave and your maidservant may rest like you.
> *(Deuteronomy 5:12–14)*

It appears that animals were to be shown concern like human beings and to be given a day's rest.

Some Jews are vegetarians through choice, but there is no religious reason why they should choose this. However, some people believe that Jews should work towards becoming vegetarian and that this was G-d's original intention for them.

There are no clear Jewish rulings on the use of animals for scientific experiments, but these experiments should be necessary and, as far as possible, suffering should be avoided.

Jewish responses to environmental issues

Every year, at the New Year festival of Rosh Hashanah, Jews give thanks to G-d for the creation of the world because, although humanity has the role of steward, the Tenakh shows that the earth is still G-d's possession:

HASHEM's is the earth and its fullness,
the inhabited land and those who dwell
in it.

(Psalm 24:1)

The scriptures also lay down regulations
about how the earth is to be treated:

When you besiege a city for many days
to wage war against it to seize it, do
not destroy its trees by swinging an axe
against them…

(Deuteronomy 20:19a)

The Jewish respect for trees is reflected in
the annual festival of **Tu B'Shevat** – New
Year for Trees, which takes place on the
15th day of the Jewish month of Shevat.
This has been especially important since
the founding of the State of Israel in 1948,
as Israelis have worked to reclaim the
desert by regularly planting trees. Jews
around the world collect money to send to
Israel for this festival.

In Israel, irrigation
schemes have 'made
the desert bloom'.

Another regulation applies to the use of the
land. It was recognised that agricultural
land needed to be rested if it was to
continue to produce good crops and the
book of Leviticus requires that once every
50 years the land should be rested in a Year
of Jubilee (see Leviticus 25:8 – 11).

At the 1986 meeting of the World Wide
Fund for Nature International held at
Assisi, Rabbi Arthur Hertzberg said that:

…when the whole world is in peril,
when the environment is in danger of
being poisoned and various species,
both plant and animal are becoming
extinct. It is our Jewish responsibility to
put the defence of the whole of nature
at the very centre of our concern. …
The encounter of G-d and man in
nature is thus conceived in Judaism as a
seamless web with man as the leader
and custodian of the natural world.
Even in the many centuries when Jews
were most involved in their own
immediate dangers and destiny, this
universalist concern has never
withered. In this century, Jews have
experienced the greatest tragedy of
their history when one third of their
people were murdered by unnatural
men and, therefore, we are today

particularly sensitive to the need for a
world in which each of G-d's creations
is what He intended it to be. Now,
when the whole world is in peril, when
the environment is in danger of being
poisoned and various species, both
plant and animal, are becoming extinct,
it is our Jewish responsibility to put the
defence of the whole of nature at the
very centre of our concern. Two men
were out on the water in a rowboat.
Suddenly, one of them started to saw
under his feet. He maintained that it
was his right to do whatever he wished
with the place which belonged to him.
The other answered him that they were
in the rowboat together; the hole that
he was making would sink both of
them.

(Vayikra Rabbah 4:6)

In the Jewish prayer book there are
berachots or blessings. Many of these are
concerned with the natural world and
show how Jews see the work of G-d in
everything around them:

Blessed are You, HASHEM, our G-d,
King of the universe,
(on seeing the ocean)
Who made the great sea
(on seeing very beautiful people, trees
or fields)
Who has such in His universe
(on smelling a fragrance)
Who creates species of fragrance
(on smelling fruit or nuts)
Who places a good aroma into fruits

Discussion

Consider how Jewish concern for the
environment has helped to 'make the
desert bloom' in Israel.

Activity

1 Explain why Jews usually show
respect for animals.

2 What are the main environmental
issues for Jews?

Practice GCSE questions

Christianity

(a) Describe Christian beliefs about how the world began. (8 marks)

(b) Explain how and why a Christian might show concern for the environment. (7 marks)

(c) 'Scientific ideas about how the universe began prove that Christianity is wrong.'
Do you agree? Give reasons to support your answer and show that you have thought about different points of view. (5 marks)

Hinduism

(a) Describe Hindu beliefs about how the world began. (8 marks)

(b) Explain how and why a Hindu might show concern for the environment. (7 marks)

(c) 'Scientific ideas about how the universe began prove that Hinduism is wrong.'
Do you agree? Give reasons to support your answer and show that you have thought about different points of view. (5 marks)

Islam

(a) Describe Muslim beliefs about how the world began. (8 marks)

(b) Explain how and why a Muslim might show concern for the environment. (7 marks)

(c) 'Scientific ideas about how the universe began prove that Islam is wrong.'
Do you agree? Give reasons to support your answer and show that you have thought about different points of view. (5 marks)

Judaism

(a) Describe Jewish beliefs about how the world began. (8 marks)

(b) Explain how and why a Jew might show concern for the environment. (7 marks)

(c) 'Scientific ideas about how the universe began prove that Judaism is wrong.'
Do you agree? Give reasons to support your answer and show that you have thought about different points of view. (5 marks)

Tips

For all four questions

In part (a), you need to be able to give an accurate description of the beliefs you have studied. You might be able to refer to some sacred texts to illustrate the points you make. Remember that not all people think alike, even if they belong to the same religion, so you might be able to show how some religious believers are happy to accept scientific views, while other people reject them and have their own beliefs instead.

In part (b) you need to think about the ways in which religious belief might affect someone's attitude and behaviour towards the environment. Why might they believe that it is important to care for the planet – how do their religious beliefs influence their opinions? You also need to say something about how they might put these ideas into practice. Perhaps there are organisations they might join, or ways in which they could care for the environment in their everyday lives.

In part (c) you need to try and think about different points of view, and the reasons why people might have different opinions about science and religion. How might a member of the religion you have been studying feel about scientific theories? Why might they hold these views? You also need to explain your own view, and say why you hold this opinion.

UNIT 4

Death and the Afterlife

Christianity

Christian beliefs about the soul

Christians believe that a person is not just made from his or her mind and body. According to Christianity, each person also has an immortal soul, which cannot be seen, and which makes people different from every other kind of animal. In the book of Genesis, when God created humanity, he set people apart from other creatures. People were made in God's image:

> So God created man
> in his own image,
> in the image of God
> he created him;
> male and female
> he created them.
>
> *(Genesis 1:27)*

People have different interpretations of what it might mean to be made 'in the image of God', but many Christians think that it means that God put something of his own divine and everlasting nature into each person, and this is called the 'soul'.

When other animals were made, according to Genesis, they were just formed '*out of the ground*' (Genesis 2:19); but when Adam was made, God did not only use the dust of the ground but gave him an extra kind of life which the animals were not given:

> the Lord God formed the man from the dust of the ground and breathed into his nostrils the breath of life, and the man became a living being.
>
> *(Genesis 2:7)*

As Christian doctrine developed and became interwoven with the ideas of Greek philosophers such as Plato, the idea was formed that people have souls, which are separate from the body and do not die when the body dies. The soul cannot be seen, but it is something that makes each individual special and sacred. Christians believe that human life is very valuable to God, because humans have souls. Animals, according to Christianity, do not have souls and this is why most Christians are happy to eat meat.

St Paul, who was one of the earliest Christians and a leading figure in the development of the church after Jesus' death, taught that the body and the soul are often in conflict. The soul wants to be with God, and to do what is right, but sometimes the body prevents this from happening. The body is only interested in pleasure, such as food and luxuries, and so the soul (sometimes called the spirit) does not achieve its aims.

Paul also taught that when people die, although the body dies, the 'spiritual body' or soul lives for ever, just as Christ lives for ever after he was raised from the dead. For Paul, the **resurrection** of Jesus was proof of life after death. Christians can expect that they, too, will be raised back to life by the power of God, because of what happened to Jesus. In his letter to the church at Corinth, Paul wrote:

> The body that is sown is perishable, it is raised imperishable; it is sown in dishonour, it is raised in glory; it is sown in weakness, it is raised in power; it is sown a natural body, it is raised a spiritual body. If there is a natural body, there is also a spiritual body.
>
> *(1 Corinthians 15:42–44)*

Paul was making the point that our physical bodies are imperfect and will die, but that our spiritual bodies, or souls, will be raised from the dead.

Understandings of heaven, hell and purgatory

Hell

In the past, belief in heaven and hell occupied a central place in Christian teaching, but today Christians tend to concentrate on belief in life after death in heaven. They usually think of hell as a poetic way of describing an eternity without God, rather than as a real place. Christians in the Middle Ages were very preoccupied with hell, and thought of it as a place of everlasting torture for people who had turned their backs on Christianity and who had committed wicked deeds. They encouraged others to join the church by threatening them with the fires of hell if they refused. Today, although there are still Christians who believe that hell is a reality for non-Christians, many focus instead on the message of a loving and forgiving God. They say that the descriptions of hell found in the Bible are symbolic, and not meant to be taken literally.

Heaven

Christians believe that when they die, the body is not needed any more, but the soul goes on to eternal life with God. This is known as 'heaven'. In Christian art and literature, heaven is often imagined as a place with angels playing on harps, but this is a way of describing something that is very difficult to put into words. The **Apostles' creed**, which is a Christian statement of belief, is said by many Christians during worship, and part of it states the Christian hope of life after death:

> I believe in … the forgiveness of sins
> The resurrection of the body
> And the life everlasting.

Christians believe that at the end of life, the soul is raised from the dead and lives on in a new kind of existence. Some Christians believe that, one day, the world will come to its Last Days, and then people's bodies will also be brought back to life. Because of this belief, they prefer to be buried rather than cremated. But most others think that there are problems with this idea, because if heaven is perfect, then people ought to be able to live with new, perfect bodies, and not need their old ones any more.

Beliefs about heaven are difficult to put into words, because heaven involves an existence that is nothing like the way that we live on the earth. Most Christians accept that they cannot know what heaven will be like, but they do believe that it will be an eternity with God, when evil and suffering no longer exist, and they find this belief comforting even if they do not completely understand what it will mean.

Purgatory

In Roman Catholic teaching, purgatory is a state after death, for people who are not completely ready to go straight to heaven. Their souls stay in purgatory until they are free from sin. Roman Catholics often pray for the souls of those who have died, in the hope that they will not have to spend too long in purgatory.

Discussion

What are your own beliefs about life after death? Do you think that people carry on existing in a new kind of way in heaven or hell after they have died, or do you believe that people are reborn back into this world, or do you think they just stop – or do you have other ideas?

Activity

1 Explain what Christians mean by:
(a) heaven, (b) hell and (c) purgatory.

2 What do you think happens to people after they die? Try to give reasons to support your answer.

In the Middle Ages Christians believed literally in heaven and hell.

God as judge

Christians believe that God knows people better than they know themselves, and will judge their actions. In particular, they believe that God will judge them on the basis of how much concern they have shown for the poor and the weak. The Parable of the Sheep and the Goats, in Matthew's Gospel, teaches that a Day of Judgement will come when God will divide people into two groups. The people who have cared about the poor and looked after those in need will be rewarded by eternal life with God, but those who have been selfish and ignored other people's needs will be sent away from God into hell.

> Then he will say to those on his left, 'Depart from me, you who are cursed, into the eternal fire prepared for the devil and his angels. For I was hungry and you gave me nothing to eat, I was thirsty and you gave me nothing to drink, I was a stranger and you did not invite me in, I needed clothes and you did not clothe me, I was sick and in prison and you did not look after me.'
>
> They also will answer, 'Lord, when did we see you hungry or thirsty or a stranger or needing clothes or sick or in prison, and did not help you?'
>
> He will reply, 'I tell you the truth, whatever you did not do for one of the least of these, you did not do for me.'
>
> Then they will go away to eternal punishment, but the righteous to eternal life.
>
> *(Matthew 25: 41–46)*

However, in spite of these warnings, Christianity also teaches that God is loving and forgiving. Christians believe that although everyone has done wrong, they will be forgiven if they are really sorry, because of their faith in Christ. When Paul wrote to the new churches in the early days of Christianity, he was keen to assure them that their Christian faith meant that they would not be harshly judged:

> Therefore, there is now no condemnation for those who are in Christ Jesus, because through Christ Jesus the law of the Spirit of life set me free from the law of sin and death.
>
> *(Romans 8:1–2)*

Christians, then, believe that there is a relationship between moral behaviour and life after death. God expects high standards of people, and will judge them because of the things that they do. But there is also the possibility of forgiveness for people who realise that they have done wrong, so that bad deeds performed in the past do not just stay there waiting to be punished, with nothing anyone can do about it once the deed has been committed. Christians believe that the death of Jesus gave people the opportunity to be forgiven, as long as they recognise the wrong they have done and make up their minds to behave better in the future.

Christian funerals

Christians, like everyone else, are sad when someone they love dies. However, a Christian funeral service reminds people that although the dead person can no longer be with family and friends, death is not the end. Christians share the hope that after death, they will be raised to eternal life with God, and the Christian funeral service reminds them of this hope. A Christian funeral begins with the words of Jesus:

> I am the resurrection and the life.

Christian funeral customs vary in different denominations. In most churches, there is a short service. A passage of the Bible is read, chosen to emphasise the hope of eternal life, and prayers are said asking for comfort for the relatives and friends, and giving thanks for the life of the person who has died. There might be a short talk about the person, to remember his or her personality and achievements, and sometimes a hymn is sung. It might be a hymn about resurrection, or one which reminds the congregation of the presence of God in times of trouble, or a hymn which was a favourite of the person who has died. Although a funeral service is always a sad occasion, the person leading the service usually tries not to allow it to become too gloomy, but emphasises the good things about the person's life, and encourages those present to be grateful to have known him or her.

Christians believe that although death is very sad, it is not the end.

After the service, the dead person might be buried in a coffin in the ground, or might be cremated. The minister will say more prayers, asking God to be merciful to the dead person's soul, and reminding people that all life is given by God and that God decides when to take it away.

When the funeral is over, those who have attended the service often go back to the house of the closest relatives, for refreshments and for a chance to express their sympathy.

Discussion

Do you think that funerals are a good idea, or do you think they just make things harder for the friends and relatives? Would it be better just to have a burial or a cremation without any speeches, readings, hymns or prayers? Give reasons for your answer.

Activity

1 Explain the main features of a Christian funeral service.

2 Why do you think that Christian funerals put so much emphasis on life after death?

ॐ Hinduism

Hindu beliefs about Atman and karma

Hindus believe that within each person, there is an eternal 'soul' known as Atman. Each person has a physical body, which is how we recognise each other. But the physical body changes and grows old; it can be damaged, and eventually it dies. The Atman, in contrast, lives on eternally. When one body is worn out and dies, the Atman is reborn into a new life as a different person. Atman is perfect. It cannot be killed, and it does not age like the physical body. It cannot become ill, or be damaged in any way.

Each Atman can be reborn through many different lives, over hundreds or thousands of years. The way that the person behaves will bring about good karma, or bad karma; the actions will have 'fruits', which then have to be lived out. As long as this chain of cause and effect continues, the Atman will carry on being reborn over and over again. This process is known as **rebirth** or **reincarnation**. Sometimes, if people go to a new place, they feel as though they have been there before, even though they never have; sometimes, people meet someone for the first time and yet feel a strong sense of recognition. There are also people such as Mozart who show great skills from a very young age; Mozart was composing music at an age when many children cannot even read. Hindus would say that these experiences are faint memories of past lives, of places visited, people met or skills learned. A few people who develop great skill in meditation and concentration can sometimes bring back much clearer memories of past lives.

Samsara and rebirth

The Hindu word **samsara** refers to the way in which the Atman wanders from one body to the next and to the next, time after time, in a long series of different lives. It is seen as a cycle of existence, just like the water cycle or the nitrogen cycle in the natural world.

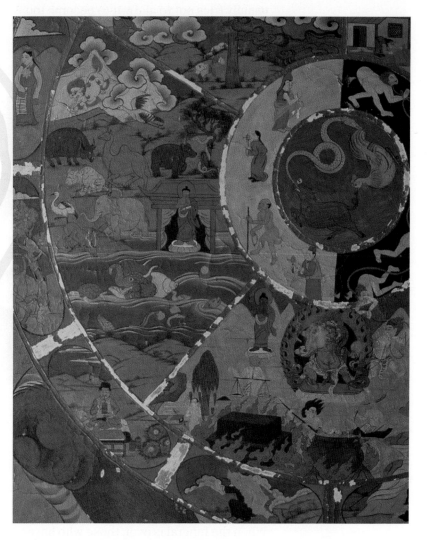

Many people who do not share Hindu beliefs still like the idea of an endless series of lives. It might be good to have the opportunity to take a different career next time, or to be born in a different part of the world and experience growing up in a different culture. But Hindus believe that the round of samsara is tiresome, and that the ideal is to escape from it. Hindus hope one day to reach **moksha**. Moksha is the name given to the release of Atman from the cycle of birth, death and rebirth, so that it no longer has to be born back into the world as another person but can become a part of God. Hinduism teaches that there are different ways to achieve moksha. One of them is by devotion to God, and another is by trying to gain wisdom and understanding.

The cycle of birth and death goes on through many hundreds of lives.

Rebirth and moral behaviour

Hindus believe that everyone's behaviour in this life affects what will happen to them in the next. Everything that a person does, in Hindu teaching, has 'fruits', or consequences, and this is known as the **law of karma**. Good deeds will bring rewards for the person who does them, and bad actions such as stealing, unkindness or greed will bring punishments. This does not always happen in the same lifetime. We can see that there are some people who live good lives, and yet bad things happen to them; and we also can see that other people who have done wrong often appear to get away with it and live happily to an old age. Hinduism teaches that the karma from one life is carried over into the next, so if someone is not rewarded or punished for their deeds straight away, it will still happen, but maybe in a future life.

Moral behaviour affects life after death because each person's fate depends on how well they have behaved. If they behave badly, then in their next life they might be born into a very poor family; or they might be born with a disability, or live a very short life, or suffer some kind of tragedy. In order to avoid this, Hindus do what they can to build up good karma. They try to make sure that they perform all their prayers properly, and that they are kind to others. They give to charity, and aim to be kind to other people whenever the opportunity arises, so that they can have a good rebirth in the next life.

Some people have argued that this kind of attitude could make Hindus treat the poor and the disabled too harshly. They say that Hindus will feel that other people's problems are their own fault, and that we should not feel too sorry for other people's misfortunes because it serves them right.

Discussion

Have you ever had an experience which might suggest past lives? Do you think that these experiences are evidence of rebirth, or do you think that there are other possible explanations?

Activity

1 Explain what Hindus mean by:
(a) Atman, (b) samsara , (c) karma and (d) moksha

2 Describe in your own words what a Hindu would say if asked about life after death.

Hindu funeral rites

For Hindus, death is not the complete end of a person. Instead, it marks the separation of the soul from the body. The body is not needed any more, and is disposed of, while the soul is set free, and rituals take place to help the soul to continue on its journey.

When a Hindu dies, the funeral takes place as soon as possible after the death, on the same day if the person has died before sunset. This is for reasons of hygiene, as in hot countries bodies decompose more quickly, and there is a danger of infection especially if the person has died because of disease. As soon as it is certain that the person is dead, the body is washed and prepared for cremation, by male relatives if the dead person is male and by women if the body is female. Cremation is the custom for most people, although burial is accepted if the dead person is a child under the age of puberty, a pregnant woman, or someone greatly admired as a saint. These people are considered to have sacred qualities which set them apart from the rest of humanity, and therefore they do not need to have their souls set free in the way that others need to.

The body is wrapped in new cloth, to represent getting rid of things which are old and worn out and preparing for something new. Then, it is carried out of the village to the piece of land that has been set aside as a cremation ground. If the Hindus live in the UK or another Western country, then they will go to the local crematorium by car. All of the family members who are able to attend join the procession to the cremation ground, and this procession is led by the eldest son whenever this is practical. Of course, in some families there may not be sons, or the son may have died before the parents, in which case the nearest male relative will take on the role instead.

When the cremation ground is reached, the eldest son walks around the funeral pyre three times. The funeral pyre is a bonfire made of scented woods, such as sandalwood, and other perfumes are added too. The body, in its cloth, is placed on top of the woodpile with its feet facing south to represent Yama, the god of death, and then more wood is added to cover it. Ghee, which is melted and clarified butter, is added to the wood to help it to burn. Then the son, or another chief mourner if there is no son, lights the fire to cremate the body.

When a Hindu dies, the body is cremated on a funeral pyre.

It is believed that cremation helps the soul to escape from the body where it once lived, and it is then free to move on and be reborn as another person.

Everyone present at the funeral stays until it is clear that the body has been cremated. Afterwards, they go home to wash and change their clothes, as a symbol of purity and beginning again. The eldest son returns to the cremation ground a day or two after the funeral, to collect the ashes. These are then sprinkled in the river Ganges, if possible, as this is a very holy place for Hindus. It represents India as a nation, the water represents life, and because the river is always flowing and is never the same from one minute to the next, it can be seen to represent the ever-changing nature of birth, life and death. Many Hindus believe that spreading the ashes in the Ganges helps the person who has died to achieve a better rebirth.

After the funeral, there are ten days of religious ceremonies, where offerings are made to help ensure that the soul finds a new body in which to live. Prayers are said for the dead, and relatives come to visit and to offer each other comfort. The eldest son has a special role to play in all of these ceremonies. It is his responsibility to make sure that they are done properly, and this role is one of the reasons why Hindus are particularly anxious to have sons. They feel that they need someone who will carry out these religious duties for them when they die, so that their souls can continue into the next life in the proper way.

To people in the West, it must seem very hard to have a funeral in which everyone watches as the body of someone they loved is cremated. People in the West are more used to funerals where the body is kept hidden, and cremation happens behind a screen out of sight. But Hindus sometimes point out that although a funeral is a very painful and emotional experience, it helps the relatives to come to terms with death, because they can see for themselves that the person really has died and that the body has become an empty shell which is no longer needed.

Discussion

Do you think that a Hindu funeral would help relatives to come to terms with a death, or do you think it would not be helpful? Give reasons for your answer.

Activity

1 What are the main features of a Hindu funeral service?

2 What do these features show about Hindu beliefs?

Islam

Muslim beliefs about heaven and hell

Muslims do not believe that people have an immortal soul but that this life is a test. When you die you stay in the grave until the Day of Judgement which will be on a date already chosen by Allah. On this day, the soul and body of each Muslim will be reunited and everyone will be raised from their graves. True followers of Allah will be 'reborn' in Paradise. For Muslims, without a belief in life after death, life on earth would be meaningless.

Muslims believe that after death there will be a Day of Judgement – **Yawmuddin**. Surah 39 describes how, on the Day of Judgement, there will be the sound of a trumpet, and people will fall down as if unconscious. The trumpet will then sound again and the dead will rise to join the living.

Islam teaches that all people who believe in God will be judged at the last day. This includes Christians, Jews and an ancient race called the **Sabians**, as well as Muslims.

> Those who believe (in the Qur'an), those who follow the Jewish (scriptures), and the Sabians and the Christians – any, who believe in Allah and the Last Day, and work righteousness – on them shall be no fear, Nor shall they grieve.
>
> *(Surah 5:69)*

Islam does not believe that it is possible to describe the afterlife as it belongs to a totally different dimension, but they do believe that it lasts forever.

This surah from the Qur'an teaches that those people who follow the words of Allah will life happily in a wonderful garden, **al-Janna** (Paradise):

> On the Day that the Hour will be established – that Day shall (all men) be sorted out. Then those who have believed and worked righteous deeds,

shall be made happy in a Mead of Delight. And those who have rejected Faith and falsely denied Our Signs and the meeting of the Hereafter – such shall be brought forth to punishment.
>
> *(Surah 30:14–16)*

People who have not followed Allah's wishes will go to the fires of Hell – **Jahannam** – where they will be punished, and good people will go to a perfect world of rest and pleasure to be with Allah for **akhirah** (life after death). However, Allah is always merciful and even a bad person may eventually reach Paradise after they have been punished. The exception will be anyone who is found guilty of shirk (see pages 35, 186) which cannot be forgiven.

Moral behaviour and life after death

Surah 17 says that true believers must follow a straight path if they are to escape punishment on Yawmuddin:

> Every man's fate we have fastened on his own neck: on the Day of Judgement we shall bring out for him a scroll, which he will see spread open.
>
> *(Surah 17:13)*

Every person is responsible for their own actions because humans have been created with free will. People can follow or reject the teachings of Islam but they will face the consequences of their decision at the Day of Judgement.

The Qur'an warns that when the Last Judgement occurs it will be too late for people to repent. The truth will be so obvious that there will be no opportunity to choose to believe with your own free will in Allah.

Like Christians and Jews, Muslims believe that you only have one chance at life and you are judged on how you live it. When the judgement of Allah finally comes he will already know everything and it will be fast and final:

> To Allah belongs the Mystery of the heavens and the earth. And the Decision of the Hour (of Judgement) is as the twinkling of an eye, or even quicker: for Allah hath power over all things.
>
> *(Surah 16:77)*

Muslims believe that they will be judged according to how well they followed the teachings of the Qur'an and the example of Muhammad ﷺ. To be judged favourably they need to have lived their lives in submission to the will of Allah and to have followed the teachings of the Five Pillars (see page 94).

When Allah makes his judgement, he will take into account not only people's deeds but also their intentions (niyyah):

> If a person intends to do something wrong but does not do it, this is a good deed.
>
> If a person intends to do something wrong and does it, this is a bad deed.
>
> If a person intends to do a good deed but cannot manage to carry it out, this is a good deed.
>
> If a person intends a good deed and carries it out, this is equal to ten good deeds.
>
> *(Hadith)*

Discussion

Do you consider that what you intend to do is as important as what you actually do?

Activity

1 Explain what Muslims mean by (a) heaven and (b) hell.

2 What do you think happens to people after they die? Try to give reasons to support your answer.

Muslim funeral rites

On their death bed Muslims will try to repeat the final words of the Prophet Muhammad ﷺ 'Allah, help me through the hardship and agony of death'. When another Muslim hears of the death they will say, 'To Allah we belong and to Allah we return', showing that they hope the person will be claimed by Allah to live in heaven.

Funerals take place within three days of death (if possible within 24 hours). The body is placed on a stretcher with the head facing Makkah. Ritual washing, ghusl, is carried out by female relatives of the dead person if it is a woman and by male relatives if the dead person is a man. The body is washed three times and perfumed with scents. It is then wrapped in a shroud, made of a single piece of unsewn cloth, and placed in a coffin. If the laws of the country permit, no coffin is used (in the United Kingdom this sort of burial is not allowed and so Muslims have to use coffins). Muslims are buried facing Makkah.

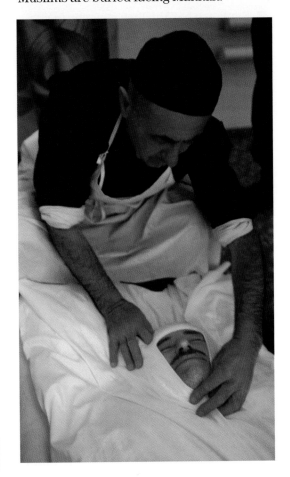

Muslims believe in a complete physical resurrection of the body and so do not approve of cremation. This verse points out that Allah will have no difficulty in putting these dead bodies back together, even including their fingerprints:

> Does man think that We cannot assemble his bones? Nay, We are able to put together in perfect order the very tips of his finger.
>
> *(Surah 75:3–4)*

> 1. **I** do call to witness The Resurrection Day;
>
> 2. And I do call to witness The self-reproaching spirit : (Eschew Evil).
>
> 3. Does man think that We Cannot assemble his bones?
>
> 4. Nay, We are able to put Together in perfect order The very tips of his fingers.
>
> 5. But man wishes to do Wrong (even) in the time In front of him.

At the graveside Surah 1, **al-Fatihah**, is recited. This is a very important statement of belief in Allah and his mercy and is always said when praying:

> In the name of Allah, Most Gracious, Most Merciful. Praise be to Allah, the Cherisher and Sustainer of the worlds; Most Gracious, Most Merciful; Master of the Day of Judgement. Thee do we worship, and Thine aid we seek. Show us the straight way. The way of those on whom Thou hast bestowed Thy Grace, those whose (portion) is not wrath, and who go not astray.

As the coffin is lowered into the ground, the mourners say the following words which show their belief that Allah will take the dead to paradise at the Day of Judgement:

> From the (earth) did We create you, and into it shall We return you, and from it shall We bring you out once again.
>
> *(Surah 20:55)*

It is traditional for the graves to be raised a little above the level of the ground to stop people walking or sitting on them, but elaborate monuments are forbidden.

It is normal for people to grieve but Islam teaches that this death should be accepted with trust and faith. The Prophet cried when his son died and it is natural for both men and women to cry at a death. However, Muslims must remember that the death is the wish of Allah. The time spent in mourning varies among different communities and can last from three days to three months and widows are permitted to mourn for longer. The community ensures that mourners are not left on their own and will visit the family, bringing food.

Discussion

'Mourning and funeral services are for the living, they serve no purpose for the person who is dead.' Consider this statement.

Activity

1 What are the main features of a Muslim funeral service?

2 What do these features show about Muslim beliefs?

Judaism

Jewish beliefs about life after death

Judaism does not have any clear teaching about the relationship between the body and soul. The distinction is not considered to be important. It is believed that G-d breathed the soul into Adam's body:

> ...and He blew into his nostrils the soul of life...
>
> *(Genesis 2:7).*

The rabbis taught that the soul leaves the body during sleep and draws refreshment from heaven. It again leaves the body at death but is reunited with it at resurrection. During Shabbat, G-d gives each body an extra soul, but takes it back at Havdalah. The **Midrash** says that the body cannot survive without the soul, but neither can the soul survive without the body.

At the time when most of the Jewish scriptures were written, Jews believed that after death everyone went to **Sheol**. This is described as a dark place where people went after death and where they stayed for eternity. This is because many Jews believe that Adam and Eve would have lived forever in the Garden of Eden but, because they disobeyed G-d, they became mortal and so, since then, everyone has grown old and eventually died.

The first mention of the resurrection of the dead comes in the book of Daniel:

> Many of those who sleep in the dusty earth will awaken: these for everlasting life and these for shame, for everlasting abhorrence.
>
> *(Daniel 12:2)*

This seems to refer to a physical resurrection although some Jews believe that the afterlife will be purely spiritual.

Beliefs in heaven and hell come much later in Jewish thought and teaching. Some say that the righteous will enter **Gan Eden** (Paradise) and the wicked will go to **Gehenna** (**Gehinnom**) only after the resurrection and last judgment; some Rabbis said that the departed would go to these places immediately after death. Gehenna is not the same as Sheol. Sheol was a place of waiting while Gehenna is Hell. When someone is judged by G-d their body and soul will be reunited, the accuser will be the soul and the body cannot blame the soul for its actions.

It is believed that this judgement will take place after the coming of the Messiah.

Moral behaviour and life after death

For a long time in their early history Jews believed that they would be punished for anything bad that their parents or grandparents had done.

> For I am HASHEM, your G-d – a jealous G-d, Who visits the sins of the fathers upon children to the third and fourth generations, for My enemies.
>
> *(Exodus 20:5)*

This belief is shown in this passage from the book of Lamentations:

> Our fathers have sinned and are no more, and we have suffered for their iniquities.
>
> *(Lamentations 5:7)*

Later, in this early period, they came to believe that it was how well they had lived their own lives which was important.

> The word of HASHEM came to me, saying: Why do you relate this parable upon the land of Israel, saying, "The fathers eat sour grapes, but the teeth of the sons are set on edge!" As I live – the word of the Lord HASHEM / ELOHIM – [I swear] that there will no longer be anyone among you who uses this parable in Israel. Behold, all souls are Mine, like the soul of the father, so the soul of the son, they are Mine. The soul that sins – it shall die.
>
> *(Ezekiel 18:1–4)*

Towards the end of the Biblical period, Jews came to the idea that there might be some eternal life with G-d after death, but they also believed that eventually G-d would judge people and that those who had not led good lives would go to hell.

In the book of Maccabees, which describes the persecution the Jews suffered from the Greeks, a man is being put to death because he refuses to say that he does not believe in G-d. He says that he would rather die knowing that he will eventually live with G-d. He also says that that the person who puts him to death will not have this resurrection.

> When he was near death, he said, 'One cannot but choose to die at the hands of mortals and to cherish the hope G-d gives of being raised again by him. But for you there will be no resurrection to life!'
>
> *(2 Maccabees 7:14)*

Although Jews believe that they may be punished or rewarded after death for the way in which they have lived their lives, there is no clear teaching about heaven and the Torah offers no suggestions as to what this might be.

The importance of life for Jews is the way in which it is lived on earth. It is thought that whatever may happen after death is in G-d's hands and should be left to G-d to arrange. Because of this thinking, Judaism is a religion that puts great stress and importance on the way people live their lives, not on how this may affect their soul.

To live a good life, Jews must follow the Ten Commandments and the 613 mitzvot, they must live a **halakhic life** (walking with G-d) and treat others well. This is the most that anyone can do – it is left up to G-d to decide what, if anything, will happen next.

Discussion

'The only important thing is how you live your life, not what you believe.'

Consider this statement.

Activity

1 Explain what Jews mean by (a) heaven and (b) hell.

2 What do you think happens to people after they die? Try to give reasons to support your answer.

The importance of life for Jews is the way in which it is lived on earth.

Jewish funeral rites

As they are dying, Jews try to say the Shema, a prayer showing belief in one G-d:

> Hear, O Israel: HASHEM is our G-d, HASHEM, the One and Only. You shall love HASHEM, your G-d, with all your heart, with all your soul and with all your resources. Let these matters, which I command you today, be upon your heart. Teach them thoroughly to your children and speak of them while you sit in your home, while you walk on the way, when you retire and when you arise. Bind them as a sign upon your arm and let them be tefillin between your eyes. And write them on the doorposts of your house and upon your gates.

When someone dies, Jews say the **Kaddish**. This is often described as the funeral prayer, but although it is said at funerals and during the period of mourning which follows, it is actually a prayer praising G-d.

> May His great Name grow exalted and sanctified in the world that He created as He willed. May He give reign to His kingship in your lifetime and in your days, and in the lifetimes of the entire Family of Israel, swiftly and soon. May His great Name be blessed forever and ever. Blessed, praised, glorified, exalted, extolled, mighty, upraised, and lauded be the Name of the Holy One, Blessed is He beyond any blessing and song, praise and consolation that are uttered in the world. May there be abundant peace from Heaven, and life, upon us and upon all Israel. He Who makes peace in His heights, may He may peace upon us, and upon all Israel.

Jews do not mourn for long periods of time. As soon as someone dies preparations must be made for burial; if possible on the same day but if not then on the following one. The body is washed and dried and dressed in **tachrichim** (a simple white shroud), and, if a man, wrapped in a **tallit** (prayer shawl). The fringes are cut from the prayer shawl to show that the man is now freed from the religious laws that bound him on earth. All these preparations are carried out by the **Chevra Kadisha** (Sacred Burial Society). The body is placed in a plain wooden coffin and this is immediately sealed. The body is never left alone from the time of death until the burial. Immediately before the burial the mourners will make a tear in their garments, **keriah,** to show their grief. No flowers are given at a Jewish funeral and the service is short and simple – everyone is equal in death. Cremation is not usually permitted amongst Orthodox Jews although Progressive communities sometimes cremate the deceased.

After burial the traditional blessing is said:

> May God comfort you among all the mourners of Zion and Jerusalem.

After the funeral the family will go home to sit Shiva 'seven'. For the next seven days a candle is kept burning and the mirrors in the house are covered. The mourners do not leave their homes, they do not shave or cut their hair and they sit on low stools. Kaddish is said three times a day and members of the community will come to the house to say it with them. Shiva is broken only by the Sabbath or a Jewish

festival which must take precedence. The 30 days after burial are the period of Sheloshim, when the bereaved do not go out for pleasure and continue to mourn. For the next 11 months (but no longer), called **Shanah**, Kaddish is said every day. After this time the dead person is remembered each year on the anniversary of their death by the lighting of a **yahrzeit** candle which burns for a full day, and by the reciting of Kaddish.

The period of mourning is carefully structured so that the relatives have time to deal with their grief but are then required to return to normal life.

Just before the first anniversary of the death, the tombstone will be placed at the grave and people often try to visit the graves of relatives during the High Holy Days, Rosh Hashanah and Yom Kippur. When people visit a Jewish grave they do not take flowers but instead place a small stone on the gravestone as a sign of respect.

Discussion

'Mourning and funeral services are for the living, they serve no purpose for the person who is dead.' Consider this statement.

Activity

1 What are the main features of a Jewish funeral service?

2 What do these features show about Jewish beliefs?

Practice GCSE questions

Christianity

(a) Describe Christian beliefs about life after death.

(8 marks)

(b) Explain how a Christian funeral might help and comfort the relatives of someone who has died.

(7 marks)

(c) 'If you behave badly in this life, you will be punished after you die.'
Do you agree? Give reasons to explain your answer, and show that you have thought about different points of view. You must refer to Christianity in your answer. (5 marks)

Hinduism

(a) Describe Hindu beliefs about life after death.

(8 marks)

(b) Explain how a Hindu funeral might help and comfort the relatives of someone who has died.

(7 marks)

(c) 'If you behave badly in this life, you will be punished after you die.'
Do you agree? Give reasons to explain your answer, and show that you have thought about different points of view. You must refer to Hinduism in your answer. (5 marks)

Islam

(a) Describe Muslim beliefs about life after death.

(8 marks)

(b) Explain how a Muslim funeral might help and comfort the relatives of someone who has died.

(7 marks)

(c) 'If you behave badly in this life, you will be punished after you die.'
Do you agree? Give reasons to explain your answer, and show that you have thought about different points of view. You must refer to Islam in your answer. (5 marks)

Judaism

(a) Describe Jewish beliefs about life after death.

(8 marks)

(b) Explain how a Jewish funeral might help and comfort the relatives of someone who has died.

(7 marks)

(c) 'If you behave badly in this life, you will be punished after you die.'
Do you agree? Give reasons to explain your answer, and show that you have thought about different points of view. You must refer to Judaism in your answer. (5 marks)

Tips

For all four questions

In part (a) you are being asked for a description of the beliefs. Try and include as much detail as you can; you might want to explain what happens to good people, and contrast it with what happens to those who have done wrong. You may be able to refer to the holy books of the religion you are studying to illustrate your answer.

For part (b) you need to think about the benefits that attending a funeral service might bring. What are the main beliefs that are being expressed in a funeral? They might be a way of telling the relatives that death is not the end; perhaps the funeral gives relatives the hope of seeing the dead person again in the next life. You might want to write about the comfort people might get just from having other family members and friends around them at a sad time.

In part (c), you need to give an evaluation. Do you agree with the statement? Perhaps you think that bad people will be punished, through rebirth or as a result of being judged by God. Or you might think that death is just the end of a person, and that nothing else happens to them. Try to explain your own point of view, and compare it with the beliefs of the religion you are studying. If you agree with these beliefs, you will need to add another point of view as well, to show that you have considered different possibilities.

UNIT 5

Good and Evil

Christianity

Why is there evil in the world?

The existence of evil and suffering in the world has always presented great problems for Christianity. Christians believe that God is perfectly good and perfectly loving; they also believe that God has the power to do anything (**omnipotence**). But there are all kinds of bad things in the world that cause people to suffer. Sometimes people are deliberately cruel, or dishonest, or uncaring – this is often called **moral evil**, which is the kind of wrong that happens because of human wickedness. At other times, suffering is caused because of **natural evil** such as floods, disease, hurricanes, fires and earthquakes. These events can cause a lot of suffering, but they do not seem to be because of any human fault. Life often seems very unfair. Terrible tragedies sometimes happen to good and innocent people, while there are others who seem to care about no-one except themselves and yet they live long and prosperous lives.

How can Christians continue to believe in an all-loving, all-powerful God, if there is so much wrong in the world? Why does God apparently do nothing to prevent cruelty to children, or cancer, or tidal waves? Did God make evil when the world was created, and can God be blamed for all that goes wrong? Or did something else create evil, and is God unable to prevent it?

Different beliefs about God and the Devil

Some Christians believe that there is evil in the world because of the **Devil**, sometimes known as Satan. The Devil is believed to be the enemy of God, who rules in hell and who tries to make humanity turn away from goodness. According to early Christian doctrine, the Devil was created good, but was jealous of God and decided to fight against God instead of being obedient.

In the creation story in Genesis, Adam and Eve were tempted to do wrong by a serpent, and some people believe that this was the Devil in disguise. In the book of Job, the Devil causes Job all sorts of suffering, as a way of trying to make him turn against God, but Job does not give up his faith. Jesus, too, before he began his teaching, was tempted by the Devil, but refused to listen:

> The devil led him up to a high place and showed him in an instant all the kingdoms of the world. And he said to him, 'I will give you all their authority and splendour, for it has been given to me, and I can give it to anyone I want to. So if you worship me, it will all be yours.'
>
> Jesus answered, 'It is written: "Worship the Lord your God and serve him only."'
> *(Luke 4:8)*

Traditionally, the Devil is shown in pictures as being red in colour, with horns and a forked tail. Some people say that, whenever there is suffering in the world, or people choose to do wrong, it is because of the power of the Devil, causing the tragedy or encouraging people to do evil.

Why does an all-powerful, all-loving God allow disasters to happen?

Not all Christians, however, believe that the Devil is a real person. Some say that this is just a poetic way of explaining how people feel pulled in different directions, and why they often want to do things even if they know they are wrong. Belief in the Devil does not provide a very good answer to the problem of evil: if God is all-powerful, why would he allow the Devil to do anything at all?

Some Christian responses to the problem of evil

Christians usually find it very difficult to explain the existence of evil. Sometimes, they say that it is the result of the Fall of Adam and Eve: because the first people rebelled against God, they brought evil and suffering into a world that was made perfect, and they spoilt the world that God had made. But this does not answer all the questions. If Adam and Eve were perfect, why did they rebel against God? Did God not know in advance what Adam and Eve would do, when they were made?

Other people say that evil and suffering are in the world as a kind of test, to help people to learn and become more mature. Christian thinkers such as Irenaeus, who lived in the second century CE, have suggested that if people never suffered and never had to choose between right and wrong, then they would be like robots, programmed to behave in a certain way and unable to choose any different. Christians sometimes argue that suffering teaches important lessons, and that we would not be able to be good unless we were faced with difficulties. For example, we could not be brave if we were never in danger, and we could not be generous if other people never needed anything. But this way of thinking, too, has its difficulties. Sometimes people suffer when they have no chance of learning anything from it, for example tiny babies sometimes die of painful illnesses, and animals suffer without being capable of learning lessons. Suffering does not always improve people, but can make them angry and bitter.

Coping with suffering through acceptance and prayer

Sometimes, Christians say that evil and suffering are a mystery. We do not know why there is evil in the world, or why people suffer, and perhaps this is something that only God can understand. However, Christians believe that God does care about people when they suffer. Christians believe that Jesus was the Son of God, and that he came into the world and suffered a terrible death on the cross, so God does not ignore suffering, but knows what it is like and shares our pain with us. Sometimes, Christians say that when they suffer, they feel closer to God because they recognise their dependence on him.

Many Christians believe that the best way of coping with suffering is through trust in God. They say that, when they are in trouble, if they pray about their difficulties they know that God is listening and they trust God to take care of them. This does not mean that things will always go the way that they want them to go; sometimes, people pray for someone who is very ill and the person still does not get better. But Christians often believe that God has plans which people cannot always understand, and that people should accept their own limitations and recognise that God does not make mistakes.

Discussion

Some people say that the existence of evil and suffering in the world proves that there is no God. Do you think that this fair?

Activity

1 Explain, with examples, the difference between 'moral' evil and 'natural' evil.

2 What might a minister or priest say to a Christian family whose child had died in an accident, to try and explain why God had allowed it to happen?

3 Do you think that Christians are right to believe in an all-loving, all-powerful God when there is evil in the world? Give reasons for your answer.

How can Christians tell right from wrong?

Christians believe that, as part of their response to God, they should try to avoid evil and to do good, because they believe that God is perfectly good and that they should try to become like God as much as they can.

But how are they to know what is right and what is wrong?

There are several different ways in which Christians can try to discover the right way to behave.

Conscience

Many people believe that they instinctively know when something is right or wrong, because their consciences tell them. They feel guilty if they do something wrong, even if they know that no-one will find out about it. They feel ashamed of themselves. In some situations, they want to do something, but know that it would be wrong, and so they decide not to do it even though they would like to, because their consciences prevent it. They know that they would not be happy if they acted against their consciences. Christians sometimes believe that the conscience is a way in which God speaks to them, particularly if they pray about their moral decisions, and ask God to help them. Other people, however, do not agree with this. They think that the conscience comes from being brought up to behave in the ways our parents like; we become so used to being told what to do and what not to do that we feel as though someone is telling us how to behave even when our parents are not around.

The Bible

The Bible, as the holy book of Christianity, is often used as a source of moral guidance. Christians study the teachings of the Bible, and try to work out how to apply it to their own lives and situations. Some of the Bible's teachings, such as the **Ten**

Commandments, are considered by many people, whether Christian or not, to contain essential truths about right and wrong.

Christians often turn to the Bible when they have difficult moral decisions to make. Many of the teachings and stories of the Bible have messages which Christians can think about, discuss with others, and try to put into practice. However, this is not always straightforward. The Bible was written a long time ago, for different people in a different culture, and it is not always easy to find teachings that relate closely to the modern world and modern circumstances. Some of the teachings of the Bible, such as 'In everything, do to others as you would have them do to you' (Matthew 7:12), mean the same thing today as they meant two thousand years ago; but other teachings are about out-dated practices like slavery and animal sacrifice, and it can sometimes be difficult to know how these are to be understood by modern people.

Many Christians turn to the Bible for reference when they have an important decision to make.

The example of Christ

Sometimes, Christians try to work out the right thing to do by imagining what Jesus would do in the same circumstances. Because Christians believe that Jesus was the Son of God, they believe that he always acted and spoke in the right way. They try to copy him; for example, they might read in the Gospels about the ways in which Jesus helped outcasts, and try to copy this by working in a shelter for the homeless. They might look at the attitude of Jesus towards wealth, or children, or women, or violence, and make an effort to adopt the same attitude themselves.

Why do Christians try to follow a moral code?

Christians believe that God is perfectly good, and that humanity was made 'in the image of God' (Genesis 1:27), with the capability to share in God's goodness. Christians, like Jews, are **ethical monotheists**; they believe in one God, who is the source of all goodness and who is interested in the way that people behave, particularly in the ways in which they treat one another. Christians believe that God has given people moral guidelines to follow, which are recorded in the Bible. The Old Testament is full of teaching about morality, in the Torah and also throughout other books. The prophets, for example, taught about the right ways to live, and the kinds of behaviour that angered God.

The teaching of Jesus, too, was often about morality. Jesus sometimes taught in **parables**, which are stories that convey a message, and many of these stories are about moral behaviour. One famous example is the Parable of the Good Samaritan, where Jesus taught that people should love each other and treat each other as neighbours, even if they are strangers or from a different race (Luke 10:25–37). Another is the Parable of the Prodigal Son, where the message of the story is about forgiveness and repentance. Many of Jesus' moral teachings have been collected together into a passage known as the

Sermon on the Mount (Matthew 5–7). In this collection of sayings, Jesus gives moral advice on all kinds of issues, such as anger, adultery, divorce, and treatment of enemies. Because they believe that Jesus was the Son of God, and Jesus taught about the right way to live, Christians consider that morality is an important part of religious life.

Christians sometimes believe that people who try to be good in this life will be rewarded after death. People used to believe that those who are good in this life will be rewarded in heaven, while those who do wrong will be punished in hell. People were encouraged to follow strict moral codes, by being threatened with the torments of hell if they did wrong. However, this view is not as popular as it once was. Many now think that descriptions of hell are not meant to be taken literally, but are poetic ways of imagining an existence without God.

Discussion

Why should people do good and not evil? As long as you are happy, why should you care about anyone else? Is there any point in behaving morally, unless you believe in God?

Activity

1 Explain what people mean when they say that they are guided by their consciences. Do you think that it is always right to do what your conscience tells you to do?

2 How might Christians use (a) the Bible and (b) the example of Jesus, when they are making moral decisions?

Hinduism

Why is there evil in the world?

According to Hinduism, God, or Ultimate Reality, contains elements of everything: creation and destruction, light and darkness, birth and death, goodness and evil. Sometimes deities are shown in more than one form, to reflect these different sides to their characters. For example, the goddess Kali is worshipped as a mother and as a protector; but at the same time, she is often shown as a frightening figure, with a necklace of skulls and a severed head in her hand, living in the graveyards. Shiva, too, is sometimes shown as a meditating saint, quiet and contemplative; but usually he is shown as 'Lord of the Dance', in a circle of flames, in eternal movement and keeping the world in motion. He is the lord of destruction, carrying a thunderbolt, and driving his chariot through the world causing havoc wherever he goes. Hindus often blame Shiva for natural disasters such as earthquakes, floods and hurricanes.

For Hindus, goodness and evil are parts of life, coming from God, just like light and shade or birth and death. Sometimes, evil and suffering are said to be the direct result of actions of the gods, and Hindus try to keep the deities happy by performing the proper rituals, so that they will not be harmed. But often, it is understood in Hinduism that good and bad can be part of the same thing, depending on how you look at it. Death, for example, can be terrible, or it can be welcome, and sometimes the same event can bring good for some people while it brings harm for others.

The doctrine of karma and rebirth

Hindus believe that each person has an eternal soul or spirit, called Atman, which is born with one physical body, but which lives on after death to be reborn as another person (reincarnation). During each life, a person performs good deeds, and bad deeds. Every action that a person does

The goddess Kali shows that both good and evil are aspects of God.

deliberately has consequences, either for good or for evil. The actions bring their own rewards and punishments, and this is called the law of karma. When we look at the people around us, we can see that it does not always happen that good people are rewarded for what they do, while bad people are punished. Some people are nearly always good, kind and truthful, and yet they have poor health or other kinds of bad luck. Other people might be cruel, selfish or deceitful, and still be rich and healthy. Hindus say that the reward or the punishment does not always come in this life. It might come in a future rebirth – the good person, for example, might be reborn into a wealthy family, and have many children, as a reward for their good deeds.

When people experience evil and suffering, therefore, it is not seen as unfair by Hindus. A Hindu would say that misfortune in this life happens because of a person's behaviour in previous lives, as a result of karma. If one person is healthier, cleverer or better looking than another, this is not because of unfairness, but is a direct result of the actions performed in previous lives. Nothing happens by accident, and if someone is suffering, it is their own fault because of their previous actions.

How do Hindus cope with evil and suffering?

Hindus believe that it is wrong to become too attached to the pleasures that the world can bring. They aim to become 'detached' from the world, recognising it for what it is: an endless cycle of birth, death and rebirth, known as samsara. Hindus try to recognise that everything in the world is only temporary, and they aim to concentrate instead on setting the Atman free from being reborn over and over again. One of the reasons why Kali is believed to be good, as well as evil, is that by causing suffering she encourages people to become more detached, as she constantly destroys the earthly pleasures that people enjoy so much. In some ways, she is evil, because she causes pain, but at the same time, she is helping people to get closer to escaping from samsara, by

making them realise that the world is not all that matters, and helping them not to be so attached to the world that they tie themselves down to future rebirths.

When Hindus suffer, therefore, they try to remember:
- Everything passes. Suffering, like pleasure, will not last forever, and the next life might bring more rewards and less pain, especially if the sufferer responds bravely and without complaint.
- Suffering happens because of actions in past lives. Even if the person in pain is a small baby, this is not unfair, because the baby must have done something in a previous life to deserve it.

Hindus try to cope with pain and suffering by becoming more devoted to God. Loving devotion to God is known as bhakti, and this is seen as one of the paths to salvation. Making offerings, saying prayers and fasting will bring rewards in the future. In this way, Hindus believe that suffering is not beyond their control, but is something that they can change by their own behaviour.

Discussion

Do you think that it is possible to be too attached to your family, or your home, or your friends, or your possessions? Give reasons for your answer.

Activity

1 Some people say that blaming suffering on past lives encourages people to take an unsympathetic view towards those in need; it is like saying that it serves them right. What do you think, and why?

2 Explain how a Hindu might explain why there is evil in the world.

How do Hindus know what is the right way to behave?

Because Hinduism is such a vast religion, including many different beliefs and many different cultures, there are also different interpretations of the right way to behave. As in all societies, the main way in which Hindus learn how to behave is through the teaching of their parents and other family members, who will bring them up to approve of some things and disapprove of others.

The most important concept in Hindu morality is the idea of dharma. Dharma is the principle of right conduct, and it is believed to be an eternal law which affects everybody, even the gods. According to the concept of dharma, there are different ways of behaving that are appropriate for different people, depending on who they are, how old they are, and the relationship they have with other people. For example, there is a dharma for daughters, and another (closely related) for wives, and another for widows.

Hindu society is divided into different groups, known as varnas, and each of the different groups has its own code of conduct. There is a dharma for **Brahmins** (the priestly class), another for **Kshatriyas** (the warrior class), another for **Vaishyas** (merchants) and another for **Sudras** (artisans):

- **Brahmins** are supposed to show qualities of ritual purity, knowledge of the Vedas, self-control and forgiveness.
- **Kshatriyas** should be brave and loyal, courageous in battle, generous, and be good leaders.
- **Vaishyas** should work hard in trade, agriculture and commerce, supporting the needs of the community and dealing honestly and fairly.
- **Sudras** should work in service to others, showing qualities of humility and care.

Hindu scriptures are a useful source of information about right and wrong. Two of the most popular Hindu texts are the

Ramayana and the Mahabharata (see pages 10, 11). These epic tales tell long stories in which the leading characters find themselves in situations where moral issues are raised. The stories show how the characters behave, and what happens as a result; for example, the Mahabharata contains an episode where gambling leads people into a difficult situation. Hindus read these stories, tell them to their children, and act them out in plays – the morals of the stories help Hindus to understand right and wrong. They can aim to be like the heroes, such as Lakshmana in the Ramayana, who showed all the right qualities of a brother by his loyalty, or Sita, who was a faithful and patient wife.

One of the most important and popular teachings about dharma can be found in the Bhagavad Gita, which is a section of the Mahabharata. In the Bhagavad Gita, one of the characters, called Arjuna, is a Kshatriya and therefore meant to fight in battles when necessary. But in the story, the battle is between two rival branches of the same family, and Arjuna is unwilling to fight because he does not want to kill his own relations. Krishna teaches him that it is his duty, according to dharma, to be a warrior, and that he should follow this and not try to follow a different path instead:

> Think thou also of thy duty and do not waver. There is no greater good for a warrior than to fight in a righteous war.
> *(Bhagavad Gita 2:31)*

> And do thy duty, even if it be humble, rather than another's, even if it be great.
> *(Bhagavad Gita 3:35)*

The **Manusmriti**, or **Laws of Manu**, is another Hindu text which contains a lot of ethical teaching. It was composed in the first century BCE in Sanskrit, and discusses rituals, dharma and moral behaviour. According to Hindu tradition, it was composed originally by Manu, the first man, who survived a great flood and went on to be the founder of the human race.

The Bhagavad Gita teaches Hindus how to follow their dharma, or right path in life. Kshatriyas should fight in battles, because this is their dharma.

Why do Hindus think it is important to try to be good?

Hindus believe that their behaviour in this life affects what will happen to them in future lives, because of the law of karma. If they do wrong in the present, then in the future they might be born into a poorer family, or have some kind of illness or disability. If they aim to follow their dharma, and behave in the right way according to the code of conduct set out for them by the eternal law, then they can expect to be rewarded in their future lives with prosperity, good health and many sons.

Hindus also try to be good as a way of pleasing the gods. Some of the deities, such as Vishnu, are believed to be particularly concerned with human morality. A person who studies the Vedas and behaves properly might help to prevent the deities from becoming displeased, and will help the family to have good luck.

Discussion

Do you agree with the idea that our behaviour in this life affects the way that we are reborn? What do you think are the best reasons for leading a good life?

Activity

1 Explain what Hindus mean by dharma, and give some examples of how dharma might be different for different kinds of people.

2 What reasons might a Hindu give to someone who wanted to know why they should behave in the right way?

Islam

Beliefs about the goodness of Allah and the nature of Shaytan/'Iblis

It is a fundamental belief of Islam that Allah is good and merciful:

> In the name of Allah, Most Gracious, Most Merciful. Prasie be to Allah, the Cherisher and Sustainer of the worlds: Most Gracious, Most Merciful.
> *(Surah 1:1–3)*

Muslims believe therefore that Allah will look after them and guide them so that they can follow his teachings and live in submission to his will. The reason that there is evil and suffering in the world is explained by the existence of **Shaytan** (**'Iblis**).

Islam teaches that Allah made Mala'ikah (angels) from nur (divine light); he created Adam, the first human, from clay; he also created spirits called Jinn and these came from fire. After Allah had made Adam, he ordered the angels and Jinn to bow down to his new creation. The angels obeyed but 'Iblis (the Devil) a Jinn, refused.

> (Allah) said: 'O 'Iblis! What is your reason for not being among those who prostrated themselves?' ('Iblis) said: 'I am not one to prostrate myself to man, whom Thou didst create from sounding clay, from mud moulded into shape.' (Allah) said: 'Then get thee out from here: for thou art rejected, accursed. And the Curse shall be on thee till the Day of Judgement.'
> *(Surah 15:32–35)*

'Iblis said that he would tempt humans for ever to choose wrong rather than right.

'Iblis is sometimes called Shaytan (the Devil – literally, the rebellious one). In his last sermon, Muhammad ﷺ warned his followers:

> Beware of Shaytan, he is desperate to divert you from the worship of Allah, so beware of him in matters of your religion.

It is Allah who allows Shaytan and the Jinns who followed him to continue to tempt people. Shaytan does this by presenting evil as an attractive thing. However, he has no power to make people do wrong, because Allah has given everyone free will.

Shaytan is not equal to Allah and although he is used to test a Muslim's faith, he cannot harm people unless Allah permits it:

> But he cannot harm them in the least, except as Allah permits; and on Allah let the Believers put their trust.
> *(Surah 58:10)*

Shaytan's first temptation was of Adam. According to the Qur'an Adam and Hawwa' (Eve) were tempted by Shaytan and ate the fruit of the forbidden tree in Al-Jannah (Paradise). Allah forgave Adam and Hawwa' their sins when they prayed to him:

They said:

> Our Lord! We have wronged our own souls: if Thou forgive us not and bestow not upon us Thy Mercy, we shall certainly be lost.
> *(Surah 7:23)*

Allah said:

> Get ye down all from here: and if, as is sure, there comes to you guidance from Me, whosoever follows My guidance, on them shall be no fear, nor shall they grieve.
> *(Surah 2:38)*

This is very different from the version of this story found in the Jewish scriptures where Adam and Eve are banished for their sin and from the Christian interpretation of this story, where the sin of eating from the tree brought the idea of Original Sin into the world. Adam and Hawwa', did not bring sin into the world and because every person is born in submission to Allah, everyone has their own responsibility to choose between right and wrong.

Islam says that during their lives people will be tempted. Life is a series of tests to which people have to find their own solutions:

> Be sure we shall test you with something of fear and hunger, some loss in goods or lives or the fruits (of your toil), but give glad tidings to those who patiently persevere – who say, when afflicted with calamity: 'To Allah we belong, and to Him is our return' – They are those on whom (descend) blessings from their Lord, and Mercy, and they are the ones that receive guidance.
>
> *(Surah 2:156–157)*

It is important for Muslims to remember that there is life after death and the next life will be better than this one. Suffering and the existence of evil in the world is a test, but people who survive this life well will have increased rewards in the afterlife. Anyone who lives according to the teaching of the Qur'an will not suffer forever even if their life is hard. It is also the responsibility of Muslims to reduce suffering for others as much as possible. Muslims cannot know why Allah permits

evil and suffering but they understand that it is all part of a larger plan that is beyond human comprehension.

> What is the life of this world but amusement and play? But verily the Home in the Hereafter – that is life indeed, if they but knew.
>
> *(Surah 29:64)*

Discussion

How do you think a Muslim might cope with suffering if it seems that prayers are not answered?

Activity

1 Explain Muslim teaching about Shaytan/'Iblis.

2 Do you think that Muslims are right to believe in an all-loving, all-powerful God when there is evil in the world? Give reasons for your answer.

Living according to the will of Allah

Muslims believe that all human beings are born without sin (**fitrah**). Therefore Muslims have free will and can choose whether to follow the will of Allah (Islam) or they can choose to do wrong. As Muslims also believe in predestination it can be difficult to understand this teaching about free will. Muslims are entirely free to make their own decisions, whether these are for good or bad, but Allah already knows what these decisions will be. There would be no purpose in Allah stopping people from making the wrong decisions, only when they have the choice can they exercise their desire to do what is right, which is submission to the will of Allah.

Allah forgives people who acknowledge that they are wrong and pray for forgiveness. Islam teaches that goodness is always better than evil:

> Nor can Goodness and Evil be equal. Repel (Evil) with what is better. Then will he between whom and thee was hatred become as it were thy friend and intimate!
>
> *(Surah 41:34)*

It is Allah who decides whether someone will be punished or forgiven. Muslims do not make public confessions of their sins.

Islam means 'submission' and living according to the Five Pillars, the teachings of the Qur'an and the example of Muhammad ﷺ, is to live according to Allah's will.

The Five Pillars are fundamental to Muslim life and a Muslim may sin against Allah by not living according to them:

- Shahadah – declaration of faith which states:

  > There is no god except Allah, Muhammad is the Messenger of Allah.

- Salah – five compulsory daily prayers for communicating with, and worshipping Allah. These are performed under specific conditions, in the manner taught by the Prophet Muhammad ﷺ and are said in Arabic. The prayers are said at fixed times and can be performed alone or with other people. Saying these prayers not only fulfils the instructions of the Qur'an and the Prophet, but also means that everyday concerns do not take over a Muslim's life. At regular intervals work has to stop and the Muslim has the opportunity to focus his or her thoughts on Allah.

- Zakah – this is literally 'the purification of wealth by the payment of an annual welfare due'. The observance of Zakah means that Muslims are protected from greed and over-concern about money. After they have given the 2.5% in zakah, the rest of their money is 'purified' for their own use.

- Hajj – pilgrimage to Makkah. The annual pilgrimage to Makkah in Saudi Arabia is an obligation on all Muslims who are able to afford it and who are fit enough to undertake it. It provides an opportunity not only to do the will of Allah but also to visit the holy places of Islam, to follow the journey taken by the Prophet and to share the experience and the prayers with other Muslims from all over the world.
- Sawm – fasting during Ramadan. The fast of Sawm is of particular importance to Muslims because, for a month, they have the opportunity to focus their thoughts on Allah because of the requirement to fast, and also to share the experience of fasting with their immediate family and also the **ummah** (the world-wide community of Muslims), all of whom are fasting at the same time.

A Muslim who believes in the statement of faith and lives his or her life according to this statement and the other four pillars is living in submission to Allah.

Islam is a religion which brings together the spiritual and everyday aspects of life and aims to control a person's relationship with God (through his or her conscience) as well as human relationships. Islam therefore affects all aspects of life, spiritual, private and public.

The combination of the words of the Qur'an and the teachings and example of Muhammad ﷺ guide Muslims in making moral decisions. Muslims study the Qur'an and the collections of Hadith in order to reach moral decisions. In this way they are following the words of Allah, given to the Prophet, and also the example of the life of Muhammad ﷺ himself. These two together give Muslims a clear idea of how Allah wishes them to behave. These provide them with the examples they need to direct their conscience and to determine 'right' from 'wrong'. Their conscience is then guided by prayer and their submission to Allah's will.

Living in submission to Allah is the way a Muslim would want to live because it shows respect to Allah and shows the Muslim is thankful for the love and care which Allah has always shown. It is also necessary if a Muslim is to reach Paradise at the Day of Judgement.

Discussion

Consider how it might be possible to believe in predestination and also in free will.

Activity

1 Explain what people mean when they say that they are guided by their consciences. Do you think that it is always right to do what your conscience tells you to do?

2 How might Muslims use (a) the Qur'an and (b) the example of Muhammad ﷺ, when they are making moral decisions?

Judaism

Beliefs about the goodness of G-d and the nature of Satan

Jews believe that G-d is good and will always protect and care for them.

This goodness is shown by the creation of the world, by the giving of the Ten Commandments so that the Israelites knew how they could live according to G-d's will, by the many occasions on which G-d saved the Israelites in the Jewish scriptures and also in the covenants which G-d made:

> And I will make of you a great nation; I will bless you, and make your name great, and you shall be a blessing. I will bless those who bless you, and him who curses you I will curse; and all the families of the earth shall bless themselves by you.
>
> *(Genesis 12:2–3)*

Judaism believes that when G-d created humans he made them so that they could chose whether to worship him or not. This is called 'free will' and it is often said that G-d would not want people worshipping him like robots who had been programmed to do this. People must follow G-d's teachings because they have decided that this is the right thing to do.

However, if we are free to choose then we will sometimes make mistakes and we will suffer because of this:

> Not to have known suffering is not to be truly human.
>
> *(Midrash)*

The story of the fall of **Lucifer**, the archangel who was to become the Devil, is not found in the Tenakh but in some of the Jewish **apocryphal books**.

According to these books, when G-d decided to create, the angels were consulted. Some said this was a good idea because he would show love and mercy whilst others were opposed to the idea because of the falsehood and strife he would create. Finally, G-d decided to create human beings. The angels were so amazed by this that they wanted to worship Adam but the man pointed upwards to G-d. All the angels were ordered to bow down to Adam and they all did so, except for Satan, who was hurled down into hell and developed an eternal hatred for human beings.

Some rabbis have taught that as G-d makes good, he also makes evil:

> [I am the One] Who forms light and creates darkness; Who makes peace and creates evil; I am Hᴀꜱʜᴇᴍ, Maker of all these.
>
> *(Isaiah 45:7)*

The common understanding of this is that the righteous undergo suffering for even the smallest sin they have committed so that they will enjoy their full reward in paradise, while the wicked are rewarded in this world for any small amount of good they have done and in the world to come they will receive the full punishment they deserve.

The story of humanity and the battle between good and evil begins with the story of Adam and Eve in the Garden of Eden:

> Hᴀꜱʜᴇᴍ G-d took the man and placed him in the Garden of Eden, to work it and to guard it. And Hᴀꜱʜᴇᴍ G-d commanded the man, saying, 'Of every tree of the garden you may freely eat, but of the Tree of Knowledge of Good and Bad, you must not eat thereof; for on the day you eat of it, you shall surely die.'
>
> *(Genesis 2:15–17)*

> Now the serpent was cunning beyond any beast of the field that Hashem G-d had made. He said to the woman, 'Did, perhaps, G-d say: "You shall not eat of any tree of the garden"?' The woman said to the serpent, 'Of the fruit of any tree of the garden we may eat. Of the fruit of the tree which is in the centre of the garden G-d has said: "You shall neither eat of it nor touch it, lest you

die."' The serpent said to the woman, 'You will not surely die; for G-d knows that on the day you eat of it your eyes will be opened and you will be like G-d, knowing good and bad.' And the woman perceived that the tree was good for eating and that it was a delight to the eyes, and that the tree was desirable as a means to wisdom, and she took of its fruit and ate; and she gave also to her husband with her and he ate.

(Genesis 3:1–6)

Although the serpent is seen as tempting Adam and Eve to do something evil (something which G-d did not want them to do) the Jewish scriptures do not describe the serpent as the devil or Satan.

Satan as an evil power does not appear in the Jewish scriptures until the book of Chronicles, where he is seen as influencing King David:

An adversary [Satan] stood against Israel, and enticed David to take a count of [the people of] Israel.

(1 Chronicles 21:1)

In the Book of Job he is seen as a sort of spy for G-d who travels around the earth and reports everyone who he sees behaving against G-d's wishes. G-d allows him to do this but sets limits on his power.

Originally Jews believed that people were punished for things which their parents or grandparents had done wrong:

For I am HASHEM, your G-d – a jealous G-d, Who visits the sins of the fathers upon children to the third and fourth generations, for My enemies; but Who shows kindness for thousands [of generations] to those who love Me and observe My commandments.

(Exodus 20:5–6)

But later the prophet Ezekiel said that people could only be punished for their own sins:

Behold, all souls are Mine, like the soul of the father, so the soul of the son, they are Mine. The soul that sins – it shall die.

(Ezekiel 18:4)

Coping with suffering

Since the Jews were driven out of Israel in 70 CE they have suffered from persecution in many times in many countries. The most famous example of suffering in the Bible is found in the book of Job. Job loses everything in a test of his faith organised by G-d and Satan. He cannot understand why he is suffering but still never loses faith in G-d. At the end of the book his suffering ends and everything is restored to him.

Therefore Jews always try to accept what happens to them as G-d's will and always continue to praise G-d for all that he has done in taking care of his people.

Jews also believe that they should apologise to G-d and to others for their behaviour and every year, in preparation for Yom Kippur, the Day of Atonement, Jews apologise to everyone whom they might have upset or hurt during the year and they also apologise to G-d for everything they have done wrong during the year. They do not make an individual apology but instead they apologise on behalf of everyone, listing all the sins that the Jewish people may have committed.

Discussion

Do you think that it really matters whether the stories of Adam and Eve and of the fall of Lucifer are true?

Activity

1 Explain Jewish teaching about Satan.

2 Do you think that Jews are right to believe in an all-loving, all-powerful G-d when there is evil in the world? Give reasons for your answer.

The Holocaust

Despite all their attempts to do what G-d wants, throughout history the Jews have been persecuted and have suffered for their religion, yet their belief in their G-d is strong despite all of this.

There are many stories of Jews being defeated in battles, being taken into slavery and being killed, simply because they were Jews. They suffered at the hands of the Egyptians and the Babylonians and, later, from the Greeks and the Romans.

The majority of the Jews were driven out of Israel in the first century CE and it did not become their own country again until 1948. During these 900 years Jews lived all over the world, at first accepted by people and later persecuted by them.

Throughout the 19th century Jews living in Russia were often the victims of **pogroms** (persecutions). They were frequently forced to leave their land and belongings because the Russian authorities wanted them and thought that the Jews were somehow not as important as other people.

The most recent disaster to hit the Jews was the **Shoah** or **Holocaust** of the Second World War. The Chancellor of Germany, Adolf Hitler, told his people that he was going to create the '**Master Race**'. This would consist of Aryan people, tall with blonde hair and blue eyes. Many German Jews were in powerful financial positions. Hitler said that they were the main cause of all Germany's problems and that they must be stopped. In an event called the **Final Solution**, he attempted to have all the Jews in Europe collected together in camps in Germany and Poland, such as Auschwitz–Birkenau, Sobibór and Treblinka, and here they were gassed. Six million Jews, together with other 'undesirables' such as gypsies, communists, Slavs and homosexuals were murdered by order of the German government in an attempt to be rid of them forever and to establish the Master Race.

Hitler was not, of course, successful and after his defeat Judaism began to grow

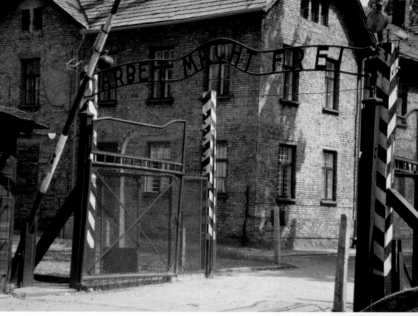

This is the gateway to Kal Nazi concentration camp Auschwitz–Birkenau The sign on the gate says 'Work Makes You Free'.

once more. It would not be surprising however if some Jews felt that their G-d had let them down. Many Jews did say that 'G-d died in Auschwitz', or that 'G-d was not in Auschwitz', but for others the tragedy served only to strengthen their faith and they believe that 'G-d was in Auschwitz' still caring for his people. Some decided that perhaps their earlier faith was too simple and that the events of the Holocaust required them to rethink how they lived, but nevertheless the belief in G-d has continued.

Making moral decisions

The Torah and the Talmud provide teachings for the Jews in the word of G-d and the interpretation of the rabbis. These teachings show the way to lead an halakhic life – a life of walking with G-d. The principles of this way of life are laid down in the Ten Commandments and the 613 mitzvot.

To live a good life, a Jew must try to follow the Ten Commandments and to observe the 613 mitzvot. In this way they can 'walk with G-d'. The many rules and regulations in the Bible are not put there to make life difficult but as a guide and a set of instructions as to how G-d wants his people to live so that they can live in a way that will enable him to love them.

These conditions were laid down in the various covenants (agreements) which G-d made with Noah, Abraham, Moses and Jeremiah.

Some of the covenants are one-sided in that G-d simply makes promises to his people, such as he does to Noah after the flood:

> And I will confirm My covenant with you: Never again shall all flesh be cut off by the waters of the flood, and never again shall there be a flood to destroy the earth.
>
> *(Genesis 9:11)*

In the later covenants G-d makes promises to his people and also places requirements on them. After he has promised to make Abraham the founder of a great nation, he says:

> And as for you, you shall keep My covenant – you and your offspring after you throughout the generations. This is My covenant which you shall keep between Me and you and your offspring after you: Every male among you shall be circumcised.
>
> *(Genesis 17:9–10)*

The first commandment was given to Adam when G-d told him to:

> Be fruitful and multiply, fill the earth and subdue it.
>
> *(Genesis 1:28a).*

Next came the Ten Commandments given to the Israelites at Mount Sinai. Jewish teaching says that as well as giving Moses the written Torah (the five books: Genesis, Exodus, Leviticus, Numbers and Deuteronomy), G-d also gave him the oral Torah. The oral Torah was an explanation and development of the ideas and teachings of the written Torah.

This was passed down through many generations by word of mouth until finally, after the destruction of the Temple, the rabbis decided that it needed to be written down. This later became the Talmud, a collection of the oral Torah together with the writings of over a thousand teachers. It is divided into **Hagaddah** (stories), **Mishnah** (laws and rulings) and Gemara (explanations of the law). Finally, the **Midrash** was produced, a rabbinic commentary and interpretation of the Scriptures which contains teachings on law, morality and religious life based on the Torah.

Jews use the Torah and Talmud to help them make ethical decisions and many will also consult their rabbis. Jews believe that the conscience is a form of spiritual pain, led by G-d's love, and that the suffering they experience may cause the conscience to make the correct ethical decisions.

Discussion

Is there any way in which the enormous suffering of the Holocaust can be explained and understood?

Activity

1 Explain what people mean when they say that they are guided by their consciences. Do you think that it is always right to do what your conscience tells you to do?

2 How might Jews use the scriptures when they are making moral decisions?

Practice GCSE questions

Christianity

(a) Describe Christian beliefs about why there is evil in the world. (8 marks)

(b) Explain how a Christian might find out the right way to behave. (7 marks)

(c) 'People should try to be happy; there is no point in trying to be good.'
Do you agree? Give reasons to support your answer, and show that you have thought about different points of view. You must refer to Christianity in your answer. (5 marks)

Hinduism

(a) Describe Hindu beliefs about why there is evil in the world. (8 marks)

(b) Explain how a Hindu might find out the right way to behave. (7 marks)

(c) 'People should try to be happy; there is no point in trying to be good.'
Do you agree? Give reasons to support your answer, and show that you have thought about different points of view. You must refer to Hinduism in your answer. (5 marks)

Islam

(a) Describe Muslim beliefs about why there is evil in the world. (8 marks)

(b) Explain how a Muslim might find out the right way to behave. (7 marks)

(c) 'People should try to be happy; there is no point in trying to be good.'
Do you agree? Give reasons to support your answer, and show that you have thought about different points of view. You must refer to Islam in your answer. (5 marks)

Judaism

(a) Describe Jewish beliefs about why there is evil in the world. (8 marks)

(b) Explain how a Jew might find out the right way to behave. (7 marks)

(c) 'People should try to be happy; there is no point in trying to be good.'
Do you agree? Give reasons to support your answer, and show that you have thought about different points of view. You must refer to Judaism in your answer. (5 marks)

Tips

For all four questions

In part (a), you need to concentrate on describing the beliefs of the religion you are studying, rather than giving your own opinion. What might a religious believer say, if asked why there is so much evil and suffering in the world? Would they blame it on God, or the Devil, or on humanity itself? What reasons would they give? For high marks, you should try and express religious ideas as clearly as you can, and perhaps give some examples.

In part (b) you should demonstrate your understanding of the issues involved. Try to think of several different ideas. You might write about the holy books and the traditions of the religion you are studying, or the ways in which religious leaders in a community might help people with decisions.

For part (c), you need to show that you realise people might have different views about this. How might a religious believer respond – what might they say about why people should bother to be good? What might a non-believer, or someone from a different religion, say in response to this question? Remember as well to give your own view. It might be the same as one of the ideas you have already expressed, or it might be another, different point of view.

UNIT 6

Religion and Human Relationships

Christianity

Christian marriage ceremonies

Christians believe that, ideally, marriage should be for life. In a Christian marriage ceremony, the priest, vicar or minister begins by explaining that marriage was created by God, and that it symbolises the relationship between Christ and the Church. The bride and groom agree in front of the congregation that they are free and willing to marry each other, and then they make promises, or vows. In these vows, they promise to love and comfort each other, to honour each other, to support each other in all different circumstances and to remain faithful to each other for the rest of their lives. They exchange rings, and the marriage is blessed. There are prayers for the couple, and usually hymns. The bride and groom have to sign the marriage register, which is a legal document, and this is witnessed by two guests.

Wedding customs in Christianity vary according to the culture of the couple. In most cultures, the bride wears a white dress, symbolising purity. She often has bridesmaids who help her with her dress and her flowers. Sometimes confetti is thrown, or sweets are given to the guests, or money is pinned to the bride; but although these customs are different depending on the culture, the main elements of a Christian marriage remain the same. Christian marriage ceremonies are designed to reflect Christian teachings about the purposes and value of marriage:

● They reflect the belief that marriage is something intended by God, from the beginning of creation.
● They show that men and women should enter a Christian marriage of their own free choice, and not because someone else has forced them into it.

● They reflect the Christian belief in **monogamy** (a faithful partnership between one man and one woman). They also show that a Christian marriage is meant to be for life.
● They reflect the belief that a permanent marriage is the best context for having children.

Christians believe that marriage is part of God's plan for humanity, and ideally should be a lifelong commitment.

The roles of men and women within a Christian family

Christians have different views about the roles that men and women should have within a family. Some Christians believe that God designed men and women to have different roles. Men and women, they say, are equally valuable to God, but they were created for different purposes.

In the book of Genesis, the creation story tells how Adam was created first, and then Eve. Eve was made because God realised that it was not good for Adam to be on his own; he needed a companion:

> The LORD God said, 'It is not good for the man to be alone. I will make a helper suitable for him.'
>
> *(Genesis 2:18)*

Some Christians might say that this shows that women are meant to be helpers for men. The duties of a man come first, and the woman should support him, because that was why she was made in the first place. In the Genesis story, Eve was the first person to sin, and she tempted Adam to copy her; so some Christians say that this shows women are weaker than men and are more likely to do wrong. They might use this to argue that men should therefore have the final say in a family, if there are differences of opinion.

In the New Testament, 1 Peter (a letter written to a newly formed Christian church) echoes these views:

> Wives, … be submissive to your husbands… Husbands, in the same way be considerate as you live with your wives, and treat them with respect as the weaker partner.
>
> *(1 Peter 3:1,7)*

Some Christians, therefore, argue that these teachings are still true today. They might say that a woman should have a different role from a man, particularly in marriage. She should look after the home, take care of the children, and support her husband in his career. If, for example, her husband is offered a promotion which involves moving house, she should be willing to go, if this is what he thinks is right.

Other Christians believe that these views belong in the past, and say that they are not appropriate for modern society. They might argue that men and women were created equally; they were both made 'in the image of God' (Genesis 1:27). Therefore there is no real difference between them, and men and women should have equal opportunities and equal responsibilities. If a married couple have children, both the mother and the father should share child-care, and both partners should be able to go out to work if this is what they want to do. They might justify these beliefs by drawing attention to Biblical passages which say that Christianity means there are no important differences between men and women:

> There is neither … male nor female, for you are all one in Christ Jesus.
>
> *(Galatians 3:28)*

In some Christian households, therefore, women take on traditional roles of child-care and housework, and consider it their job to support their husbands in their careers. Other Christian households have a more modern view, where men and women have more similar and equal roles.

Discussion

Do you think that there are jobs at home, or in the world of work, that are more suitable for one gender than for the other?

Do you think that today, when people often live for more than 75 years, it is reasonable to expect that they should stay married for life? Give reasons to support your argument.

Activity

1 Describe the main features of a Christian wedding ceremony.

2 Explain why Christians still believe that marriage is important – try to give several reasons.

Christian beliefs about the ethics of divorce

All Christians realise that sometimes marriages do not work, and a married couple might end up making each other unhappy. However, within Christianity, there are very different views about the ways in which Christians should behave if they no longer wish to stay with the person that they married. The teaching in the Bible is not completely clear on the subject of divorce. In Matthew's Gospel, Jesus teaches that a man is only allowed to divorce his wife if she has been unfaithful to him (Matthew 5:31–32), but in Mark's Gospel, divorce is not allowed at all, under any circumstances (Mark 10:11–12). Christians have come to different conclusions about which is the right teaching to follow.

The **Roman Catholic Church** teaches that married couples may live apart, if that is what they want to do, but they may not divorce. Catholics believe that marriage is a **sacrament**; it is a sign of something holy and special done by God, and it cannot be undone, any more than a baptism or taking part in Mass can be undone. Roman Catholics, therefore, cannot marry a new partner if their first husband or wife is still alive. But sometimes, in serious situations, a marriage can be **annulled**, which means that it is agreed that the marriage bond never really existed, perhaps because one of the partners was forced into the marriage or did not understand what was happening. It is not easy for a Roman Catholic couple to have their marriage annulled, and usually they have to choose between staying married, or divorcing without the agreement and recognition of the Church.

Other Christian denominations, such as the **Church of England**, have different ideas. They believe that if the couple sincerely believe that there is no possibility they will ever want to live together again, divorce can be allowed, and both partners are then free to marry other people. If either of them wants to marry a new partner in church after they have been divorced, then it is up to the vicar or minister to decide whether they are taking Christian marriage seriously enough for this to be allowed.

The Christian Churches agree that they should do all that they can to help couples who are having difficulties in their relationships. They often have special classes for people who are about to get married, and groups that married couples can join to talk about how they can work towards a happy and successful married life. Some churches also run counselling services to help people who are thinking about separating or divorcing.

Christian beliefs about sexual relationships and contraception

Within Christianity, there are many different opinions about sexual relationships. Many Christians believe that sex is only appropriate between people who are married to each other. This means that sex before marriage, homosexual relationships and affairs outside marriage are all considered to be wrong. They argue that the Bible teaches that the human body is a 'temple of the Holy Spirit':

> Do you not know that your body is a temple of the Holy Spirit, who is in you, whom you have received from God? You are not your own; you were bought at a price. Therefore honour God with your body.
>
> *(1 Corinthians 6:19)*

and that it should be treated with respect. They might also say that sex was designed by God for a purpose – to create children and to strengthen the love between married people. If sex is used only for pleasure and not for the reasons God made it, then this behaviour spoils something that was meant to be very special.

Other Christians believe that these views are old-fashioned. They say that the main message of Christianity is love, and that sex is morally acceptable within any relationship that is committed and loving, whether or not the people involved are married to each other. Some Christians, then, might accept sexual relationships between a committed homosexual couple, or between two people who are living together on a permanent basis, but they would still think that it is wrong for people to have sex if they have only just met and if they do not particularly care about each other or plan to stay together in a lasting relationship.

Contraception (birth control)

The Roman Catholic Church teaches that artificial contraception is wrong. It is acceptable for Roman Catholics to use 'natural methods' to plan their families, such as only making love at the times of the month when a woman is at her least fertile, but it is not acceptable to use artificial methods such as the Pill or condoms. This is taught because Roman Catholics believe that the main reason why God created sex was so that children could be brought into the world, and they say that using artificial contraception goes against God's plans.

Some people, however, including some Roman Catholics, disagree with this teaching. They argue that it could sometimes be a good idea for people to use contraception, especially if they do not have enough money to support a large family.

Other Christian Churches, such as the Church of England and the Methodist Church, give very different teachings. They say that using contraception is the responsible thing to do. People should be free to choose when to have children, and how many they want to have, so that every child brought into the world is wanted by its parents. Family planning using contraception is therefore encouraged.

Discussion

Why do you think couples today often choose to live together without getting married? Do you think that people should marry if they want to have to children, or do you think that it doesn't matter?

Activity

1 Explain two different Christian views about (a) divorce and (b) contraception. Which do you agree with, and why? (If you agree with neither, say why and explain your own view instead.)

2 Do you think that sex should only happen between heterosexuals who are married to each other? Give reasons for your answer, and explain what a Christian might say.

Roman Catholics believe that the main purpose of sex is so that children can be brought into the world.

Hinduism

Hindu marriage ceremonies

Hindus believe that marriage is an important duty for men and women; choosing to stay single is not encouraged. In Hindu society, a marriage does not just join together a man and a woman, but brings together two entire extended families. This can have a large impact on a community, particularly in a village, and so it has often been the practice for Hindu parents to arrange a marriage for their son or daughter, or at least to help them to find someone suitable by organising meetings with people who might make suitable partners.

There are many different marriage customs within Hinduism. Customs vary between one region of India and another, and also they depend on the circumstances of the wedding. A widow who is getting married for the second time will have a much quieter, less elaborate ceremony than a young bride, for example.

Hindu weddings take place at a time carefully chosen, after horoscopes of both partners have been consulted. There are many preparations and celebrations in the bride's home, where cooking and parties will begin several days before the wedding itself. Traditionally, the wedding ceremony takes place in the home of the bride, but often a hall is hired so that enough guests can be accommodated, and a small altar is set up in the middle. The bride and her family wait in the hall to welcome the groom and his relations. Blessings are said and sung by the two families and the priest. Then the bride is given away in marriage by her parents, who join the couple's hands. The priest lights a sacred fire, in honour of the god Agni, and recites sacred chants, called **mantras**, in the holy language of Sanskrit, and the groom also repeats sacred words which ask for the marriage to be blessed with children. The end of the bride's sari is tied to her new husband's scarf, as a symbol that they are joined together.

In many traditions, the bride places her foot on a stone, which symbolises her willingness to perform her duties as a wife and to use all her strength to try to overcome any problems the couple might have. Then the couple walks seven steps around the sacred fire, with the groom's right hand on the bride's right shoulder, and at every step a prayer is said for a special blessing:

1 for food
2 for strength
3 for wealth
4 for wisdom and happiness
5 for children
6 for good health
7 for friendship.

The groom's family helps him to make offerings of barley to the fire, and the guests and priest bless the couple with good wishes for a long, happy marriage with children and grandchildren.

These wedding rituals symbolise that in Hinduism, marriage is for life. The husband and wife have duties to perform towards one another, and have the support of the whole community.

The 'seven steps' around the sacred fire are the most important part of a Hindu marriage.

Contraception (birth control)

Until relatively recently, birth control was an idea which went completely against the thinking of Hindus. Children born to families in India had a high chance of dying in infancy, and adults needed to have children in order to provide a work force if they were unable to afford to pay someone to help them. It was also seen as a sign of great blessing for a family to have many sons; and therefore, it was quite common for there to be as many as eight or ten children in a family, although not all of them would survive to become adults. The sacred writings of Hinduism encourage people not to limit the number of children that they have, and it was much more usual for Hindus to worry about being childless, rather than about having too many children.

However, in modern times, the situation has changed. In general, people have better food, and better access to medical care and immunisation, and, as a result of this, a higher proportion of children reach adulthood. World population has risen dramatically, and the population of India has grown faster than that of many other countries. The Indian government has encouraged people to use contraception and to limit their families to two or three children, and Hinduism as a religion does not object to this policy. Many Hindus use some form of birth control, although there is still the pressure to produce sons, and so a couple with daughters is likely to want to keep on having children until at least one son is born. When people do not use contraception, it is usually because they are uneducated and illiterate, and do not understand what is available to them. The government continues to promote the idea of smaller families, and sends health workers into poorer areas to teach people about how to obtain and use contraceptives.

Discussion

Do you think that it is all right for Hindus to value sons more highly than daughters, if that is their culture, or do you think something should be done to try and change this attitude?

Activity

1 Explain the ways in which a Hindu woman's expectations of married life might be different from those of a Western woman.

2 Why is divorce quite rare amongst Hindus?

3 Explain (a) why the Indian government works to promote contraception, and (b) why some Hindus still have large families.

Muslim marriage ceremonies

A Muslim marriage ceremony is a very simple one. There is a declaration to the witnesses of the marriage that the bride and groom are marrying of their own free will. A marriage contract is signed which specifies the mahr (dowry) which the groom is giving to the bride and then there are prayers and readings and a ceremonial sermon usually led by the imam.

Almighty God created humanity, male and female, each in need of the other, and established the institution of marriage as a means of uniting souls in blessed bond of love…

Some Muslims in the United Kingdom now include specific vows in their marriage ceremony and these include promising that, in accordance with the teaching of the Qur'an, they will work to make the marriage an act of obedience to Allah and a relationship of mercy, love, peace and faithfulness.

The nature of marriage is laid down in the Qur'an:

Among His signs it is that, that He created you from dust; and then – Behold, ye are human beings scattered (far and wide). And among His signs is this, that He created for you mates from among yourselves, that ye may dwell in tranquillity with them, and He has put love and mercy between your (hearts): verily in that are Signs for those who reflect.

(Surah 30:20–21)

They are your garments and ye are their garments.

(Surah 2:187)

Marriage and the family are the basis of Islamic society:

It is He Who has created man from water: then has He established relationships of lineage and marriage.

(Surah 25:54)

No institution in Islam finds more favour with God than marriage.

(Hadith)

Many Muslim marriages are arranged by families. Courtship or 'going out with each other' is not permitted and the couple who may be married are only allowed to meet each other when members of their families are present. Although marriages like this may be arranged by families, no one can ever be forced to marry someone in Islam and if this did happen then the marriage would be invalid.

The father or any other guardian cannot give in marriage a virgin or one who has been married before without her consent.

(Hadith)

Men are urged to be careful about who they marry:

A woman is taken in marriage for three reasons; for her beauty, for family connections or the lure of wealth. Choose the one with faith and you will have success.

(Hadith 4:235)

Under normal circumstances a Muslim man has only one wife but the Qur'an does permit polygamy under certain circumstances.

If ye fear that ye shall not be able to deal justly with the orphans, marry women of your choice, two, or three, or four; but if ye fear that ye shall not be able to deal justly (with them), then only one.

(Surah 4:3)

The roles of men and women within a Muslim family

Islam teaches that men and women are equal and that Allah will judge them equally according to the way in which they have lived.

To help men value women for who they are, rather than for their bodies, women wear garments that leave only the hands and face exposed (see Surah 33:59).

Many non-Muslim Westerners cannot understand Islamic teachings about women and feel that the need for women to be covered up in public and the way in which they are brought up is wrong.

According to Islam, the rights and responsibilities of a woman are equal to those of a man, but they are not identical and, therefore, they should be complementary to each other rather than competitive. However, it appears in the Qur'an that a final decision is to be taken by the husband (see Surah 2:228, 4:34).

In Islam this difference is seen as both natural and desirable. Men must support the family while women bear and rear children. Women have the right to study, refuse a marriage, to divorce, to inherit, to keep their own names, to own property, to take part in politics, and to conduct business, whether they are married or unmarried.

Some governments, saying that they are Islamic, impose harsh and repressive laws on women but these are not part of Islamic teaching.

Muhammad ﷺ stressed the respect which should be shown to women:

> Paradise lies at the feet of your mother.
> *(Sunan An-Nasa'i)*

> A man asked Prophet Muhammad ﷺ, 'O Messenger of Allah! Who deserves the best care from me?' The Prophet said, 'Your mother.' The man asked, 'Who then?' The Prophet said, 'Your mother.' The man asked yet again, 'Who then?' Prophet Muhammad ﷺ said, 'Your mother.' The man asked once more, 'Who then?' The Prophet then said, 'Your father.'
> *(Sahih Al-Bukhari)*

The great importance of the way in which a husband and wife live together is stressed in the Qur'an:

> Among His signs is this, that He created for you mates from among yourselves, that ye may dwell in tranquillity with them, and He has put love and mercy between your (hearts): verily in that are Signs for those who reflect.
> *(Surah 30:21)*

Usually, within a Muslim marriage the wife stays in the home while the husband goes out to work but there is no rule about this and it simply follows from the 'normal' practice of society. Men are expected to help at home however, because Muhammad ﷺ is known to have helped his wives.

Discussion

Do you think that there are jobs at home, or in the world of work, that are more suitable for one gender than for the other? Give reasons to support your argument.

Activity

1 Describe the main features of a Muslim wedding.

2 Explain why Muslims still believe that marriage is so important – try to give several reasons.

Muslim beliefs about the ethics of divorce

Although the principles of Muslim marriage are supported by Islam and are a common belief between the couple, Muslims realise that sometimes marriages break down. Marriage is a legal contract between two people and therefore it can be ended. This is done if continuation of the marriage brings misery to the couple and to their children and close relatives.

In the Hadith it says: 'Among all lawful things, divorce is most hated by Allah'. However, divorce is lawful, it is not forbidden by Islam.

The Qur'an says that:

> If a wife fears cruelty or desertion on her husband's part, there is no blame on them if they arrange an amicable settlement between themselves; and such settlement is best; even though men's souls are swayed by greed.
>
> *(Surah 4:128)*

A man cannot seek a divorce from his wife until it is certain that she is not pregnant, as it is possible that he might then change his mind. Once the divorce is announced there is a period of three months called **'iddah**, this is a period in which reconciliation should be attempted. If there is no reconciliation then the divorce takes place. A man and a woman can remarry twice, but after a third divorce remarriage to each other cannot take place unless the woman has been married to another man in the meanwhile (see Surah 2:230–231).

The wife can free herself completely from the marriage by returning her mahr. During the period of 'iddah, she must stay in her husband's house and he must provide everything for her. He is not allowed to evict her. It is hoped that, in this way, there may eventually be a reconciliation (see Surah 65:1).

A woman is also able to obtain a divorce, either by an agreement with her husband (**khul**) or because of his treatment of her.

Children are regarded as illegitimate if their parents are not married and, according to Shari'ah, the father has no legal responsibility.

Muslims have rules about 'marrying out'. A Muslim man may marry a Jewish or Christian woman but a Muslim woman is forbidden to marry anyone except a Muslim.

Muslim beliefs about sexual relationships and contraception

For Muslims sexual intercourse is an act of worship which fulfils emotional and physical needs as well as being the means of procreation. Children are the means by which humans can contribute towards Allah's creation. Sexual intercourse is seen as a gift from Allah and must only take place within a married relationship (see Surah 25:24).

Marriage includes the responsibility of both husband and wife to meet each other's sexual needs.

Men are forbidden from being alone with women except for their wives in case they are tempted by them:

> Let no man be in privacy with a woman who he is not married to, or Satan will be the third.
>
> *(Hadith)*

It could be said that Islam has a very realistic attitude towards sex and realises that both men and women can be tempted to have sexual relationships outside of marriage.

Sexual activity of any kind outside of marriage is forbidden. Adultery by the husband or the wife is a serious crime:

> Nor come night to adultery: for it is a shameful (deed) and an evil, opening the road (to other evils).
>
> *(Surah 17:32)*

and the Qur'an clearly specifies the punishment.

The woman and the man guilty of adultery or fornication – flog each of them with a hundred stripes: let not compassion move you in their case, in a matter prescribed by Allah, if ye believe in Allah and the Last Day: and let a party of the Believers witness their punishment.

(Surah 24:2)

Homosexual and lesbian relationships are forbidden by Islam as unnatural. In practice it is often ignored, though some Islamic lawyers have argued that it should be punished with the death penalty because it is unpure (Surah 26:165–166, 4:16).

Contraception

Islam teaches that Allah created the world and everything in it. Life is therefore a special gift.

For Muslims, the birth of a child is not an 'accident' and does not happen by mistake, it is a gift of life from Allah.

> He bestows (children) male or female according to His Will (and Plan), or He bestows both males and females, and He leaves barren whom He will. For He is full of knowledge and power.
>
> *(Surah 42:49–50)*

Because of this view, contraception is not welcomed. However, in 1971, the Conference on Islam and Family Planning agreed that safe and legal contraception was permitted under certain circumstances:
- if there was a threat to the mother's health
- if the use of contraception would help a woman who already had children
- where there was a chance of the child being born with mental or physical deformities
- where the family did not have the money to raise a child.

Generally Muslims prefer the use of the rhythm method of contraception: intercourse only takes place at the time of the month when the woman is known to be least fertile. Other, artificial methods of contraception such as condoms or the Pill are used in preference to permanent sterilisation or vasectomy.

Discussion

Do you think that today, when people often live for more than 75 years, it is reasonable to expect that they should stay married for life? Try to support your answer with reasons.

Activity

1 Explain Muslim views about (a) divorce and (b) contraception.

2 Do you think that sex should only happen between heterosexuals who are married to each other? Give reasons for your answer, and explain what a Muslim might say.

Jewish marriage ceremonies

Marriage and the family have always been at the very centre of Jewish life. Many of the ceremonies of Jewish worship take place within the home and so **kiddushin** (marriage) is seen as being of very great importance. The Talmud says that:

> A man without a woman is doomed to an existence without joy, without blessing, without experiencing life's true goodness, without Torah, without protection and without peace.

A Jewish wedding may take place in a synagogue or anywhere else, the important feature is that the bride and groom must stand under a **huppah** (wedding canopy) which represents their new home together.

A very important part of the wedding is the **Ketubah**. This is a marriage contract in which the groom makes promises about how he will look after his wife. This is often a very beautifully decorated document and may hang over the bed in the new couple's home.

Traditionally many Jews had an arranged wedding in which the couple were introduced to one another by a **shadchan** (matchmaker).

The importance of marriage in Judaism is seen as lying in the first book of the Torah, Genesis:

> Therefore a man shall leave his father and mother and cling to his wife and they shall become one flesh.
> *(Genesis 2:24)*

This is explained in the Midrash:

> G-d created the first human being half male, half female. He then separated the two parts to form a man and a woman.

The Jewish teacher, Maimonides said:

> Through the sanctification of marriage, a husband and wife become the closest of relatives.

A Jewish wedding ceremony is very short. At the centre lies the vow made by the man to the woman as he gives her a ring:

> Behold, you are consecrated to me by means of this ring, according to the rituals of Moses and Israel.

After this the **Sheva Berachos** (Seven) Blessings are said over a glass of wine.

The Seven Blessings

Blessed are You, HASHEM, our G-d, King of the universe, Who has created everything for His glory.

Blessed are You, HASHEM, our G-d, King of the universe, Who fashioned the Man.

Blessed are You, HASHEM, our G-d, King of the universe, Who fashioned the Man in His image, in the image of his likeness. And prepared for him – from himself – a building for eternity. Blessed are You, HASHEM, Who fashioned the Man.

Bring intense joy – and exultation to the barren one – through the in-gathering of her children amidst her in gladness. Blessed are You, HASHEM, Who gladdens Zion through her children.

Gladden the beloved companions as You gladdened Your creature in the Garden of Eden from aforetime. Blessed are You, HASHEM, Who gladdens groom and bride.

Blessed are You, HASHEM, our G-d, King of the universe, Who created joy and gladness, groom and bride, mirth, glad song, pleasure, delight, love, brotherhood, peace, and companionship. HASHEM, our G-d, let there soon be heard in the cities of Judah and the streets of Jerusalem the sound of joy and the sound of gladness, the voice of the groom and the voice of the bride, the sound of the grooms' jubilance from their canopies and of youths from their song-filled feasts. Blessed are You, Who gladdens the groom with the bride.

Blessed are You HASHEM, our G-d, King of the universe, Who creates the fruit of the vine.

During the ceremony the groom smashes a glass under his foot. The reason for this ritual is unknown. Some people say that it shows that marriage can be fragile, others that it represents the destruction of the Jerusalem Temple in 70 CE and reminds people that life is not perfect and of the sadness of much of Jewish history.

The roles of men and women within a Jewish family

The family is a very important part of Judaism. When Abraham was a very old man he was promised that he would have many descendants:

> Gaze, now, towards the Heavens, and count the stars if you are able to count them!… So shall your offspring be.
> (Genesis 15:5)

Many Jews still have very large families and the family is the centre of all Jewish life and worship. It is often said that the home, rather than the synagogue, is the centre of Jewish worship.

Judaism also has very strict rules concerning the relationships between husband and wife. A married couple is considered to be a complete organism whereas men and women on their own are incomplete, lacking the qualities of each other. Marriage sanctifies the relationship.

Judaism has usually seen the role of a woman as being that of helpmate, wife, mother, homemaker but still definitely subservient to her husband who 'rules over her.'

Traditionally Jewish women have no status in public prayer and worship and were not permitted to study the Torah. The woman's responsibility was seen as observing the mitzvah of lighting the candles that welcome in Sabbat and the religious holidays, observing the laws of purity and those of kashrut. All these duties rely, of course, on the woman being married; an unmarried Jewish woman has no religious status.

On the other hand, the responsibility of the man is to provide for his family, to care for his wife and children and to observe all his religious duties.

These traditional views are still important within Judaism but they are beginning to change and many Jewish wives now go out to work as well as look after their family, and within Progressive Judaism, women have taken on more religious responsibilities in the synagogue, with some becoming rabbis.

Discussion

Do you think that there are jobs at home, or in the world of work, that are more suitable for one gender than for the other? Give reasons to support your argument.

Activity

1 Describe the main features of a Jewish wedding.

2 Explain why Jews still believe that marriage is so important – try to give several reasons.

Jewish beliefs about divorce

Although Jews believe that marriage is for life, they do accept that sometimes divorce is inevitable. In these circumstances a man must issue his wife with a **get**, this is a divorce documents from a **Beth Din** (Rabbinical Court). This is the rule which is found in the book of Deuteronomy:

> If a man marries a woman and lives with her, and it will be that she will not find favour in his eyes, for he found in her a matter of immorality, and he wrote her a bill of divorce and presented it into her hand, and sent her from his house.
>
> *(Deuteronomy 24:1)*

A divorce is not allowed to take place for three months, in order to ensure that the woman is not pregnant.

Without a get neither a man nor a woman can remarry. No one can be forced to issue a get and so, even if a husband has left his wife, he can still refuse to divorce her. In these circumstances even though the woman may obtain a civil divorce she is still married according to Jewish law. However, people would not respect a man who refused to give his wife a get in these circumstances.

Because this could be seen as unfair and sexist, Progressive Jews may allow the woman to obtain a get.

In the past, most Jewish communities lived close together, often the areas in which they lived were known as **ghettos**. Here they mixed almost entirely with other Jews and so they married other Jews. Today, many young Jews live and work outside of such a closely-knit community and they may meet and fall in love with someone who is not Jewish. Very Orthodox Jews do not permit such marriages and the father of a young man or woman who finds that they intend to marry someone who is not Jewish may disown their child and say the Kaddish (the prayer said at funerals), showing that to them their child is dead (see Deuteronomy 7:3–4).

> You shall not intermarry with them; you shall not give your daughter to his son, and you shall not take his daughter for your son, for he will cause your child to turn away from after Me and they will worship the gods of others; then HASHEM's wrath will burn against you and He will destroy you quickly.
>
> *(Deuteronomy 7:3–4)*

As an increasing number of people do marry non-Jews, the number of Jewish weddings and of people taking an active part in their religion has continued to fall.

Jewish beliefs about sexual relationships and contraception

Jewish moral behaviour is laid down by mitzvot (rules) found in the Torah and the Talmud (oral Torah). Judaism has a very natural and realistic view of sexuality. Sexuality plays a very important part in human relationships. Judaism recognises the strength of sexual desire but also sees that this must be carefully controlled. It may only be expressed within a marriage.

Judaism does not believe that procreation is the only purpose for sex and says that it is a physical way in which two married people can show their love for one another even when they are too old to have children.

Adultery is forbidden by the seventh commandment and this law is very strictly observed. Also, although some of the Jewish leaders found in the Bible had several wives, Jews today may only be married to one person.

Unlike in Christianity, the idea of religious celibacy does not exist within Judaism. It is believed that G-d wished men and women to serve him by living together and producing families as the leaders in the Bible such as Abraham, Jacob and Moses did. Therefore Jewish tradition would see it as 'abnormal' for people to live celibate lives like monks or nuns.

An ancient mikveh.

Within marriage, sex is 'controlled' or regulated by the laws of niddah (sexual purity). During a woman's monthly menstrual period she is not allowed to have sex with her husband. This then continues for a further week. After this time she goes to a ritual bath called a mikveh where she 'cleans' herself. After this she and her husband can resume normal sexual relations until her next period. This is mentioned in the Torah and the Talmud:

> You shall not approach a women in her time of unclean separation, to uncover her nakedness.
>
> *(Leviticus 18:19)*

> A wife returning from the mikveh is as fresh to her husband as on their wedding day.
>
> *(Talmud)*

Although the rules of niddah are observed by most Orthodox Jews, most Progressive Jews feel that they are now out of date.

Homosexuality is forbidden in the Jewish tradition. Male homosexuality is clearly wrong according to the Torah:

> You shall not lie with a man as one lies with a woman, it is an abomination.
>
> *(Leviticus 18:22)*

Lesbianism is not mentioned in the Torah but it is forbidden in the Talmud. Orthodox Jews adhere strictly to these rules. It is believed that homosexuality is a condition which is learnt or brought about by circumstances, and that people can be helped out of it.

Contraception

Sexual relationships within a marriage are a very important part of Judaism where they are seen as a husband's duty and a woman's right, therefore the question of contraception is very important.

A passage from Genesis says that people should, 'Be fruitful and multiply, fill the earth...'. This is one of the reasons that Judaism is opposed to the use of birth control. This idea is repeated much later in Isaiah when Isaiah says:

> For thus said HASHEM, Creator of the heavens; He is the G-d, the One Who fashioned the earth and its Maker; He established it; He did not create it for emptiness; He fashioned it to be inhabited.
>
> *(Isaiah 45:18)*

However, any restriction on the use of contraceptives can be lifted if a married woman would be placed at risk, either physical or psychological, by becoming pregnant.

Contraception is not allowed when people are not married or simply feel that they do not want a child: this is viewed as interfering with G-d's plan.

When contraceptives are used, they are usually taken by the woman so that sexual intercourse is still as natural as possible. Condoms are thought to interfere with the physical relationship between couples.

Of course, the use of condoms is now recommended to help prevent the spread of the HIV virus, but they are not generally permitted by Jewish teaching. In the same way, neither sterilisation or vasectomy are permitted as they are seen as mutilating the body.

Discussion

Do you think that today, when people often live for more than 75 years, it is reasonable to expect that they should stay married for life? Try to support your answer with reasons.

Activity

1 Explain Jewish views about (a) divorce and (b) contraception.

2 Do you think that sex should only happen between heterosexuals who are married to each other? Give reasons for your answer, and explain what a Jew might say.

Practice GCSE questions

Christianity

(a) Describe Christian beliefs about the use of birth control (contraception). (8 marks)
(b) Explain how the beliefs of Christians might affect their attitudes towards divorce. (7 marks)
(c) 'People should only have sex if they are married to each other.'
Do you agree? Give reasons to support your answer, and show that you have thought about different points of view. You must refer to Christianity in your answer. (5 marks)

Hinduism

(a) Describe Hindu beliefs about the use of birth control (contraception). (8 marks)
(b) Explain how the beliefs of Hindus might affect their attitudes towards divorce. (7 marks)
(c) 'People should only have sex if they are married to each other.'
Do you agree? Give reasons to support your answer, and show that you have thought about different points of view. You must refer to Hinduism in your answer. (5 marks)

Islam

(a) Describe Muslim beliefs about the use of birth control (contraception). (8 marks)
(b) Explain how the beliefs of Muslims might affect their attitudes towards divorce. (7 marks)
(c) 'People should only have sex if they are married to each other.'
Do you agree? Give reasons to support your answer, and show that you have thought about different points of view. You must refer to Islam in your answer. (5 marks)

Judaism

(a) Describe Jewish beliefs about the use of birth control (contraception). (8 marks)
(b) Explain how the beliefs of Jews might affect their attitudes towards divorce. (7 marks)
(c) 'People should only have sex if they are married to each other.'
Do you agree? Give reasons to support your answer, and show that you have thought about different points of view. You must refer to Judaism in your answer. (5 marks)

Tips

For all four questions

In part (a) you are being asked to display your knowledge of religious attitudes towards birth control (contraception). You need to be able to show what the views are, as well as why they are held. Remember that within a religion, there might be different opinions; for example, Roman Catholic and Protestant Christians are likely to hold different views, and Orthodox and Reform Jews are also likely to have different attitudes on this issue.

For part (b), you need to be able to demonstrate your understanding. Try and say something about what marriage means in the tradition of the religion you are studying, and how this affects opinions about divorce. Again, there might be different opinions within the religion, and you could explain what these are. Try to apply the beliefs to everyday life; how might a religious believer who was unhappily married respond to the issue of divorce, and why might he or she think in this way?

In part (c), you need to evaluate the issue of sex outside marriage. You could include discussion of sex between people who are single, and also adultery. Remember that you need to refer to the religion you are studying, as well as giving your own view. You should try to support the views you give with reasons, and show that you understand how people who disagree with you might feel.

UNIT 7

Religion and Medical Ethics

Introduction

Medical ethics is about issues of right and wrong which arise in the context of health care. Often, the issues deal with life and death; should a person be kept alive in all circumstances, even if they are severely disabled or in great pain? Should babies be born even if no-one wants them, or if they will have serious health problems? Does everyone have the right to have a child, with the help of doctors when necessary? Medical staff have to deal with this sort of problem every day.

Many religious people have strong opinions about medical ethics. This is because these issues deal with life and death, and most religions teach that life comes from God and is 'sacred' or holy. When people are talking about the way in which human life is special to God, they often use the phrase **the sanctity of life**, to show how important they believe these issues are.

Abortion

An **abortion** is when a foetus leaves the mother's uterus and dies before it is ready to be born. When this happens naturally, which it often does, it is called a 'miscarriage'. But usually, when people talk about abortion, they are referring to 'procured abortion', when someone makes the choice to end a pregnancy which would probably otherwise have ended with the birth of a baby.

There are many reasons why a woman might want an abortion. She might be very young, or have become pregnant by accident, or have been raped. She might have wanted the pregnancy at first, but then her circumstances might have changed, for example her partner might have lost his job, or she might have lost hers, or their relationship might have ended. She might find out, through medical tests, that the developing foetus has serious health problems and that the baby would be disabled in some way. Whatever the reason for considering abortion, it is hardly ever an easy choice to make. The woman has to persuade two doctors that her mental or physical health would suffer if the pregnancy continues, and she has to make her decision as early in the pregnancy as she can. Abortion is only legal in the first 24 weeks of the pregnancy. After 28 weeks of development, the foetus is considered 'viable', which means it could live outside the womb if it was born, and then abortion is not an option.

Some people believe that abortion is the same as murder. They think that a foetus is a human life, whether it has been born or not. Others hold the view that a woman should not be expected to go through pregnancy and birth if this is not what she wants.

Fertility treatment

This is the name given to medical treatments which are tried when people want to have babies, but are unable to conceive naturally. There are lots of reasons for infertility; sometimes the man does not produce healthy sperm, or sometimes the woman does not ovulate, for example. If people very much want to have their own children, infertility can be extremely upsetting.

There are different medical procedures which can be used to help people conceive, depending on the cause of the problem. The success rate is not always very high, but when it does work, it can bring people great happiness. One of the most common treatments is known as IVF, which stands for **in vitro fertilisation**; 'in vitro' means

Medical staff often have to make important decisions about life and death.

'in glass', and people sometimes refer to this process as 'test tube babies'. A human egg and some healthy sperm are brought together outside the womb in a laboratory by doctors, and if the treatment works, embryos are formed and then carefully placed inside the woman's uterus where they can continue to develop until it is time for the baby to be born. Often, to make sure that at least one of the embryos survives, more than one egg will be fertilised. This can create 'spare' embryos, because the couple might want a single child or twins but may not want to take the risk of a multiple pregnancy where there is a much higher chance of miscarriage or prematurity. Religious people, and others with no religious beliefs, are often worried about what happens to these spare embryos that are not implanted. Do they count as 'people', or as 'human life', and would it be murder to throw them away if they are not needed?

Another problem that can arise is if one of the partners in the couple cannot produce healthy sperm or eggs at all. Is it all right to

use 'donor' sperm or eggs, from someone else unknown to the couple, or does this go against the idea of a man and woman being faithful to each other?

Euthanasia

Euthanasia comes from two Greek words: 'eu' meaning 'good' and 'thanatos' meaning 'death'. It is used to refer to situations where someone is 'helped' to die more quickly than they might have done naturally. It is different from suicide, because it is for people who are not capable of taking their own lives, because they are too ill or too disabled.

Sometimes people think that euthanasia is the right choice for them, because they are in a lot of pain or they are suffering from an illness which is taking away their dignity and independence. Sometimes, they are very brain-damaged or have become very confused, and they cannot make this decision. If someone asks for euthanasia, it is called **voluntary euthanasia**, but if the person has not asked or is not capable of asking, then it is called **involuntary euthanasia**. Someone else decides whether that person's quality of life is so bad that it would be better if they were dead.

When a person is helped to die by being giving an injection of strong drugs, this is known as **active euthanasia**, because a positive action was taken to bring about the death. This is against the law.

Passive euthanasia is not against the law. In cases of passive euthanasia, nothing is done deliberately to make death come more quickly, but the people involved decide not to give treatments that might prolong life. Doctors, patients, nurses and relatives might decide that it is better to allow a person to die naturally, rather than continue with extra treatment and maybe more operations just to help them live a little longer.

Some people think that euthanasia ought to be an option for those who want it. They say that it is unkind to make people continue to suffer when they are terminally ill, if it is possible do something to help them to die more quickly. They say that we would do the same for a pet who was suffering, and would allow it to be 'put down' because this is the kindest thing to do. But many religious people, and others, think that euthanasia is a form of murder, and that decisions about the end of life should be left to God.

Suicide

A **suicide** is when someone deliberately ends his or her own life. Sometimes it is called 'self-murder'. In the past in many countries suicide was treated as a crime, and if someone tried but failed to commit suicide then they would be severely punished. Today, most people recognise that if someone wants to commit suicide, this is often because they are very depressed or suffering from another kind of mental illness. Religious teaching about suicide often dates back to times when people understood a lot less about mental illness than they do today.

Animal research

For a long time, animals were used in all kinds of experiments: for cosmetics, for cleaning products, for food additives and in many other ways. This still goes on, although people are made more aware of it today from people who support animal rights, and some make an effort to avoid buying products that have used animal testing. There are strict government guidelines about how the animals should be treated, and how different companies should share the results of their experiments so that the number of animals used can be reduced.

Some people prefer to buy cosmetics that have not been tested on animals.

Testing on animals is an important part of medical research. Many of the drugs people use today have been tested on animals, and many medical and surgical procedures, such as the use of artificial feeding tubes and heart surgery, have been tried on animals before they have been used to save human life. Most medical scientists argue that, unless these tests had taken place, we would not have the safe and essential medicines that we now rely on. We can now diagnose and treat illnesses that once killed thousands of people. Animal experiments were used in the discovery of vitamins, in the understanding of how embryos develop, in the development of anaesthetics and in the understanding of how diabetes can be treated. Tests on animals have helped to produce a vaccine for polio, drugs for the treatment of asthma, and new ways of helping very premature babies to survive. These are just a few examples. Today, experiments using animals continue, in the hope of discovering ways of curing cancers and finding treatments to prevent Alzheimer's disease.

Some people believe, however, that it is wrong to use animals in this way. Many of the tests are painful for the animals. Some people argue that an animal has just as much of a right to life as humans do, and that we should not treat them in this way

just for our own benefit. They say that scientists should find other ways of testing drugs and procedures which do not involve the use of animals.

Many people prefer to buy cosmetics and other products that have not been tested on animals.

Discussion

Would you be prepared to use new medicines that had not been tested on other animals first?

Activity

Explain what is meant by:
(a) abortion, (b) euthanasia,
(c) suicide, (d) sanctity of life and
(e) animal experimentation.

 # Christianity

Different Christian attitudes towards abortion

Christian attitudes towards abortion vary widely, and the teaching of the Christian Churches has changed over the centuries. In the first 200 years after the beginning of Christianity, abortion was common, and so was the practice of killing young babies (infanticide) if they were unwanted or their parents could not afford to bring them up. In those days, the Christian Church was interested in discussing '**ensoulment**'; they argued about when it was that a developing foetus received its soul. If a foetus did not yet have a soul, abortion could be acceptable, as it did not count as murder. The conclusion was that the soul was given at 40 days if the foetus was a boy, and at 80 days if it was a girl, so abortion was allowed in the very early stages of a pregnancy, but not later, and infanticide was not allowed at all.

Today, the Roman Catholic Church is the only Christian church to give absolute, firm teaching on the subject of abortion. According to the Roman Catholic Church, abortion is never allowed, even if the pregnancy is the result of rape or the pregnant woman is very young. The only circumstances in which abortion is allowed is when it is absolutely necessary in order to save the life of the mother. Roman Catholics believe that the developing foetus is a person, with all the rights of any other person. They believe that its life is sacred and should never be deliberately destroyed.

Other Christians from different traditions might agree with this view, and believe that abortion is always wrong. They might agree that life is sacred, and consider that abortion treats human life too cheaply. Sometimes, Biblical ideas are used to support this view. For example, in the Old Testament, Jeremiah the prophet is told by God:

'Before I formed you in the womb I knew you, before you were born I set you apart; I appointed you as a prophet to the nations.'

(Jeremiah 1:5)

This verse and others might be used to demonstrate a belief that God forms each individual human life, and has a plan for each person. Abortion might be seen as a deliberate attempt to spoil the plans that God has made for people.

But the other Christian Churches teach that this issue is very much up to the conscience of the individual. Sometimes, a woman or a couple might want to terminate a pregnancy if there is a serious risk that the baby would be born with severe disabilities. Perhaps the mother is very young and became pregnant by accident. Perhaps, if the baby were born, it would put great emotional or financial strains on the rest of the family; or perhaps it would just be unloved and unwanted. Some Christians believe that the most important Biblical reference to use is the Golden Rule:

So in everything, do to others what you would have them do to you, for this sums up the Law and the Prophets.

(Matthew 7:12)

They might try to put into practice the Christian principle of **agape** (unconditional love) and try to imagine what they would want if they were faced with the same situation. They might come to the conclusion that, in some circumstances, abortion could be the kindest and most loving solution to the situation.

Christian attitudes to fertility treatment

There is no teaching in the Bible which refers explicitly to fertility treatment, because it is something that was not possible in the time when the Bible was

Fertility treatment, when it works, gives people the opportunity to enjoy all the benefits of becoming parents.

So in everything, do to others what you would have them do to you, for this sums up the Law and the Prophets.
(Matthew 7:12)

Other Christians, however, are not sure that fertility treatment is always acceptable. They might argue that if people have no children, this is God's way of saying that he has different plans for them. Perhaps fertility treatment is going too far, and trying to make things happen which were not part of God's intentions. Many Christians are also worried about the kinds of fertility treatment that create 'spare' embryos (see page 121) because, if it is believed that these embryos count as 'persons' individually created and loved by God, then destroying them is the same as murder. Methods of treatment that involve eggs or sperm from anonymous donors are also against the beliefs of some Christians because it can be seen as introducing a third person into a relationship, when God meant it to be between just two. Roman Catholics, in particular, are often against artificial methods of fertility treatment.

written; doctors did not have the technology. If people had no children, then they were often very unhappy, but there was nothing they could do about it. In the Bible, if someone cannot have children, this is believed to be God's decision:

Hannah had no children… because the Lord had closed her womb.
(1 Samuel 1:2,6)

Fertility treatment, like abortion, is an area where not all Christians agree. Many couples want to have children, and if they find that they cannot conceive, it can bring a great deal of unhappiness. Some Christians believe that if these couples can be helped, with medical treatment, to have the family that they have always wanted, then the treatment should be encouraged. They think that giving fertility treatment would be the most loving way to behave, and will bring about the creation of new human life which is a good thing. It is following the example of Jesus as a healer, and is keeping the commandment given by Jesus about treating other people in the way that you would like to be treated yourself:

Discussion

Do you think that there should be rules about who should or shouldn't be allowed to have fertility treatment – for example, should women aged over 50, or gay couples, or disabled people, be helped to have babies if they are unable to conceive naturally?

Activity

1 Explain why Christians might have different views about abortion.

2 Do you think that fertility treatment should be allowed for couples who are unable to have children, even if 'spare' embryos have to be destroyed? Give reasons for your answer.

Christian attitudes to euthanasia and suicide

According to Christian belief, all human life is sacred. People were made as God's special creation, and each individual person is known by God, who plans their lives and decides how long they should live:

> your eyes saw my unformed body.
> All the days ordained for me
> were written in your book
> before one of them came to be.
> *(Psalm 139:16)*

Many Christians therefore believe that euthanasia and suicide are wrong. They believe that God gave the gift of life, and that it is not for humans to choose when to take it away. Sometimes, they argue that both euthanasia and suicide are a sign of a complete lack of faith in God. Christians should trust God to know when it is the right time for them to die, and they should not feel the need to make that decision for themselves, as God will always know what is best.

Christians often point out that there is a difference between killing someone (active euthanasia) and letting them die rather than trying to extend the life with extra treatment (passive euthanasia). For many Christians, killing another person is always wrong, even when the person doing the killing is trying to be kind and save someone from suffering. But letting someone die, rather than making him or her have endless treatment and operations, is often agreed to be acceptable. Life does not have to be preserved at all costs; there is a time when we must realise that we have to die, and we should try to come to terms with that, rather than struggling to keep people alive in all circumstances.

When members of different Christian denominations have met to discuss the moral issue of euthanasia, they have all come to the same conclusions: deliberate killing is wrong, but no-one has to try and keep a life going on and on unnecessarily.

Doctors are allowed to decide to stop treatment, even though they are not allowed to kill.

The Roman Catholic Church teaches a principle known as '**double effect**'. According to this principle, euthanasia is only allowed if it happens as a kind of side-effect of treatment that is meant to help. For example, a patient with a terminal illness who was in a lot of pain might need doses of the drug morphine as a painkiller. The principle of double effect says that the morphine can be given to ease the pain, even if a side-effect of the drug is that death comes more quickly. This is acceptable to the Roman Catholic Church, because the intention is to help the patient, not to kill.

Many Christians believe that a dignified death can be achieved if a person goes into a **hospice** for care. Hospices do not practice euthanasia, but instead they give special care to help make a dying patient as comfortable as possible (this is called **palliative care**). They help the patient and the relatives and friends to come to terms with death, and they help everyone to sort out financial problems or anything else that is worrying them, so that when death comes, it is peaceful and as painless as possible.

Most Christians also realise that suicide is the result of great unhappiness, rather than wickedness. People who want to take their own lives are helped, as gently as possible, to deal with whatever is making them unhappy. Some Christians volunteer to help with organisations such as The Samaritans, which offer counselling services to people who are desperately unhappy.

Christian beliefs about the use of animals in medical research

Christians believe that humans are God's most important creation, and that other animals were made for humanity to control and to rule:

God blessed them and said to them, 'Be fruitful and increase in number; fill the earth and subdue it. Rule over the fish of the sea and the birds of the air and over every living creature that moves on the ground.'

(Genesis 1:28)

Animals are not believed to have a 'soul', or to be capable of having a special relationship with God, and most Christians are happy to eat meat and to keep animals as pets or in zoos. Throughout most of Christian history, animal rights have not been considered, but more recently, as people have become aware of the issues involved in human treatment of animals, Christians have looked again at their beliefs. Many Christians now think that animals deserve respect and have value, as part of God's creation. Treating animals with cruelty is a misuse of the special responsibilities that God gave to humanity.

However, most of the Christian churches agree that the use of animals for medical research is sometimes necessary. The Church of England states:

> The Church recognises the need for animals to be used in certain research to improve medical understanding, veterinary or behavioural knowledge, and to test for the safety of chemicals, and understands that such testing is a requirement of law. It also, however, affirms that responsible stewardship of the natural world requires all animals to receive careful and sympathetic treatment, both during their lives and in the manner of their dying.
>
> *(What the Churches say, CEM)*

The Roman Catholic Church takes a similar view, saying that animal experiments are tolerable as long as the experiments are reasonable, and as long as the intention is to improve the quality of human health or to save lives. It is also acceptable, in Catholic teaching, to use animals for food and clothing. The Roman Catholic Church emphasises that people should not give animals exaggerated attention and care when there are humans who are suffering in the world. They believe that it is wrong to spend a lot of money on expensive dog foods while ignoring starving people in other countries.

Roman Catholics believe that it is wrong to make too much fuss of pets while doing nothing about the starving people of the world.

In Christianity, then, the majority view is that the use of animals in medical research can be useful and acceptable, although people should take care to avoid causing unnecessary suffering.

Discussion

Christians believe that humans are more important than other animals. What do you think of this view?

Activity

1 Explain why most Christians believe that euthanasia and suicide are wrong.

2 What might Christians do to help people who are thinking about euthanasia or suicide?

ॐ Hinduism

Hindu attitudes towards abortion

Many Hindus believe that abortion is not acceptable, and neither is any other form of birth control. They believe that marrying and having children is an important part of an adult's life, and is a duty laid down for everyone in the eternal law of dharma. Abortion is considered a crime in many Hindu sacred texts. It goes against Hindu teaching about **ahimsa** (non-violence) because it fails to respect the life of the growing foetus. It also prevents the rebirth of the soul (**Atman**) living in the foetus. Hindus believe that all life is sacred, and that it brings bad karma if a person decides to terminate a pregnancy.

However, in practice, abortion does happen among Hindus, and the majority of the Hindu population of India is in favour of it being a legal possibility for people who want to make that choice. Many believe that it is better for a child not to be born, than to be brought into a family where there is poverty and where the child is not going to be welcome. Some Hindus might also choose to terminate a pregnancy if the foetus has serious abnormalities, or if there is a risk to the health of the mother, or if the woman has been raped.

There has always been a great deal of pressure for Hindu couples to produce sons, as they are considered a greater blessing than daughters. Daughters are still considered to be a problem, because in some cultures a dowry has to be found for them when they marry, and this can be a great financial burden for parents. A girl is the responsibility of her parents until she marries, whereas a son is much more likely to be able to earn his own living and to support his parents in their old age. It is now possible for doctors to determine the sex of the foetus, by looking at scans or by testing the amniotic fluid which surrounds the foetus in the womb. Sometimes, Hindu couples who already have daughters, or who want only one child, might choose to

terminate the pregnancy if they find out that the foetus is female. The test is quite cheap, and easily available, not only in the cities but also in local clinics in the countryside.

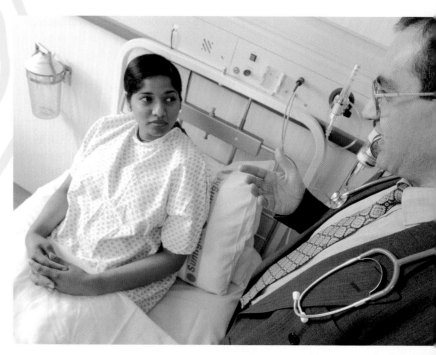

Some states in India now forbid the tests during pregnancy which tell the sex of the foetus, so that parents cannot choose to have abortions just because they do not want daughters. Nevertheless, female foetuses are far more likely to be aborted than male, even though this is a practice which goes against Hindu teaching. It causes Hindus and the Indian government a great deal of concern.

Hindus and fertility treatment

Fertility is an important part of Hinduism. Married couples are keen to produce at least one son, because the son has important religious duties to carry out, especially when his parents die and he has the responsibility of carrying out the proper rituals in lighting the funeral pyre. If a couple have been married for some time, and they have not managed to conceive,

Sometimes, Hindus who find out that they are expecting a female child will have the pregnancy terminated, because they would prefer to have sons. This is against Hindu teaching and is discouraged by the Indian government.

this can be seen as grounds for a divorce, and a woman with no children is often pitied and sometimes looked down upon. It is part of the dharma, or right code of conduct, for a man to be the father of sons.

If a Hindu couple want children but are having difficulty conceiving, then fertility treatment is often welcomed as a way of helping them to achieve this important religious duty. Hindus are often uneasy about methods of fertility treatment that involve the donation of sperm or eggs from another person outside the marriage, because it is important in Hinduism to carry on a line of inheritance through the father. Many Hindus are also concerned about **caste** (social class) and would not be happy about having a child who might have the genes of a different group from those of the rest of the family.

Some, too, might prefer not to use fertility methods which involve the production of 'spare' embryos which are then destroyed; but most Hindus consider that bringing a child into the world is important enough to outweigh the disadvantages. Hindus who have difficulty conceiving are likely to welcome the possibility of having a child with the help of medical technology. They would be particularly keen to try methods such as IVF using the eggs and sperm from both partners.

In many parts of India, fertility treatment is not a possibility. It is something which is available for the rich, and for people who live in the cities with access to the hospitals. Poorer people and those who live in villages who are desperate to have children sometimes adopt a child from elsewhere in the family, especially from relations who have many children and cannot afford to look after all of them. This is often seen as a good way of resolving the situation.

Discussion

Do you think that parents should be allowed to choose the sex of their children? What do you think that most people would choose?

Activity

1 Do you think that some forms of fertility treatment are more acceptable than others? Explain why.

2 Explain in your own words how the Hindu obligation to have sons affects attitudes towards (a) abortion and (b) fertility treatment.

Hindu attitudes towards euthanasia and suicide

Because Hindus believe that all of life is sacred, they disagree with the idea of euthanasia. One of the most important principles in Hinduism is ahimsa or harmlessness. It is always considered wrong to take life, even when someone else is ill or in pain. If someone is suffering, this is believed to be the results of karma. The person is suffering because they have performed wrong actions in the past, either in this life or in a previous life, and it is necessary for the suffering to follow its natural course rather than be brought to a quicker end – otherwise the rest of the bad karma will still have to work itself out in the person's next life. People who are caring for terminally ill patients should do all they can to help them and make them more comfortable, but they should not end the patient's life.

In Hinduism, it is not unusual for someone who is very old or very ill to decide for themselves that the right time has come for death, and to stop eating or drinking, so that they bring about their own deaths. 'Renouncing' (or 'giving up') the world and everything in it is a way that some Hindus show their recognition that this world is not as important as it appears. Understanding the nature of God and the eternity of the soul are the keys to wisdom, and giving up the world is just one step further than deciding to become a **sannyasin**, or holy man, who gives up all his family and possessions and goes and lives alone. This way of bringing death more quickly is not seen as wrong, but is often admired as a sign of great holiness. It is not the same as euthanasia, because it does not involve anyone apart from the person who wishes to die; no-one else is asked to help with the death, or to make any decisions about it.

Suicide is not acceptable in Hinduism when it involves people taking their own lives because of hopelessness and depression. However, when people take their own lives as self-sacrifice, or because they cannot bear to be parted from someone who has just died, this is accepted, and even approved of, by Hindus. **Suttee,** sometimes spelt **sati,** is an example of this kind of suicide; it is the name given to a custom in which Hindu widows used to throw themselves onto the flames of their husbands' funeral pyres as a way of showing their faithfulness and devotion. It was believed that this death would earn the women great karma and so bring about good fortune in the next life. The custom was made illegal in 1829, because of its cruelty, and because sometimes women were forced into suicide by their relatives, who made it clear that they did not want to have the responsibility of looking after a widow.

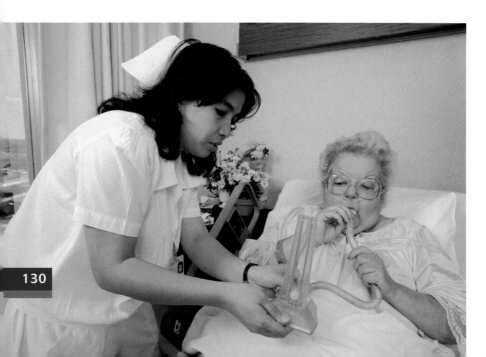

Hindus believe that everything should be done to make ill people more comfortable, but this should not involve the taking of a life.

Hindu beliefs about the use of animals in medical research

Unlike many other religious believers, Hindus do not often believe that people are much more important than other kinds of animals. Hindu beliefs include respect for all living things and a recognition of how all the different elements of nature work together to form a whole. Some animals are frequently used in Hindu images of the deities, as an aid to worship. For example, the bull is often associated with the god Siva, the tiger with the goddess Durga, the monkey with Hanuman and the elephant with Ganesha. The cow is especially important in Hinduism, as a sacred animal (see page 30). Animals are treated with great care and respect, and many Hindus will not eat meat or meat products because of their respect for animals.

The Hindu principle of ahimsa (see page 54) involves doing no harm to other living creatures. Hurting or destroying animal life leads to bad karma, and the person who has done the damage can expect that, in the future, something similar will happen to them.

For all of these reasons, Hindus are opposed to any kind of cruelty to animals. Using animals unnecessarily in experiments is completely against Hindu teaching. However, some Hindus do accept that there are times when experiments on animals are essential for human health, and therefore some might agree that when absolutely necessary, animals could be used in medical research. In India, medical research involving animals does take place, but not on the same scale as in the West. Many people are without even the most basic health care, and the question of testing medicine and other procedures on animals does not arise except in the largest cities. People cannot afford to buy any medicines of any kind, whether they have been tested on animals or not.

Discussion

What do you think of the Hindu idea that people are not much more important than any other kind of animal?

Activity

1 How might a Hindu doctor or nurse answer someone who asked for an overdose of pain-relieving drugs, to make death come more quickly?

2 Do you think that humans have the right to use other animals for food and in medical experiments? Give reasons for your answer.

Muslim attitudes towards abortion

Although contraception is permitted in some circumstances, generally Islam will not allow abortion. It is thought of as a crime against a living human being and so, if an abortion is carried out, blood money can be payable for the loss of life.

However, abortion is allowed if a doctor is convinced that continuation of the pregnancy will result in the mother's death. The later in the pregnancy that an abortion takes place, the more human is the foetus and so the greater the crime. Some Muslims believe that for the first four months of pregnancy the mother's rights are greater than those of the child, while after this time they have equal rights.

Imam Al-Ghazzali (born 1058, died 1111) distinguished between contraception and abortion by saying:

> Contraception is not like abortion. Abortion is a crime against an existing being. Existence has various stages. The first is the settling of the semen in the womb and its mixing with the secretions [egg] of the woman. It is then ready to receive life. Disturbing it is a crime. When it develops further and becomes a lump, abortion is a greater crime. When it acquires a soul and its creation is complete the crime becomes even more grievous. The crime reaches its maximum seriousness after the foetus is separated from its mother alive.

In Arabia, before the time of Muhammad ﷺ unwanted baby girls were often buried alive and the Qur'an has very strict rules against this which are now also applied to the issue of abortion:

> Kill not your children for fear of want: We shall provide sustenance for them as well as for you. Verily the killing of them is a great sin.
>
> *(Surah 17:31)*

and the innocence of the child is stressed:

> When the female (infant) buried alive, is questioned – For what crime she was killed?
>
> *(Surah 81:8–9)*

If a pregnant woman is sentenced to death for a crime, she cannot be executed until after the baby is born.

There are different beliefs among Muslim writers about when a foetus becomes a person.

> We believe that the soul is breathed in by the first 42 days of pregnancy. What has led us to this opinion is the hard fact of embryology, that all stages – seed, clot of blood and morsel of flesh occur in the first 40 days of life.

Before 120 days from conception, the foetus lacks a human soul. Only at the end of 120 days is the foetus ensouled. To consider in the same light abortions that are performed before the 120-day period and after, as the Anti-Abortion lobby does, is therefore both ridiculous and unIslamic. Muslim jurists prohibit, absolutely, any abortion taking place after ensoulment when the soul enters the body, but many of them permit it before 120 days under certain conditions, for example the poor health of the mother, in the case of rape, etc.

Muslim attitudes to fertility treatment

The procreation of children is a very important part of a Muslim marriage. Therefore, it is very difficult for a couple when they find that they cannot have children of their own.

Islam often looks to the women in the Qur'an and in the life of Muhammad ﷺ as examples of how people have coped with infertility. For example, Sara, the wife of Ibrahim, was barren until she was 90. Then her future pregnancy is announced by angels:

They said, 'Fear not,' and they gave him glad tidings of a son endowed with knowledge. But his wife came forward (laughing) aloud: she smote her forehead and said: 'A barren old woman!' They said, 'Even so has thy Lord spoken: and He is full of Wisdom and Knowledge.'

(Surah 51:28–30)

Zakariya also prays to the Lord for a child and his elderly wife Ishba is cured of her barrenness and gives birth to a child, Yabya:

And (remember) Zakariya, when he cried to his Lord: 'O my Lord! leave me not without offspring, though Thou art the best of inheritors.' So We listened to him: and We granted him Yabya: we cured his wife's (barrenness) for him. These (three) were ever quick in emulation in good works; they used to call on Us with love and reverence, and humble themselves before Us.

(Surah 21:89–90)

Children are a very important part of a Muslim marriage.

Women who cannot have children might argue that although Sara and Ishba were very old, they still had children eventually.

Muslims also look at the example of Muhammad ﷺ who had children with his first wife Khadijah, but none with any of his other wives: Sawda, Aisha, Hafsa, Umm Salamah, Zaynab bint Jahshm Juwayriyya, Rayhana, Umm Habiba, Safiyya, and Maymuna.

The possibility, in Islam, of a man having more than one wife, is sometimes suggested as a way around a fertility problem but this is not a common practice in many Muslim countries and still does not deal with the suffering of the wife who wants children and cannot have them.

Although some Muslims believe that people should simply accept Allah's will if they cannot have children, others see infertility as a disease and argue that Muslims have a duty to seek treatment for any disease.

IVF is one possibility for Muslims. Although not all the fertilised eggs are placed in the uterus and some therefore eventually die, this is not seen as a problem. Muslims argue that these embryos are not human beings and therefore their death is not seen in the same way as an abortion. From Muslim tradition it might be argued that these 'spare' embryos could be used for stem cell research to cure other conditions. However, the embryos cannot be donated to another woman as any child born in this way would be viewed as illegitimate and break Muslim teaching about lineage.

It is He Who has created man from water: then has He established relationships of lineage and marriage: for thy Lord has power (over all things).

(Surah 25:54)

Discussion

Consider whether a woman has a right to have a child or whether they should see this as a gift from God.

Activity

1 Explain why Muslims might disagree about abortion.

2 Do you think that fertility treatment should be allowed for couples who are unable to have children? Give reasons for your answer.

Muslim attitudes to euthanasia and suicide

Muslims are opposed to euthanasia and also to suicide.

> O ye who believe! Seek help with patient Perseverance and Prayer: for Allah is with those who patiently persevere … Be sure we shall test you with something of fear and hunger, some loss in goods or lives or the fruits (of your toil), but give glad tidings to those who patiently persevere – who say, when afflicted with calamity: 'To Allah we belong, and to Him is our return.'
>
> *(Surah 2:153–156)*

Because every soul is created by Allah, life is sacred. To kill yourself is therefore forbidden.

> Nor kill (or destroy) yourselves: for verily Allah hath been to you most Merciful!
>
> *(Surah 4:29)*

The sufferings people have to endure are a test of their iman (faith). Nothing which happens to a person, no matter how painful, is a good enough reason to end life, whether by suicide or euthanasia.

The Prophet Muhammad ﷺ said that anyone who killed themselves would go to hell:

> Anyone who throws themselves down from a rock and commits suicide will be throwing themselves into Hell. A person who drinks poison and kills themselves will drink it for ever in Hell. A person who stabs themselves will stab themselves for ever in Hell.
>
> *(Hadith)*

Muslims say that the time when someone will die can only be decided by Allah:

> When their Term expires, they would not be able to delay (the punishment) for a single hour, just as they would not be able to anticipate it (for a single hour).
>
> *(Surah 16:61)*

> Nor can a soul die except by Allah's leave, the term being fixed as by writing.
>
> *(Surah 3:145)*

If anyone does commit suicide, they have taken their life which did not belong to them and also it shows that the ummah has failed to take care of this individual.

Because of these teachings, euthanasia is forbidden in Islam. Euthansia is therefore **zalim**, wrongdoing against Allah, other people, or yourself. Everyone has the responsibility to preserve and prolong life and although suffering is not seen as a good thing in its own right and everything possible should be done to relieve it, nevertheless it can help people to grow spiritually.

Muslim beliefs about the use of animals in medical research

The Qur'an states that all life, animal and human belongs to Allah:

> He has created man from a sperm-drop and behold this same (man) becomes an open disputer! And cattle He has created for you (men): from them ye derive warmth, and numerous benefits, and of their (meat) ye eat. And ye have a sense of pride and beauty in them as ye drive them back home in the evening, and as ye lead them forth to pasture in the morning. And they carry your heavy loads to lands that you could not (otherwise) reach except with souls distressed: for your Lord is indeed Most Kind, Most Merciful.
>
> *(Surah 16:4–7)*

> There is not an animal (that lives) on the earth, nor a being that flies on its wings, but (forms part of) communities like you. Nothing have we omitted from the Book, and they (all) shall be gathered to their Lord in the end.
>
> *(Surah 6:38)*

Humans have a duty towards all living beings.

It is clear that humans have a duty towards all living beings.

Islam is not opposed to necessary animal experimentation when it safeguards humans but it does stress the importance of animals as part of Allah's creation:

> Seest thou not that it is Allah Whose praises all beings in the heavens and on earth do celebrate, and the birds (of the air) with wings outspread? Each one knows its own (mode of) prayer and praise. And Allah knows well all that they do.
>
> *(Surah 24:42)*

This respect is shown in the life of Muhammad ﷺ. During his travels he saw an army of ants heading towards a fire so he ordered the fire to be put out so that the ants would not be harmed. Islam also teaches that when Muhammad ﷺ was travelling from Makkah to al-Madinah and hid from his pursuers in a cave, a spider spun a web across the entrance and a dove nested on a ledge outside in order to protect him.

In the 13th century a Muslim lawyer called Izz ad-Din ibn Abd as-Salam drew up a bill of legal rights for animals based on Shari'ah (Muslim law).

At the World Wide Fund for Nature International in 1986, the Muslim representative, Dr Abdullah Omar Nasseef, stressed that humans had a responsibility to look after the earth and the animals:

God created mankind – a very special creation because mankind alone was created with reason and the power to think and even the means to turn against his Creator ... mankind's role on earth is that of a khalifa, a viceregent or trustee of God. We are God's stewards and agents on Earth. We are not masters of this Earth; it does not belong to us to do what we wish. It belongs to God and He has entrusted us with its safekeeping ... His trustees are responsible for maintaining the unity of His creation, the integrity of the Earth, its flora and fauna, its wildlife and natural environment.

Discussion

Consider whether there are any circumstances when religious people might say that someone was right to commit suicide.

Activity

1 How might a Muslim doctor or nurse answer someone who asked for an overdose of pain-relieving drugs, to make death come more quickly?

2 Do you think that humans have the right to use other animals for food and in medical experiments? Give reasons for your answer.

Judaism

Jewish attitudes towards abortion

Jews believe that, as G-d created human beings, therefore G-d is in charge of when they live and when they die. Judaism considers that abortion not only interferes with G-d's plan for the world but also destroys what has the potential to become a human being. However, according to the Jewish scriptures, the life of a human being is more important than the life of the unborn child. This is shown in this passage from Exodus:

> If men shall fight and they collide with a pregnant woman and she miscarries, but there will be no fatality, he shall surely be punished as the husband of the woman shall cause to be assessed against him, and he shall pay it by order of judges. But if there shall be fatality, then you shall award a life for a life; an eye for an eye, a tooth for a tooth, a hand for a hand, a foot for a foot; a burn for a burn, a wound for a wound, a bruise for a bruise.
>
> *(Exodus 21:23–25)*

This passage from Exodus is often misunderstood. It does not suggest that these penalties should be paid literally but that money should be exchanged to the value of what is lost. It also limits what money people can ask for.

Rabbis have argued that killing is allowed in certain circumstances. For example, enemies may be killed in battle, meat is slaughtered, insects are killed and plants are cut down or dug up. The argument is therefore when a foetus becomes a human being or when the soul enters its body. The decision made was that the foetus became a person at the moment of birth, not at conception. Therefore, abortion is not murder.

> If a woman is in difficult labour (to the point that her life may be in danger) her child must be cut up while it is still in her womb since the life of the mother is more important than the life of the foetus. But if the greater part of the child has already emerged it may not be damaged, since one life cannot be more important than another.
>
> *(Mishnah)*

Many Jews now accept that there are some instances when abortion is permissible. The life and well being of the mother is the most important issue and abortion is acceptable if the mother or child is at risk either physically or mentally or if the pregnancy is the result of rape. The mother must be the person who decides in these circumstances. Abortion would never be approved simply for the sake of convenience, and the later in the pregnancy the mother is the more difficult it becomes for Judaism to sanction it.

Jewish attitudes to fertility treatment

There is no teaching in the Bible which refers explicitly to fertility treatment, because it is something that was not possible in the time when the Bible was written; doctors did not have the technology. If people had no children, then they were often very unhappy, but there was nothing they could do about it. In the Bible, if someone cannot have children, this was believed to be G-d's decision:

> Hannah had no children … for HASHEM had closed her womb.
>
> *(1 Samuel 1:2,6)*

However, Judaism sees children as not only a blessing to a family but as a commandment:

> Whoever adds even one Jewish soul is considered as having created an (entire) world.
>
> *(Maimonides)*

Some Rabbis have argued that when procreation cannot take place through normal sexual intercourse, other means are acceptable. If the husband's sperm can be used in order for the woman to become pregnant, then the father has fulfilled his obligation to have children. In some circumstances, it may be permissible for the sperm to come from a donor. Although the donor remains the father according to Jewish law, no sin has been committed and the child is still seen as fully legitimate.

Discussion

Consider whether a woman has a right to have a child or whether they should see this as a gift from G-d.

Activity

1 Explain why Jews might disagree about abortion.

2 Do you think that fertility treatment should be allowed for couples who are unable to have children? Give reasons for your answer.

Jewish attitudes to euthanasia and suicide

According to Jewish belief, all human life is sacred. People were made as G-d's special creation, and each individual person is known by G-d, who plans their lives and decides how long they should live:

> your eyes saw my unformed body.
> All the days ordained for me
> were written in your book
> before one of them came to be.
>
> *(Psalm 139:16)*

The Torah was given to humans 'so that they might live'. Therefore, suicide is a sin. 'One who intentionally takes one's life has no share in the world to come.' Jews who commit suicide are not allowed the normal burial rites and are not buried near other Jews. There are examples in the Torah of people taking their own life. Samson pulls down the columns of the temple, killing himself and his enemies. Saul falls on his sword and dies rather than risk being captured alive by the Philistines and the consequences that this might have for the morale of his soldiers. The Rabbis have said that, in circumstances such as these, suicide is permissible because of the over-riding reasons which are to fight enemies and protect others. However, suicide carried out because someone is 'fed up' with life is not permissible.

Therefore, in general terms, Judaism cannot approve of euthanasia because only G-d can decide when a person should die.

According to the Talmud, someone who shoots a man as he falls off a cliff to certain death is still guilty of murder, as they have hastened the death.

However, the teaching of Rabbi Moses Isserles is sometimes used to argue that life-support machines should be turned off if there is not hope of the patient's recover:

> If there is anything which causes a hindrance to the departure of the soul … then it is permissible to remove it.

Jewish beliefs about the use of animals in medical research

According to the Jewish scriptures, after the Creation of the world, G-d said:

> Let us make Man in Our image, after Our likeness. They shall rule over the fish of the sea, the birds of the sky, and over the animals, the whole earth, and every creeping thing that creeps upon the earth.
>
> *(Genesis 1:26)*

> G-d said, 'Behold, I have given to you all the herbage yielding seed that is on the surface of the entire earth, and every tree that has seed-yielding fruit; it shall be yours for food.'
>
> *(Genesis 1:29)*

The Jewish scriptures do not have very much to say about animal rights. Animals are seen as very valuable and they were offered as sacrifices to G-d in the Temple in Jerusalem.

However it is clear that the early Jews were concerned about their animals. G-d gave Adam control over all the animals and:

Samson pulling the columns of the temple.

Now, HASHEM G-d had formed out of the ground every beast of the field and every bird of the sky, and brought them to the man to see what he would call each one; and whatever the man called each living creature, that remained its name. And the man assigned names to all the cattle and to the birds of the sky and to every beast of the field…

(Genesis 2:19–20)

Knowing the name of a person or animal was believed to give you special power over them.

That animals are to be shown respect is shown in several passages:

You shall not muzzle an ox in its threshing.

(Deuteronomy 25:4)

The righteous one knows [the needs of] his animal's soul…

(Proverbs 12:10)

Animals are also mentioned in the Ten Commandments:

Safeguard the Sabbath day to sanctify it, as HASHEM, your G-d, has commanded you. Six days shall you labour and accomplish all your work; but the seventh day is Sabbath to HASHEM, your G-d; you shall not do any work – you, your son, your daughter, your slave, your maidservant, your ox, your donkey, and your every animal, and your convert within your gates, in order that your slave and your maidservant may rest like you.

(Deuteronomy 5:12–14)

Here the animals were to be shown concern like human beings and to be given a day's rest.

At the 1986 meeting of the World Wide Fund for Nature International held at Assisi, Rabbi Arthur Hertzberg said that:

…when the whole world is in peril, when the environment is in danger of being poisoned and various species, both plant and animal are becoming extinct. It is our Jewish responsibility to put the defence of the whole of nature at the very centre of our concern.

Although animals are important and should be respected and treated well, nevertheless they are seen as less important than humans. Their purpose is to be of use to humans and this is the reason they were created. There are no clear Jewish rulings on the use of animals for scientific experiments but these experiments should be necessary and, as far as possible, suffering should be avoided.

The use of animals in organ transplants is welcomed by many Jews. This avoids the difficulties of doctors having to decide when someone is clinically dead before removing organs for transplant. Even the use of pigs, normally regarded as unclean, is not seen as a problem for transplants.

Discussion

Consider whether there are any circumstances when religious people might say that someone was right to commit suicide.

Activity

1 How might a Jewish doctor or nurse answer someone who asked for an overdose of pain-relieving drugs, to make death come more quickly?

2 Do you think that humans have the right to use other animals for food and in medical experiments? Give reasons for your answer.

Practice GCSE questions

Christianity

(a) Describe Christian attitudes towards fertility treatment. (8 marks)

(b) Explain how a Christian might respond to someone who was thinking about euthanasia. (7 marks)

(c) 'People should make up their own minds about issues of life and death.'
Do you agree? Give reasons to support your answer, and show that you have thought about different points of view. You must refer to Christianity in your answer. (5 marks)

Hinduism

(a) Describe Hindu attitudes towards fertility treatment. (8 marks)

(b) Explain how a Hindu might respond to someone who was thinking about euthanasia. (7 marks)

(c) 'People should make up their own minds about issues of life and death.'
Do you agree? Give reasons to support your answer, and show that you have thought about different points of view. You must refer to Hinduism in your answer. (5 marks)

Islam

(a) Describe Muslim attitudes towards fertility treatment. (8 marks)

(b) Explain how a Muslim might respond to someone who was thinking about euthanasia. (7 marks)

(c) 'People should make up their own minds about issues of life and death.'
Do you agree? Give reasons to support your answer, and show that you have thought about different points of view. You must refer to Islam in your answer. (5 marks)

Judaism

(a) Describe Jewish attitudes towards fertility treatment. (8 marks)

(b) Explain how a Jew might respond to someone who was thinking about euthanasia. (7 marks)

(c) 'People should make up their own minds about issues of life and death.'
Do you agree? Give reasons to support your answer, and show that you have thought about different points of view. You must refer to Judaism in your answer. (5 marks)

Tips

For all four questions

In part (a) you are being asked to display your knowledge of religious attitudes towards fertility. You need to be able to show what the views are, as well as why they are held. Remember that within a religion, there might be different opinions; for example, Roman Catholic and Protestant Christians are likely to hold different views, and Orthodox and Reform Jews are also likely to have different attitudes on this issue.

For part (b), you need to be able to demonstrate your understanding. Try and say something about the beliefs on euthanasia in the tradition of the religion you are studying, and how this affects people's attitudes. Again, there might be different opinions within the religion, and you could explain what these are. Try to apply the beliefs to everyday life; how might a religious believer who was suffering from incurable pain react and why?

In part (c), your answer could include beliefs in the sanctity of life, as given by God, and the concept that each individual has a purpose. Different circumstances under which taking life might be acceptable could be included, alongside contrasting points of view. Remember that you need to refer to the religion you are studying, as well as giving your own view. You should try to support the views you give with reasons, and show that you understand how people who disagree with you might feel.

UNIT 8

Religion and Equality

Christianity

Biblical teaching about equality

The Bible teaches that all people are equally valuable to God, because they are made 'in the image of God' (Genesis 1:27). The book of the Acts of the Apostles, for example, teaches that God does not have favourites:

> Then Peter began to speak: 'I now realise how true it is that God does not show favouritism but accepts men from every nation who fear him and do what is right.'
>
> *(Acts 10:34)*

Christians believe that God loves all of humanity unconditionally; it does not matter whether the people are men or women, black or white, rich or poor, attractive or unattractive. They believe that it is important that people should show the same kind of love for each other. They should be concerned about other people's welfare, whoever they are. In the letter to the Galatians, Paul teaches people that they should not look for differences between people but should recognise that their Christian faith unites them:

> There is neither Jew nor Greek, slave nor free, male nor female, for you are all one in Christ Jesus.
>
> *(Galatians 3:28)*

Christian attitudes towards racism

Christianity was for centuries strongest amongst white, Western people, but today there are Christians of all different colours and nationalities. According to Christianity, because all people are made by God and are equally valued by God, they should all be treated as equally important. Racism is the belief that some people are better than others because of the colour of their skin or their ethnic origin, and Christianity teaches that racism can never be right.

Jesus was once asked what a man should do to inherit eternal life. He asked the man what the Jewish Law said on the subject, and the man told him:

> 'Love the Lord your God with all your heart and with all your soul and with all your strength and with all your mind'; and, 'Love your neighbour as yourself.'
>
> *(Luke 10:27)*

The person asking the question was still confused; he wanted to know which people he should treat as his neighbours, and which people were not important and could be ignored. Jesus answered by telling the parable of the Good Samaritan. At the time of Jesus, Samaritans were treated as an inferior race, and no-one wanted to mix with them. The parable of the Good Samaritan teaches that people should treat each other as neighbours and look after them, even if they are strangers or from a different nationality.

This does not mean that Christianity has always taken a firm stand against racism. Sometimes, people who call themselves Christian have been responsible for encouraging racist attitudes; for example, some Christians in the past have been slave-owners or enthusiastic supporters of **apartheid** in South Africa. But there have also been many Christians who have devoted their lives to the struggle against racism, because they believed that helping to get rid of racism is an important way of putting Christian beliefs into practice.

Martin Luther King was a Christian who lived in America at a time when black people and white people were often kept apart (segregated). Black people were not allowed to use the same schools, restaurants or swimming pools as white people, and they were not allowed to sit down on buses if a white person wanted the seat. Martin Luther King was black, and his Christian beliefs led him to campaign against racism by leading non-violent protests against racist rules. He was a very powerful speaker, and hundreds of people gathered to hear him and to join in the protests. Although he was often threatened, his beliefs in the love and power of God encouraged him to continue his work. Martin Luther King was shot dead when he was 39, but it is now against the law in America to discriminate against people because of their race.

Trevor Huddleston and **Desmond Tutu** campaigned in South Africa to try and break down the system of apartheid. In South Africa, there used to be laws which made black people live in poor areas with very few rights, while the white people owned land, factories and mines. Black people often had to live in hostels, separated from their families, so that they could get work. Trevor Huddleston and Desmond Tutu both put Christian beliefs into action by becoming part of the movement to end apartheid. They helped to publicise the things that were happening, and encouraged the rest of the world to pressurise South Africa until it changed its laws.

Desmond Tutu is a Christian who puts his beliefs into action by campaigning against racial discrimination.

The role of women in Christian society

Within Christianity, there are many different opinions about whether men and women should have different roles, duties and responsibilities, or whether they should be the same. Some Christians believe that men and women were always intended to be partners for each other, but that they have different skills and abilities. Men are physically stronger; women can become pregnant and breastfeed their children. Some Christians say that God made men and women in different ways because they are meant to do different things with their lives. Men should do the physical work, and take care of their families by providing them with an income.

Women should support their husbands, and should take care of the children and of the home. In the Bible, there are passages that agree with this view of different roles for men and women.

Other Christians, however, hold different views. They believe that God created men and women to be equal, to share the same opportunities and to use the talents they have been given, whether they are male or female. They argue that it is old-fashioned to expect women to stay at home with the children while their husbands go out to work. Women and men should share childcare, if they are parents, and should both have equal choice about whether or not to go out to work.

Many Christians believe that only men should become priests, and that this is not an appropriate role for women. The Roman Catholic Church, for example, teaches that the priest represents Christ during the Mass, and that it would be wrong for a woman to try and do this. Women are not regarded as inferior in the Roman Catholic Church, but their role is not the same as the role of men. In some Churches, however, women have always been allowed to take leadership roles.

Discussion

Do you think that men and women should have exactly the same opportunities, or do you think that they should recognise their different skills? Give reasons for your answer.

Activity

1 Explain why Christians believe that racial prejudice is wrong.

2 Look up the Parable of the Good Samaritan, in Luke 10, and make a summary of the story and its meaning.

3 Choose either Martin Luther King, Trevor Huddleston or Desmond Tutu, and find out more about their work to fight racism. Write two or three paragraphs explaining how they put their Christian beliefs into practice.

Christian attitudes towards other religions

Christians hold very different views about non-Christian religions. Some people believe that only Christianity holds the truth about God, and all other religions are false. They believe that members of other religions should abandon their wrong ideas and convert to Christianity. This belief is based on a passage from John's gospel:

> Jesus answered, 'I am the way and the truth and the life. No-one comes to the Father except through me.'
>
> *(John 14:6)*

Some Christians interpret this to mean that eternal life with God is only for Christian believers. They say that there would be no point in the death and resurrection of Jesus if there were already lots of other ways to reach God, and therefore Christianity is the one and only true religion. In the past, Christians used to travel to other countries as missionaries, with the aim of changing the religion of the people they met and persuading them to become Christians instead. Today, there are many Christians who believe that this is right, and who go overseas to tell people about Christianity and to try and establish churches throughout the world, although missionary work is not as popular as it once was.

Christianity is an **evangelical** religion. Christians believe that it is important that they share their beliefs with other people, and that they try to persuade others to become Christians. From the earliest days of Christianity, Christians have told others about their faith by preaching in public places. Today, some Christians visit people in their homes or distribute leaflets to try and encourage their neighbours to find out more about converting to Christianity.

Other Christians, however, hold different views. They believe that everyone who is genuinely trying to follow God is doing the right thing, whichever religion they happen to belong to. They encourage members of different faiths to worship together, and to meet for discussions so that they can try to understand each other better, but they do not try to convert others who already have sincere religious beliefs of their own. They say that religious belief often depends on where in the world someone was born, and they say that a loving and forgiving God is not going to reject someone just because he or she was born into a non-Christian religious tradition.

Within the Christian Church, there are also differences and prejudices. Sometimes, Roman Catholics and Protestants have serious disagreements about issues like the authority of the Pope or whether women should be ordained as priests. In each branch of the Church, there are people who think that theirs is the only right way to worship, and that Christians from other denominations are wrong. Some Christians are very concerned about these differences, especially when they lead to extreme situations such as the Troubles in Northern Ireland. They work towards uniting all the different groups within Christianity, by reminding them that they should think of themselves as one body sharing a common aim. This kind of work is known as the **ecumenical movement**.

Christian beliefs about forgiveness and reconciliation

Christianity teaches that people should not hold grudges, and should not keep remembering for many years their differences and arguments. Instead, they should try to be forgiving, and aim to copy the forgiveness of God. The Lord's Prayer, taught by Jesus and used every day by Christians around the world, reminds people that they should be forgiving if they expect God to forgive them:

> Our Father, who art in heaven
> Hallowed be thy name.
> Thy kingdom come, thy will be done on earth as it is in heaven.
> Give us this day our daily bread, and forgive us our trespasses, as we forgive those who trespass against us.
> And lead us not into temptation, but

deliver us from evil.
For thine is the kingdom, the power
and the glory, for ever and ever, Amen.

There are some Christian centres which focus on forgiveness and reconciliation. Coventry Cathedral, which was bombed to ruins during the Second World War and then rebuilt, encourages its visitors to think about ways in which peace can be promoted. **Taizé** in France is an ecumenical centre, where Christians from different denominations and different parts of the world can meet together for prayer and worship.

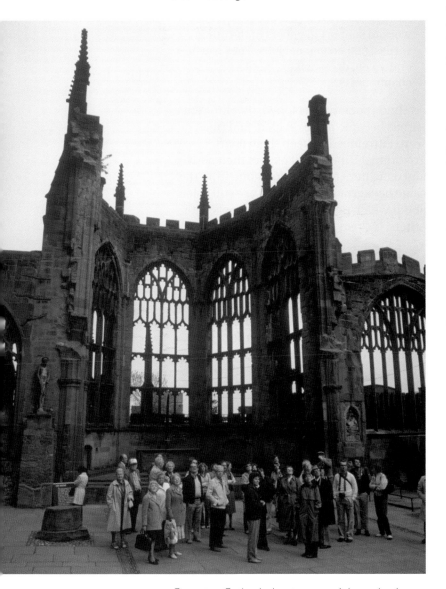

Coventry Cathedral puts a special emphasis on peace and forgiveness.

In the Roman Catholic Church, if a person wants to be forgiven for something wrong they have done, they can go to confession (the **Sacrament of Reconciliation**) and tell a priest about whatever it is that is making them feel guilty. The priest acts on behalf of God in showing the person how to repent and be forgiven.

Christians believe that the service of Holy Communion, also called Mass or the Lord's Supper, is a way of making all believers recognise that they are part of the same Church in spite of their differences of opinion. They believe that when they share the bread and wine, they are joining together like different parts of the same body. Most services of Holy Communion include the words:

Though we are many, we are one body, because we all share in one bread.

This shows the Christian belief that people should forget their differences and work together.

Discussion

Do you think that it is right to try to forgive everyone who does wrong, or do you think that there are some things which should never be forgiven? Try and give reasons for your answer.

Activity

1 Explain why Christians might have different views about whether there is any truth in other world religions.

2 Explain how and why Christians try to become more united.

ॐ Hinduism

Varnashramadharma

Hindu life and behaviour is dominated by the social group to which a Hindu belongs, and by the stage of life that the Hindu has reached. The social groups are called varnas, and the stages of life are called **ashramas**. Each varna and each ashrama has a special code of conduct associated with it (dharma), so a Hindu will always know how to behave.

A Hindu will be born into a varna and will stay a member of that group for all of his or her life, until he or she is reborn. Then, according to how well or how badly the person has behaved, the next life might change things. Someone who has behaved well, followed the right rules and been kind to others will be reborn into a higher social group, while someone who has neglected their duties and been selfish will be born into a lower group.

In Hinduism, there are four main varnas, which are believed to have existed from the beginning of time, ever since the world was created. An ancient text called the **Purusha Sukta**, in the **Rig Veda**, tells of how the different varnas were formed from different parts of the body of the first 'cosmic man':

> His mouth became the Brahmin; his arms were made into the Warrior, his thighs the People, and from his feet the Servants were born.
>
> *(Rig Veda 10.90)*

The four varnas

1 Brahmins – This is the priestly group. They have the duties of keeping up the traditions of Hindu worship, and of performing ritual sacrifices when necessary. They are responsible for studying the Hindu scriptures and for making sure they are passed on to future generations. They have jobs in the professions, teaching and guiding other Hindus.

2 Kshatriyas – This is the warrior and leadership group. Their main duty is to protect and defend the rest of society. They are responsible for government and decision-making.

3 Vaishyas – This is the group which provides the main source of income for society. They run farms and businesses, trading with other nations, and producing wealth for the benefit of the whole community.

4 Sudras – This is the servant group. They work to support members of the other varnas, and do manual jobs. They can be craftsmen, dressmakers, cooks or chauffeurs etc.

As Hindu society developed, the different varnas became more divided, and rules were introduced to keep them apart. Traditional Hindus still expect their sons and daughters to marry someone from the same background, and there are still rules about which people can share meals with others.

Hindus often say that all of the different groups are equal. The groups are not based on wealth or status, but all work together at different but equally important tasks, so that Hindu society can function as a whole. But in practice, the different groups have been given different amounts of respect by Hindus. Most people, given the choice, would prefer to be Brahmins, who have the best opportunities for education and for living a wealthy lifestyle. Sudras do not have the same chances to become rich or to be educated or travel. A special Hindu initiation rite called the Sacred Thread ceremony is performed for Brahmins, Kshatriyas and Vaishyas, but never for Sudras; and Sudras are not allowed to study the Vedas. In some parts of India, members of lower groups are not allowed to go into the temples for worship, because it is believed that they are 'unclean' and that their presence will pollute the temple for everyone else.

Hindus from lower social groups perform services for others, and do the jobs which other Hindus believe are unclean.

In the past, some people were believed to be so unclean that they were outside the varna system altogether. They had jobs which involved dealing with the dead and with clearing away rubbish, and they were known as 'outcastes' or 'untouchables'. These people were often treated very badly and were not allowed to mix with everyone else. MK Gandhi felt particularly strongly that this was wrong, and he renamed the untouchables **harijans**, or 'children of God'. Today they prefer to call themselves **dalits**, which means 'oppressed'. Gandhi published a pamphlet explaining his objections to this discrimination, and because of his work and the work of many other Hindu leaders, it became illegal to treat people as untouchable.

Although it might seem to Western people that these different social groups are unfair, because they give privileges to some but not to others, Hindus argue that everyone has control over which group they belong to, because of karma and rebirth. The way in which someone behaves in this life will determine how they are reborn; so if someone is reborn as a Sudra, then they should work hard and behave well in service to others in the hope of a higher rebirth the next time. Their position in life is their own fault, based on their deeds in former lives, and so is not unfair at all.

Ashramas are the different stages of life through which each Hindu passes, according to tradition. Each stage has its own special duties, or dharma. The first stage, after childhood, is that of the student (**brahmacarya**), when a young person is meant to study the Vedas and be taught by a **guru**. The next stage is that of the householder (**grihastha**), where the responsibilities are to have sons and to work for a living so that the rest of the community can have financial support. Once the children are grown and no longer need to be supported, the Hindu is supposed to give up possessions and family ties, in a stage known as **vanaprastha**. Finally, the elderly Hindu becomes a **sannyasin** or wandering hermit, living alone and concentrating on meditation and devotion to God, in the hope of being released from the continual round of birth and rebirth.

Discussion

Hindus sometimes say that when a society is divided into groups like this, everyone knows how to behave and it encourages peaceful living. Do you think that this is a fair point? Give reasons for your answer.

Activity

1 Explain (a) the responsibilities and (b) the privileges of each of the four varnas.

2 What do you think of the view that someone's status in life is their own fault, because of their previous lives? Give reasons for your answer.

3 If you were writing a pamphlet explaining objections to untouchability, what would be the main points you would make?

Hindu attitudes towards racism

India is a multi-racial society, and co-operating peacefully with members of other races has always been an important part of being a Hindu.

Hindus believe that all people share a common link. All of the world is part of one unified whole. The plants, other animal species, and humans are all part of the ever-changing stream of life, so that in some ways, harming another living thing is the same as harming yourself. Therefore, many Hindus believe that it is wrong to be prejudiced against someone else just because of their ethnic origin, as the differences between people matter a lot less than the similarities.

However, in practice, there are prejudices in Hindu society just as much as in any other group. Hindus traditionally classify non-Hindus as being inferior to members of the higher Hindu groups (Brahmins, Kshatriyas and Vaishyas), and many Hindus prefer not to eat with foreigners in case it makes them ritually impure. There are still many prejudices within Hinduism between people of different skin colours, and when people are looking for a husband or wife, they often specify that they want a partner with a light skin colour. These sorts of prejudices take a long time to overcome.

The role of women in Hindu society

In Hinduism, men and women have different roles and duties, as each has a different dharma to follow. In the past, men and women lived very different kinds of lives, and this is still the case in more rural parts of India and more traditional families. If a family cannot afford to send all of their children to school, they will choose to educate the boys rather than the girls, because the boys are expected to support the family financially while the girls have domestic jobs to do. Although this might seem unfair, Hinduism teachers would say that if a woman performs her duties well, she could be reborn as a man.

Women are expected to be good wives and mothers, to be faithful and supportive of their husbands, and to take care of the home and of the cooking. They are meant to try to copy the example of Sita, the wife of Rama, who faithfully followed her husband through all kinds of hardships without complaining. Women are responsible for worship in the home, so in this way they have a very special role to play. They are the ones who bring up the children to follow in the ancient traditions. All women are expected to marry, and if possible, to have sons. In India, when a woman gets married, she often lives at the home of her parents-in-law and helps with the household chores until she has children of her own, after which she and her husband move to their own house. Women are believed to be the property of their fathers when they are young, and then they belong to their husbands, and then to their sons in their old age. They have a duty to protect her, but she is not really regarded as equally independent.

Sita is believed to be the ideal example of a Hindu wife, faithfully following and supporting her husband Rama in everything he does.

Modern Hindus sometimes have less traditional ideas about the role of women. Education for women is becoming more widely accepted, and people looking for marriage partners for their sons often want well-educated girls. Both India and Pakistan have had female Prime Ministers. But if a woman never marries, she is still regarded as rather a failure; her duty in the home comes first.

Hinduism attitudes towards other religions

Although Hinduism teaches tolerance, in the past there have been conflicts based on race and religion. There has been prejudice between Hindus and Muslims especially, partly because of struggles over ownership of land and partly because each holds beliefs that the other finds particularly difficult to accept. Hindus worship many different deities, which Muslims think is wrong because of their belief in one God, Allah. Hindus object to the Muslim practice of slaughtering and eating beef, because of their beliefs that the cow is a sacred animal. These differences sometimes make it difficult for Hindus and Muslims to accept each other.

Hinduism contains many different beliefs. Some Hindus follow Krishna as their god, while others follow Ganesha or a different deity, and some Hindus do not believe in God at all, but they are all still counted as Hindus. Hindus therefore have no problem in accepting that members of other religions want to worship in their own way and have their own beliefs. This is because there is no one 'right way' to believe or worship, according to Hindus; there are lots of different paths to God, and everyone should be able to worship in the way that he or she chooses. Hinduism is not a religion that tries to persuade other people to join it, and sometimes Hindus resent the efforts of Christians and Muslims to try and convert other people to share their beliefs. Hindus are tolerant of other beliefs, and they find it difficult to accept that members of other religions are less tolerant.

The **Ramakrishna Mission** began as an attempt to show that Hindus do not need to convert to other religions, but can continue as Hindus whatever they choose to believe. Ramakrishna lived in the 19th century, at a time when many Christian missionaries were being sent to India. He taught that all religions were paths to God, and so there was no need to abandon the religion that had always been a part of Indian culture. Ramakrishna and his followers worked hard to show people in the West that Hinduism has a lot to offer; they were so successful that many began to question whether it was right to send Christian missionaries to India at all.

Hindu beliefs about forgiveness

Because Hindus believe that every action has 'fruits', this means that if someone is the victim of injustice, they know that the person who treated them badly will one day be punished. Holding a grudge against someone else is not really necessary, because the other person will get what they deserve. Hindus believe that to hold grudges and to look for revenge is damaging to the person who has these feelings. It is better to adopt an attitude of 'detachment' rather than to be angry, because anger can cause bad karma.

Discussion

Do you agree that all religions are equally true (or false) or do you think that one religion is better than all the others? Give reasons for your answer.

Activity

1 Explain Hindu ideas about the role of women. What do you think a Hindu might say to someone who thought that this was unfair?

2 Explain why Hindus do not go out as missionaries, or try to convert other people to their own beliefs.

Islam

Muslim teachings about equality

The Qur'an teaches that all people are created by Allah and are therefore equal:

> And among His Signs is the creation of the heavens and the earth, and the variations in your languages and your colours; verily in that are Signs for those who know.
>
> *(Surah 30:22)*

> O mankind! We created you from a single (pair) of a male and a female; and made you into nations and tribes, that ye may know each other (not that ye may despise each other). Verily, the most honoured of you in the sight of Allah is (he who is) the most righteous of you. And Allah has full knowledge and is well-acquainted (with all things)
>
> *(Surah 49:13)*

Muslim attitudes towards racism

Muslims are not a particular racial group: followers of Islam can be found all over the world and so there can never be any excuse for racism or prejudice. A person will see themselves as a Muslim first, regardless of their colour of nationality.

In his last sermon Muhammad ﷺ said:

> All mankind is descended from Adam and Eve, an Arab is not better than a non-Arab and a non-Arab is not better than an Arab; a white person is not better than a black person, nor is a black person better than a white person except by piety and good actions. Learn that every Muslim is the brother of every other Muslim and that Muslims form one brotherhood.

The first muezzin, chosen by Muhammad ﷺ, was an Ethiopian slave called Bilal. Racism has become an issue for many Muslims, not because they are racist, but because of the way in which they are often treated by non-Muslims.

Muslims may fight racism but must obey those in authority unless they are required to go against the will of Allah.

> The Prophet invited us so we swore allegiance to him; and among the conditions which he laid down on us to follow was this: that he had a promise from us to hear and obey, whether we liked or disliked an order, and whether we were in adversity or ease, even if our rights were not granted; and that we should not dispute the authority of those entrusted with it adding, 'Unless you see an act of open disbelief in which you have a clear argument from Allah.'
>
> *(Hadith)*

The role of women in Muslim society

Islam teaches that men and women are equal and that Allah will judge them equally according to the way in which they have lived.

To help men value women for who they are, rather than for their bodies, women wear garments that leave only the hands and face exposed.

> O Prophet! Tell thy wives and daughters, and the believing women, that they should cast their outer garments over their persons (when abroad): that is most convenient, that they should be known (as such) and not molested. And Allah is Oft-Forgiving, most Merciful.
>
> *(Surah 33:59)*

Many non-Muslim Westerners cannot understand Islamic teaching about women and feel that the need for women to be covered up in public and the way in which they are brought up is wrong. Some Muslim women, however, say that being covered is

Some Muslim women say that being covered is a statement of freedom.

a statement of freedom because they feel that they are protected from being stared at and so are free to lead their lives without hindrance from men.

According to Islam, the rights and responsibilities of a woman are equal to those of a man, but they are not identical and, therefore, they should be complementary to each other rather than competitive.

> And women shall have rights similar to the rights against them, according to what is equitable; but men have a degree (of advantage) over them. And Allah is Exalted in Power, Wise.
>
> *(Surah 2:228)*

> Men are the protectors and maintainers of women, because Allah has given the one more (strength) than the other, and because they support them from their means. Therefore the righteous women are devoutly obedient, and guard in (the husband's) absence what Allah would have them guard. As to those women on whose part ye fear disloyalty and ill-conduct, admonish them (first), (next), refuse to share their beds, (and last) beat them (lightly); but if they return to obedience seek not against them means (of annoyance): for Allah is Most High, Great (above you all).
>
> *(Surah 4:34)*

In Islam this difference is seen as both natural and desirable. Men must support the family while women bear and rear children. Women have the right to study, refuse a marriage, to divorce, to inherit, to keep their own names, to own property, to take part in politics, and to conduct business, whether they are married or unmarried.

Some governments, saying that they are Islamic, impose harsh and repressive laws on women but these are not part of Islamic teaching.

Muhammad ﷺ stressed the respect which should be shown to women:

> Paradise lies at the feet of your mother.
>
> *(Sunan An-Nasa'i)*

> A man asked Prophet Muhammad ﷺ, 'O Messenger of Allah! Who deserves the best care from me?' The Prophet said, 'Your mother.' The man asked, 'Who then?' The Prophet said, 'Your mother.' The man asked yet again, 'Who then?' Prophet Muhammad ﷺ said, 'Your mother.' The man asked once more, 'Who then?' The Prophet then said, 'Your father.'
>
> *(Sahih Al-Bukhari)*

Discussion

Consider whether there are any reasons why women should not be treated equally to men.

Activity

1 Explain Muslim ideas about the role of women. What do you think a Muslim might say to someone who thought that this was unfair?

2 Find an example of a Muslim who has worked to combat racism and describe their work.

Muslim attitudes towards other religions

Like Christianity, Islam sees itself as the only true religion and Muslims believe that they have a duty to lead other people into the faith.

> Strongest among men in enmity to the Believers wilt thou find the Jews and the Pagans; and nearest among them in love to the Believers wilt thou find those who say, 'We are Christians': because amongst these are men devoted to learning and men who have renounced the world, and they are not arrogant.
>
> *(Surah 5:82)*

> If anyone desires a religion other than Islam (submission to Allah), never will it be accepted of him; and in the Hereafter he will be in the ranks of those who have lost (all spiritual good).
>
> *(Surah 3:85)*

Muslims believe that all people are born with a natural instinct to be Muslims – this is called '**fitrah**'. People may belong to other religions but this is because of the way they were brought up. Therefore, when someone 'converts' to Islam, they are reverting or coming back to the religion into which they were born.

Muslim beliefs about forgiveness and reconciliation

Allah forgives people who acknowledge that they are wrong and pray for forgiveness. Islam teaches that goodness is always better than evil:

> Nor can Goodness and Evil be equal. Repel (Evil) with what is better: then will be between whom and thee was hatred become as it were thy friend and intimate!
>
> *(Surah 41:34)*

Islamic law Shari'ah is based on the Qur'an and says how people are to be punished for crimes which they commit against other people.

However, Shari'ah has very strict rules and procedures to safeguard the person who is being judged, to ensure that they have a fair trial and that the punishment is only that specified for the crime committed:

- people must be tried by a legal court
- murder of a robbery victim is punished by death
- bodily harm of a robbery victim is punished by cutting off a hand and a foot
- less serious crimes are punished by prison sentences.

Shari'ah Islamic law is based on the Qur'an and the belief that Allah is a forgiving judge.

Allah is a merciful and forgiving ruler and judge and Muslims are required to follow this example:

> Hold to forgiveness; command what is right; but turn away from the ignorant.
> *(Surah 7:199)*

> Those who are kind and considerate to Allah's creatures, Allah bestows His kindness and affection on them.
> *(Abu Dawud, Tirmidhi)*

So Muslims must follow the will of Allah and also follow his example in being forgiving to others.

Discussion

Consider whether there are circumstances where even religious people might not feel that they were able to forgive a criminal.

Activity

1 Explain Muslim ideas about forgiveness and reconciliation.

2 Do you agree that all religions are equally true (or false) or do you think that one religion is better than all the others? Give reasons for your answer.

Judaism

Jewish teachings about equality and racism

Jewish teaching about how other people should be treated is very clear:

> When a proselyte dwells among you in your land, do not taunt him. The proselyte who dwells with you shall be like a native among you, and you shall love him like yourself, for you were aliens in the land of Egypt – I am HASHEM, your G-d.
>
> *(Leviticus 19:33–34)*

Judaism believes that the aim is to live at peace with other people.

This passage from Isaiah shows the hope for peace:

> It will happen in the end of days: The mountain of the Temple of HASHEM will be firmly established as the head of the mountains, and it will be exalted above the hills, and all nations will stream to it. Many peoples will go and say, 'Come let us go to the Mountain of HASHEM, to the Temple of the G-d of Jacob, and He will teach us of His ways and we will walk in His paths'. For from Zion will the Torah come forth, and the word of HASHEM from Jerusalem. He will judge among the nations, and will settle the arguments of many peoples. They shall beat their swords into plowshares and their spears into pruning hooks; nation will not lift sword against nation and they will no longer study warfare.
>
> *(Isaiah 2:2–4)*

The Rabbis taught that when G-d created Adam, he took soil from the four corners of the earth and used dark, light, red and yellow soil to create the first human. This means that as everyone is descended from Adam, no-one can say 'my father is better than your father'. Different languages are explained by the story of the Tower of Babel (Genesis 11:6–9) and it is suggested that the three sons of Noah founded the three races: black, caucasian and semitic.

Although the Jews are described as a 'chosen people' this simply means that they have a special role to play in setting an example for others and therefore have to work harder to fulfil G-d's will. The Talmud is clear that 'The righteous of all nations will inherit the World to Come' and that it is the responsibility of society to ensure that everyone, of every colour, race, religion, disability, wealth or poverty should be equal.

Despite this teaching, Jews have themselves been the victims of persecution for 2,000 years. Jews were driven out of Israel at the time of the Exile in Babylon, sixth century BCE and after the destruction of the Temple in 70 CE. They were driven out of Spain in 1492 CE and massacred during the Shoah (Holocaust) of the Second World War 1939–45 when six million Jews were killed. All these incidents are blamed on anti-semitism, 'hatred of the Jews'. Nevertheless, Judaism is totally opposed to racism and Jews work actively to oppose it.

In the Shabbat service a husband tells his wife how valuable she is to him.

The role of women in Jewish society

Some people say that the traditional Jewish attitude towards women is sexist. In Orthodox Judaism, women sit separately from men in synagogue services and cannot take part. Only men are bound by the 613 mitzvot (laws).

At the Shabbat service on Friday night, the husband tells his wife how valuable she is to him:

> An accomplished woman who can find? Far beyond pearls is her value. Her husband's heart relies on her, and he shall lack no fortune. She bestows goodness upon him, never evil, all the days of her life.... Her children have risen and praised her; her husband, and he extolled her: 'Many women have amassed achievement, but you surpassed them all.' Grace is false, and beauty vain; a woman who fears HASHEM, she should be praised. Give her the fruits of her hands; and let her be praised in the gates by her very own deeds.
>
> *(Proverbs 31:10–31)*

Some Jewish women feel that even statements such as these stress that they are still subservient to men and are not treated as equals. Some people claim that this attitude dates back to the punishment of Eve in the Garden of Eden when she picked the fruit of the Tree of Knowledge and gave it to Adam:

> To the woman He said, 'I will greatly increase your suffering and your childbearing; in pain shall you bear children. Yet your craving shall be for your husband, and he shall rule over you.'
>
> *(Genesis 3:16)*

Progressive Jews, believe that the scriptures should be interpreted for the 21st century and so they make no distinction between the way in which men and women are treated. They pray and worship together and women can become rabbis.

Discussion

Do you think telling someone how valuable they are is the same as treating them equally? Which would you prefer?

Activity

1 Explain Jewish attitudes towards racism and equality.

2 Find an example of a Jew who has worked to combat racism and describe their work.

Jewish attitudes towards other religions

Jews say that all people should follow their own religion and in doing so will please G-d. They do believe, however, that everyone should follow the **Noachide Code**. These seven commandments were given to Noah by G-d after the flood:

- Worship only G-d
- Do not blaspheme
- Do not murder
- Do not steal
- Do not commit adultery
- Do not be cruel to animals
- Establish a system of law and order so that everyone can live together in harmony.

Judaism believes that all humans are descended from Adam and Eve:

> The man called his wife's name Eve, because she had become the mother of all the living.
>
> *(Genesis 3:20)*

and recalls when they were living in a strange country:

> You shall not reject an Edomite, for he is your brother; you shall not reject an Egyptian, because you were a sojourner in his land. Children who are born to them in the third generation may enter the congregation of HASHEM.
>
> *(Deuteronomy 23:8–9)*

Jews believe that although they have their own religion, they should work in every way possible to help other people and especially as they seek to serve G-d:

> I am HASHEM; I have called you with righteousness; I will strengthen your hand; I will protect you; I will set you for a covenant to the people, for a light to the nations; to open blind eyes; to remove a prisoner from confinement, dwellers in darkness from a dungeon.
>
> *(Isaiah 42:6–7)*

Judaism actively discourages converts. Jewish belief is that people should follow their own religion, provided that they are guided by the Noachide Code and that only people who are born Jews (the children of a Jewish mother) are required to follow the

People who are born Jews are required by Judaism to follow its mitzvot and customs.

mitzvot and customs of Judaism. If someone is insistent on conversion they have to study Hebrew and Jewish laws and customs. They have to go to the mikveh and, if the convert is a man, he has to be circumcised. Finally, the convert has to go to a Beth Din (Jewish Court) to be tested by three rabbis before they are accepted as a Jew. Once a person has become a Jew their previous religion and their conversion is never referred to.

Jewish beliefs about forgiveness and reconciliation

The rabbis taught that everyone should repent their sins on the day before they died. Asked how you could know when you were about to die, he answered, 'Exactly, so you must repent every day'. Jews are told:

> You shall not hate your brother in your heart; you shall reprove your fellow and do not bear a sin because of him. You shall not take revenge and you shall not bear a grudge against members of your people; you shall love your fellow as yourself – I am HASHEM.
> *(Leviticus 19:17–18)*

Criminals should be brought to justice but this must be sought in a properly constituted court and that justice accepted.

Jewish experience of pogroms over many centuries, and of the 20th-century holocaust should, perhaps, make them especially aware of prejudice, discrimination and persecution.

Jews believe that they should forgive other people but that they cannot forgive on behalf of others. When he was asked if he could forgive the Nazis for the Holocaust, Rabbi Hugo Gryn said that only G-d could forgive their crimes.

Discussion

Consider whether there are circumstances where even religious people might not feel that they were able to forgive a criminal.

Activity

1 Explain Jewish ideas about the role of women. What do you think a Jew might say to someone who thought that this was unfair?

2 Do you agree that all religions are equally true (or false) or do you think that one religion is better than all the others? Give reasons for your answer.

Practice GCSE questions

Christianity

(a) Describe and explain Christian beliefs about the truth of other world religions. (8 marks)

(b) Explain how Christian beliefs might affect someone's attitude towards people of other races. (7 marks)

(c) 'People are not the same; there is no point in trying to make everyone equal.'
Do you agree? Give reasons to support your answer, and show that you have thought about different points of view. You must refer to Christianity in your answer. (5 marks)

Hinduism

(a) Describe and explain Hindu beliefs about the truth of other world religions. (8 marks)

(b) Explain how Hindu beliefs might affect someone's attitude towards people of other races. (7 marks)

(c) 'People are not the same; there is no point in trying to make everyone equal.'
Do you agree? Give reasons to support your answer, and show that you have thought about different points of view. You must refer to Hinduism in your answer. (5 marks)

Islam

(a) Describe and explain Muslim beliefs about the truth of other world religions. (8 marks)

(b) Explain how Muslim beliefs might affect someone's attitude towards people of other races. (7 marks)

(c) 'People are not the same; there is no point in trying to make everyone equal.'
Do you agree? Give reasons to support your answer, and show that you have thought about different points of view. You must refer to Islam in your answer. (5 marks)

Judaism

(a) Describe and explain Jewish beliefs about the truth of other world religions. (8 marks)

(b) Explain how Jewish beliefs might affect someone's attitude towards people of other races. (7 marks)

(c) 'People are not the same; there is no point in trying to make everyone equal.'
Do you agree? Give reasons to support your answer, and show that you have thought about different points of view. You must refer to Judaism in your answer. (5 marks)

Tips

For all four questions

In part (a), you need to describe and explain how members of the religion you are studying feel about other world religions. Perhaps they think that their religion is the only true one, and that they have a duty to work as missionaries and to try to gain converts. Perhaps they think that other religions also hold some truth, and that people should be free to worship in the way that they want. You need to explain their views, and give reasons where you can.

For part (b), you should think about how religious beliefs might affect someone's attitude to issues of race. You might write about attitudes towards racial prejudice, and the reasons why religious believers hold these attitudes. You might be able to support your points with quotations from sacred texts, or with the example of well-known people who have dealt with the issue of racism.

In part (c) you are being tested on your evaluative skill. You should think about whether equality means that everyone has to be the same, or whether it means something different. You need to explain how a religious believer would answer this question, and also give your own point of view, backed up with reasons explaining why these are your opinions.

UNIT 9

Religion, Poverty and Wealth

Introduction

The causes of hunger, poverty and disease

In the teaching of many religions, concern for the poor means caring for people nearby. Hindus, Jews, Christians and Muslims are taught how they should behave if they see someone in need, and, when the holy books were written, people understood the teaching to apply to people who were poor and lived in the same neighbourhood. However, today, people are much more aware of the needs of people who live much further away, people they will probably never meet. Television, newspapers, radio and the Internet give people a far greater awareness of how others live. If there is a famine in Africa or an earthquake in India, people in the UK know about it. They see pictures of the victims and hear them interviewed. We are much more aware today that there are huge differences between our own lifestyles and those of other people in developing countries. Religious believers have come to understand that poverty is not just a local issue, but a global one. If they are rich, the way that they shop, and where they bank, and the way that they vote and the care they take of the environment can affect people on the other side of the world.

The North-South divide

The world today is sharply divided between rich and poor. In general, the rich people live North of the Equator, and the poor live in the South (although there are rich countries in the South, such as Australia, and poor countries in the North, such as Mali and Albania). The huge differences in lifestyle between the rich and the poor have become known as the North-South divide. The poorer developing countries used to be called the Third World, but people have started to look for different names because 'Third World' implies that these people are inferior to those in the First World. Sometimes the poorer countries are known as the Developing World.

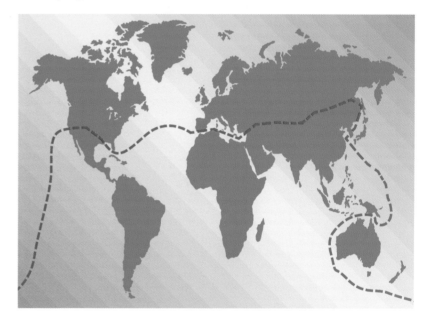

Countries in the North are, in general, much more rich and powerful than those in the South.

The difference is enormous between the lifestyles of people in rich and poor countries. People in rich countries have problems with overeating, and often have to make an effort to lose weight by eating less. Housing is safe and warm, and everyone has access to clean water. People have different clothes for different occasions, which they throw away when the fashions change. They can be educated for as long as they want, and usually have a choice of jobs to go to. If they are ill, health care is available nearby.

In developing countries, there is a daily struggle for food, which is often inadequate. People suffer from starvation or from diseases caused by malnutrition;

1.1 billion people do not have access to safe, clean water. Many live in shacks made from other people's rubbish, or in overcrowded and unsafe conditions, or have no home at all but wander as beggars or refugees. Many never receive any education, and remain illiterate; this is a particular problem amongst women. Health care is scarce and often involves long journeys which make the sick person worse. Basic medicines such as antibiotics are not available. Diseases such as measles, which are only a nuisance in the North, can kill. Problems such as cleft palates or poor sight, which can often be easily corrected in the North, can become major disabilities. In the poorest countries, a quarter or more of all children die before reaching the age of five.

Poverty soon becomes a vicious circle. If the population of a country is poor, then families tend to have more children, to help them with the work and avoid the expense of having to employ people, and to make sure that enough survive to look after the parents when they become old. When the population is poor, the need for health care is much greater because diseases spread quickly and few children are immunised, so the country has to spend a lot more on health provision. In a poor country, disasters such as drought and flood cause enormous damage because the people have no insurance and no emergency supplies.

When the rich countries make changes to the world economy, such as charging high rates of interest on debts, or dropping the price of goods such as bananas, the poor countries do not have the power to do anything about it, and they are exploited so that they end up owing the rich countries money.

The causes of world poverty are very complex, but there is no escaping the fact that the majority of the world's population is poor because the rich are unwilling to change their way of life. The rich countries have all the power. They have the factories, they own the mines, and they run the banks, making the decisions about which goods are worth the most and how much interest countries should pay. Because the rich countries run the ways world trade operates, everything works in favour of the rich countries. The things owned by the rich countries increase in value, while the poor get steadily poorer, and whenever they have to borrow money in order to survive, they end up owing more and more. Aid agencies, whether they are religious organisations or not, often emphasise that the rich countries will have to change their attitudes and their laws before anything can improve for the poor.

Christianity

Christian teaching about concern for the poor

Christianity teaches that caring for the poor is an obligation, not an option, for all those who love God. It is a central issue, not an extra. In the Bible, when people are taught about the right ways to behave, the main theme is the way in which they treat each other, and in particular, the way they treat people in need. They are taught that God will judge them on the basis of whether or not they care for the poor; the parable of the Sheep and the Goats in Matthew's Gospel (Ch. 25) clearly illustrates this point.

In the Old Testament, the prophets often preached a warning of the punishment in store for people if they did not treat the poor with more consideration. The laws that the people were given after the Exodus gave clear guidelines about how to care for the poor and avoid exploiting them:

> If one of your countrymen becomes poor and is unable to support himself among you, help him as you would an alien or a temporary resident, so that he can continue to live among you. You must not lend him money at interest or sell him food at a profit.
>
> *(Leviticus 25:35,37)*

When Jesus began his teaching, according to Luke's gospel he made a statement in which he quoted from the Old Testament, telling everyone why he had come, and what he was planning to do:

> The Spirit of the Lord is on me, because he has anointed me to preach good news to the poor. He has sent me to proclaim freedom for the prisoners and recovery of sight for the blind, to release the oppressed, to proclaim the year of the Lord's favour.
>
> *(Luke 4:18–19)*

All of the gospel writers show that Jesus taught about caring for the poor, but Luke in particular emphasised this. Luke wanted to show that, for Jesus, the poor were just as important as the rich, and that the message of Christianity included the poor as equals with everyone else. When Luke recorded some of Jesus' teachings, he opened with the words:

> Looking at his disciples, he said: 'Blessed are you who are poor, for yours is the kingdom of God. Blessed are you who hunger now, for you will be satisfied. Blessed are you who weep now, for you will laugh.'
>
> *(Luke 6:20–21)*

The teaching of the Bible is focused on the poor people who live in the same community as everyone else, the widows and the beggars who might live in the same village. Today, now that communication is so much better and we are much more aware of what is happening on the other side of the world, Christian concern about the poor includes everyone, whether they live in the same street as we do or on a different continent. The Bible teaches that it is impossible to have a genuine love for God while at the same time ignoring people in need:

Christianity teaches that people cannot be true believers if they do nothing to help the poor.

If anyone has material possessions and sees his brother in need but has no pity on him, how can the love of God be in him?

(1 John 3:17)

Giving to charity in Christianity

Christians give to charity in a variety of ways. Some donate money on a regular basis, and set aside a certain amount every month which they pay to the charities they have chosen to support. This is a particularly good way of giving, because it means that the charities know in advance how much money to expect, and they can plan projects in the confidence that they will be able to fund them.

In a letter to one of the newly formed churches in the earliest days of Christianity, Paul wrote to the Christians in Corinth advising them to put aside money for others on a regular basis, and to make a habit of it:

On the first day of every week, each one of you should set aside a sum of money in keeping with his income, saving it up…

(1 Corinthians 16:2)

Some Christians keep small collecting boxes in their homes, as a reminder that there are people in the world who have less, and they put money into it whenever they remember. They might also give money to the local church whenever they go to services, and some of this money is set aside for helping the poor. As well as giving money to charities, Christians often work for charity in other ways too. They might work as volunteers in local charity shops, or bake cakes for a charity stall in the local market, or knit small garments for babies in developing countries. Jesus taught that the size of the gift is not as important as the generous spirit behind the giving:

As he looked up, Jesus saw the rich putting their gifts into the temple treasury. He also saw a poor widow put in two very small copper coins. 'I tell you the truth,' he said, 'this poor widow has put in more than all the others. All these people gave their gifts out of their wealth; but she out of her poverty put in all she had to live on.'

(Luke 21:1–4)

There are many different charities registered in the UK, which aim to help a wide variety of causes. Some support sick animals, for example, or aim to provide care for children whose parents cannot support them, or give grants to medical research. When they are choosing a charity to support, Christians are likely to look for something that has a basis in Christian principles, or which is consistent with Christian teaching. They might choose a charity such as Christian Aid, CAFOD or Tearfund, all of which are Christian agencies working in developing countries.

Discussion

Christianity teaches that people should sell all they have and give the money to the poor. Do you think that this is practical or possible for people who live in rich countries?

Activity

1 Explain Biblical teaching about concern for the poor. You might want to look up the following, and include some of the ideas in your answer: Matthew 25:31–46; Mark 10:21; James 2:14–17

2 Find out more about the work of a Christian aid agency, such as CAFOD, Christian Aid or Tearfund.

Christian teaching about the right uses of money

Christianity, like many other religions, teaches that although obviously people need to feed and clothe themselves and their families, money can easily become a central focus and make people greedy. Because they want too much for themselves, they forget about other people who might be less well off. They can also reach a point where they forget about God because they are too interested in getting more money. In the Sermon on the Mount, Jesus taught:

> No-one can serve two masters. Either he will hate the one and love the other, or he will be devoted to the one and despise the other. You cannot serve both God and Money.
>
> *(Matthew 6:24)*

The early churches, too, were told:

> For the love of money is a root of all kinds of evil. Some people, eager for money, have wandered from the faith and pierced themselves with many griefs.
>
> *(1 Timothy 6:10)*

In New Testament times, people often believed that wealth was a sign of God's blessing. If someone had a lot of money, it showed that God was pleased with him or her, and the wealth was a reward. In contrast, people who were poor were considered inferior and were treated with less respect.

Jesus taught that it was wrong to be too satisfied with wealth. Money can give people very happy and comfortable lives, but it does not last for ever, and when a rich person dies, he or she cannot take their money on into the next life.

> Then he said to them, 'Watch out! Be on your guard against all kinds of greed; a man's life does not consist in the abundance of his possessions.'

> And he told them this parable: 'The ground of a certain rich man produced a good crop. He thought to himself, "What shall I do? I have no place to store my crops."

> 'Then he said, "This is what I'll do. I will tear down my barns and build bigger ones, and there I will store all my grain and my goods. And I'll say to myself, 'You have plenty of good things laid up for many years. Take life easy; eat, drink and be merry.'"

> 'But God said to him, "You fool! This very night your life will be demanded from you. Then who will get what you have prepared for yourself?"

> 'This is how it will be with anyone who stores up things for himself but is not rich towards God.'
>
> *(Luke 12:15–21)*

In Mark's Gospel, a story is told of when a rich young man asked Jesus what he should do in order to have eternal life. He told Jesus that he had tried all his life to be good and to keep the commandments.

> Jesus looked at him and loved him. 'One thing you lack,' he said. 'Go, sell everything you have and give to the poor, and you will have treasure in heaven. Then come, follow me.' At this the man's face fell. He went away sad, because he had great wealth.
>
> *(Mark 10:21–22)*

Some people think that when Jesus said this, he was exaggerating in order to make a point, and that he did not mean it literally but meant that people should try not to be too greedy. However, other people think that Jesus really did mean that they should sell all they have and give the money to the poor. Some Christians, such as St Francis of Assisi, have followed this teaching and have given all their money to the poor so that they can devote their lives to God instead. Monks and nuns usually take a vow of poverty, and give up all their possessions except for a few clothes and religious objects, as a way of putting Jesus' teaching into practice.

St Francis of Assisi came from a rich family, but because of his Christian faith he gave all his wealth to the poor. His father was furious with him.

Christian teaching about moral and immoral occupations

Christianity does not specify particular jobs which are allowed or not allowed, but many Christians try to choose careers that reflect their beliefs. Not everyone has much choice about the career which they follow; if they live at times of high unemployment, or if they are disabled, or for other reasons, they may find that they have to accept a job which they would not have chosen if they had more freedom. But if they have a choice, they might try to find a job that is directly involved in helping other people; for example, they might become doctors or nurses or care assistants, or they might work with children in teaching, or they could work as a solicitor or a police officer trying to get fairer treatment for people. Christians are unlikely to choose jobs that exploit others, such as jobs involving gambling or pornography.

The Internet is a useful source of information about the ethical record of different companies. It is possible to discover whether a company uses animal testing, or whether it has a clear policy on environmental issues, or whether it allows fair working conditions for its employees, and people can look at these records and make up their own minds. A Christian might investigate the behaviour of a company before he or she applies to work there.

Whether Jesus' teaching was meant to be taken literally or not, Christians believe that the main use of money should be for helping other people. Christians should only spend what they need on themselves, and any extra should be given to someone who has less. Of course, people find this very difficult to put into practice, and have very different ideas about how much money is essential.

Sometimes Christian churches are criticised for owning land, expensive buildings and gold and silver. Some people think that Christians should sell all this and give away the money; but others say that it is important to show respect to God with beautiful things, and that the churches need money in order to provide people with a place of worship and properly trained ministers.

Discussion

Do you think people today treat the poor with less respect than the rich? Why might this happen?

Activity

1 What does Christianity teach about money and greed?

2 Do you think that Christians should sell all they have and give the money to the poor? Give reasons for your answer.

ॐ Hinduism

Hindu teaching about moral and immoral occupations

In Hinduism, there is a social system where people are divided into different groups, known as varnas, and each of these groups has its own code of conduct, known as dharma. The different varnas have existed since the earliest days of Hinduism, and someone belongs to one group or another because of birth. A family will stay in the same varna for generations, and marriage between the different groups is not encouraged, especially in more traditional families.

The Brahmins are the priests and the teachers. The Kshatriyas are the warriors, rulers, and leaders of society. The Vaishyas are traders, merchants and involved in commerce, and the Sudras work in manual jobs such as building and agriculture. A 'good' job for a Hindu is the job that is appropriate for the class into which he or she is born. Many trades and businesses are handed down through the generations of a family, and most people in India do the same kind of work that their fathers and grandfathers did before them. In a village, the different families depend on each other for different skills, such as carpentry, farming, pottery and so on; everyone recognises that they need each other. But at the same time there are very definite views about which jobs are 'higher' than others, and everyone knows the status of everyone else and looks down on the people below them. To Hindus, this is not unfair, because someone who performs his or her tasks well and with the right attitude can expect to be born into a higher group in the next life.

The Bhagavad Gita sets out the different duties and qualities appropriate for different kinds of Hindus. It is believed that, because of their different varnas, Hindus have different skills which make them better suited to different kinds of work:

The works of Brahmins, Kshatriyas, Vaishyas and Sudras are different, in harmony with the three powers of their born nature.

The works of a Brahmin are peace, self-harmony, austerity and purity; loving-forgiveness and righteousness; vision and wisdom and faith.

These are the works of a Kshatriya: a heroic mind, inner fire, constancy, resourcefulness, courage in battle, generosity and noble leadership.

Trade, agriculture and the rearing of cattle is the work of a Vaishya. And the work of the Sudra is service.

A 'right' job is one which matches someone's dharma, so it would be right for a Brahmin to be a priest and wrong for him to be a shoemaker, and it would be right for a Sudra to drive a bus but wrong for him to become a teacher. A 'wrong' job is one which takes the Hindu outside the traditions of his or her own group, although this idea is breaking down now and there are more opportunities for people from lower groups to enter the professions, especially in the cities. Today, in the cities, there are some places reserved in the professions for 'dalits' (members of the lowest, oppressed group).

But some kinds of occupation go against Hindu ideas of right and wrong for members of any group. Hindus believe that women should dress modestly, and so a Hindu woman is unlikely to become a fashion model. Most Hindus are vegetarian, and so it is rare to find a Hindu butcher, and where they do exist, they are of a very low social status.

Hindu teaching about the right use of money

One of the four aims of life in Hinduism, called purushartas, is to earn and enjoy money. It is the duty of everyone at the householder stage of life, in between being

Lakshmi, the goddess of wealth and prosperity, is worshipped at Divali in the hope that she will bring financial gains to the worshipper.

minimum. He is meant to appreciate that the most important things in life cannot be bought. Instead, he should learn wisdom, devotion to God, and the right ways to behave towards other people. Then, when he goes on to become a householder, he will remember this and will earn money to support his family members, including elderly relations and others who need financial help. In Hindu society, wage-earners often have a large number of people to support, because they are expected to take care of elderly and disabled relatives as well as their own immediate families. Many Hindus who have settled in other countries still send some of their earnings back to India for the people who are dependent on them.

Hindu literature teaches that money alone will not bring perfect happiness, especially if it is kept rather than shared with the poor. In later life, the Hindu is expected to become less interested in money and possessions, and to become more concerned with leading a religious life. Money is good and necessary in the right place, but it should not be allowed to take over.

a student and becoming a monk, to work hard and to earn enough to support the people who depend on him. This aim is called **artha**. It is quite acceptable for Hindus to pray for money, and at the festival of Divali Hindu businessmen make offerings to the goddess Lakshmi, asking for her help to make them prosperous.

But this does not mean that Hindus can be greedy, or think about money more than they think about other important things. When a Hindu is a student, he is meant to live a very simple life without any luxuries, and this is supposed to make him aware that it is perfectly possible to live with the

Discussion

Are there some kinds of jobs that you would never do, because you think they are morally wrong? Explain your reasons.

Activity

1 Explain how Hindus divide society into different groups to do different work. Do you think that this system would make people more content, or more unhappy? Give reasons for your answer.

2 Explain Hindu views about the right attitude towards money.

Giving to charity in Hinduism

Giving to the poor is a way of life for Hindus in India. Many people are very poor indeed, and anyone who has a little more than he or she needs is expected to share it with those who have less. It is expected that people will employ the less well-off whenever they can, to provide them with an income, and so many Indian households have servants even when they are not particularly wealthy themselves. Poorer people are employed to sweep the yard, to do the washing and so on, whenever a family can afford it, as it is believed to be better to provide someone with a job than to make them rely entirely on charity. There is no unemployment benefit in India, and people who refuse to employ servants and do all their own housework instead are thought to be very mean. It is expected that servants will be treated with respect. The employer should pay for their medicines if they become ill, and might give the servants' families clothes and books which their own children have outgrown.

One of the best ways in which Hindus can build up good karma for themselves, so that they will be rewarded in future lives, is by giving to the poor. Beggars are a common sight on the streets of India, and giving them some money benefits the giver as well as the beggar, because the giver will be rewarded for this good deed in later life or in a future rebirth.

Many Hindus believe that if people are poor, it is their own fault because they must have behaved badly in a former life. But this does not mean that Hindus are allowed to ignore people in need of their help. Poverty is an enormous problem in India, where large numbers of the population are unable to provide their families with the basics they need for survival. **Dana**, or giving, is a part of everyday life. Many Hindus make a small donation to the poor before their own main meal each day, to remind themselves of the need to share what they have with others. Hindus rarely throw away clothes or shoes that they are tired of wearing, because

Hindus in India see people who live in poverty every day. They believe that in a former life, a beggar might have been their own brother or sister.

there is always someone nearby who would be glad to have them. The beggar in the street outside might, after all, have been the wealthy person's brother or sister in a former life.

MK Gandhi taught that it is wrong to think that a poor person is only getting what he or she deserves. He believed that every person was a part of God, and that everyone should recognise that they belong to the same world and should take care of one another. Gandhi taught that service to others was the best way to find God and understand more fully what it means to be human.

In India, there are many different charitable organisations set up to try and help those in need, although the problems are still far greater than India can cope with. Some are founded by Hindus, and some by other religious groups, but Hindus are meant to do their best to support charities whenever they can. Rich Hindus often contribute large amounts of money to schools or hospitals, and Hindus in other countries often send money back to India to try and help people there who are poor.

The Hindu Mission Hospital in Chennai, India, for example, aims to provide health care for people whether or not they can pay. They run an immunisation programme for children, a clinic for fitting artificial limbs, an eye clinic, and a screening programme for the early detection and treatment of leprosy. In-patients are given free food if they are poor, even though in most Indian hospitals food has to be provided by the patients' relatives. The hospital staff also runs a rural mobile clinic, taking medicines and health education out to people in the villages who are unable to travel to hospital.

Prison Fellowship India is a charity that works to help prisoners and their families. It runs children's homes, to take care of children whose parents are in prison, and organises rehabilitation and training in a trade for prisoners after their release, to help them find their way back into society. Without this sort of help, ex-prisoners and their families would have very few chances of making a decent life for themselves, and would probably end up as beggars or committing more crimes because they would not be able to find work.

Disasters, floods and famines are not unusual in India. On 26 January 2001, a severe earthquake hit Gujerat in India, and left hundreds of people dead and many more homeless. Organisations such as CAF India have been working to provide emergency medicines, food and shelter for the victims, and this, too, is the sort of charitable work that Hindus might choose to support.

Discussion

If you were surrounded every day by beggars and people who obviously did not have enough to eat, do you think your attitude to the poor would change? Would you become more caring, or do you think you would stop noticing them?

Activity

1 Explain why Hindus believe that it is important to give to the poor.

2 Do you think it is right, or wrong, for rich Hindus to have servants? Give reasons for your answer.

Muslim teaching about poverty and zakah

To Muslims, all wealth and riches come from Allah and are for the benefit of all humanity. Central to Islamic belief in this matter is zakah (purification of wealth by payment of welfare due) which is one of the Five Pillars.

> And be steadfast in prayer and regular in charity: and whatever good ye send forth for your souls before you, ye shall find it with Allah: for Allah sees well all that ye do.
>
> *(Surah 2:110)*

Zakah purifies the wealth that you have left so that no harm can come to you from it. Zakah itself is 2.5% of the income and savings of all Muslims after they have taken care of their families. It is not a charitable donation which people can choose to make but an obligation on all Muslims. However, the rich pay more than the less well off and very poor people pay nothing at all.

The calculations for zakah are complex and made after all essential bills, personal expenses and family expenditure have been allowed for.

Zakah	
Money and savings	2%
Produce from naturally irrigated land	10%
Produce from artificially irrigated land	5%
Cattle	one per 30 animals
Goats and sheep	one per 40 animals
Five camels:	one sheep or goat
Precious metals:	7%
Mining produce	20%
Rent	2%

In an Islamic state zakah is a form of social security: it ensures that food, clothing, housing, medicine and education can be provided for every person.

> Alms are for the poor and the needy, and those employed to administer the (funds); for those whose hearts have been (recently) reconciled (to the Truth); for those in bondage and in debt; in the cause of Allah; and for the wayfarer.
>
> *(Surah 9:60)*

Mullahs offer bread and water to pilgrims during the Id al-Fitr

Extra zakah is given at the festivals of Id-ul-Fitr and Id-ul-Adha. Additional voluntary charity called sadaqah can also be given when someone is in need.

> It is not righteousness that ye turn your faces towards East or West; but it is righteousness – to believe in Allah and the Last Day, and the Angels and the Book, and the Messengers; to spend of your substance, out of love for Him, for your kin, for orphans, for the needy, for the wayfarer, for those who ask, and for the ransom of slaves; to be steadfast in prayer, and practise regular charity, to fulfil their contracts which ye have made; and to be firm and patient, in pain (or suffering) and adversity, and throughout all periods of panic. Such are the people of truth, the God-fearing.
>
> *(Surah 2:177)*

Charity should always be given privately:

> There is a man who gives charity and he conceals it so much that his left hand does not know what his right hand spends.
>
> *(Hadith)*

This shows that it is much better to give charity privately – people should not boast about how much they give. The only exception to this would be when the giver is setting an example to encourage other people to give.

> Every day, each person has two angels near him who have descended from heaven. One says, 'O Allah!, compensate the person who gives to charity,' the other says, 'O Allah! Inflict a loss on the person who withholds his money.'

Discussion

Do you think that it is better to choose when to give money to others and how much, or are there advantages in having a religious obligation to give a certain amount of money?

Activity

1 Explain Muslim teaching about concern for the poor.

2 Find out more about the work of a Muslim aid agency.

Muslim teaching about moral and immoral occupations

Muslims are required to live according to the teachings of the Qur'an and therefore some occupations and activities are forbidden.

Money-lending where the lender benefits from **riba** (interest) is forbidden:

> That which ye lay out for increase through the property of (other) people, will have no increase with Allah.
>
> *(Surah 30:39)*

When people do owe money, Muslims are encouraged to be sympathetic to the debtor:

> If the debtor is in a difficulty, grant him time till it is easy for him to repay. But if ye remit it by way of charity, that is best for you if ye only knew.
>
> *(Surah 2:280)*

There are Muslim banks which have set up special facilities so that Muslims are able to borrow money without the bank making interest on the loan.

Along with not lending money at interest, all forms of gambling and activities such as lotteries are also forbidden in Islam:

> O ye who believe! Intoxicants and gambling … are … Satan's handiwork; eschew such (abomination) that ye may prosper.
>
> *(Surah 5:91)*

This has sometimes led to problems in countries where there are lotteries and the money is given to charitable causes. Many Muslims feel that they cannot take charitable donations towards, for example, building a new mosque or school, if the money has come from gambling or a lottery.

Because of their beliefs, Muslims in the United Kingdom will take an active part in raising money for their mosque where it is distributed to the poor; many will send money to Muslim communities abroad. Muslim charities such as Muslim Aid and Islamic Relief work to help people in developing countries.

> The generous man is near God, near Paradise, near men and far from Hell, and the ignorant man who is generous is dearer to God than a worshipper who is miserly.
>
> *(Hadith)*

Work is an essential part of Islamic life. This is stressed in the Qur'an:

> But Allah has created you and your handiwork!
>
> *(Surah 37:96)*

The Qur'an also records the ways in which Muslims should not earn their living. Muslims cannot profit from alcohol or gambling, from brothels or prostitution:

> Women impure are for men impure, and men impure for women impure, and women of purity are for men of purity, and men of purity are for women of purity.
>
> *(Surah 24:26)*

nor from lying, fraud or burglary:

> And do not eat up your property among yourselves for vanities, nor use it as bait for the judges, with intent that ye may eat up wrongfully and knowingly a little of (other) peoples' property.
>
> *(Surah 2:188)*

The two Pillars of Salah (prayer) and Sawm (fasting from sunrise to sunset through the month of Ramadan) are also important elements in Muslim teaching about work.

Praying five times a day at fixed times means that work is put into perspective when Muslims stop their normal activities to think about Allah. This is particularly true of Salat-ul-Jumu'ah, the weekly prayers at noon on Fridays. Islam does not have a day of rest but all Muslims should try to attend these prayers each Friday and hear the Khutbah (talk) given by the Imam. In a similar way, the fast of Ramadan brings people closer together in Ummah (the world Islamic community) and helps them to focus on God when they are also controlling their bodies.

Discussion

Consider Muslim arguments about not accepting money that has come from gambling or a lottery. Do you think that religious principles should come before the possible benefits to people and to the community?

Activity

1 What does Islam teach about money and greed?

2 Do you think that Muslims should give more than 2.5% of their income to the poor? Give reasons for your answer.

Salah (prayer) puts work and leisure activitites into perspective.

 Judaism

Jewish teaching about poverty and tzedaka

Jewish teaching on poverty and wealth is found in the Tenakh.

Jews are expected to give a tenth of their wealth as **tzedaka** (righteousness). This money is owing to the poor and so not to give it to them is seen as being the same as robbery. Even the very poorest people should try to give something as tzedaka.

The worst way to give tzedaka is to hand someone the money; the best way is to lend it to them indefinitely and without interest. Judaism teaches that by doing this you are saving people the embarrassment of taking a gift. The hope is that this money will help a poor person to become self-supporting so that they no longer need help.

> The best way of giving is to help a person help themselves so that they may become self-supporting
> *(Maimonides)*

> If there shall be a destitute person among you, any of your brethren in any of your cities, in your land that HASHEM, your G-d, gives you, you shall not harden your heart or close your hand against your destitute brother. Rather, you shall open your hand to him; you shall lend him his requirement, whatever is lacking to him.
> *(Deuteronomy 15:7)*

At home, many Jews have collection boxes called **pushkes** and children are encouraged to use these so that they can give part of their pocket money to charity.

As well as tzedaka, Jews should try to ensure that any excess wealth is also used for the poor:

> When you reap the harvest of your land, you shall not complete your reaping to the corner of your field, and the gleanings of your harvest you shall not take. You shall not pick the undeveloped twigs of your vineyard;

and the fallen fruit of your vineyard you shall not gather; for the poor and the proselyte shall you leave them – I am HASHEM, your G-d.
> *(Leviticus 19:9–10)*

Everyone should try to give something as tzedaka.

The Talmud teaches that people must never waste or give away so much money as to make themselves poor. This is wrong because it makes other people then become responsible for you.

> It is better to make your Sabbath like a weekday than to need other people's support.

Although Judaism believes that it is wrong to make yourself poor it is totally opposed to materialism.

> Do not weary yourself to become rich; forbear from your own understanding.
> *(Proverbs 23:4)*

> As goods increase, so do those who consume them; what advantage, then, has the owner except what his eyes see?
> *(Ecclesiastes 5:10)*

Love of money can eventually lead people away from God:

THEY'RE NOT ASKING FOR A TON OF MONEY TO SURVIVE THE WINTER.

JUST A TON OF COAL.

Over 100,000 elderly Ukrainian Jews face a desperately difficult winter, where the temperature will go as low as 30 degrees below freezing point. If they spend their tiny pensions (£11 a month) on fuel, they have no money for food.

In the words of 82 year-old Ludmilla Kornikov: "We never had a fancy life, but now it is real poverty. The inflation meant our savings became worthless and now we only have money either

for a loaf of bread and a glass of milk or to buy a little coal. Our conditions are very difficult. We have no money to live."

World Jewish Relief is launching an Emergency Winter Relief Appeal which will pay for fuel and other life-saving supplies. Just £40 will buy a ton of coal, which will provide elderly

WORLD JEWISH RELIEF

Jews like the Kornikovs with the fuel they're missing for the winter.

Don't leave Ukrainian Jews out in the cold. Please give as generously as you can using the coupon.

WJR EMERGENCY WINTER RELIEF APPEAL
☐ I am sending you a donation of £ _____
Name _____
Address _____

Postcode _____ Tel _____
Please make your cheque payable to World Jewish Relief (Regd. Charity 290 767).
Send this coupon to: World Jewish Relief, Drayton House, 30 Gordon Street, London WC1H 0AN.

Gemilut Hasadim is another form of Jewish charity. Literally it means 'kind actions' and covers all sorts of charitable work. This might be organisations for Jews such as Jewish Care or the Norwood Orphanages, soup kitchens to feed the hungry and homeless or more global organisations such as Tzedek, which works to improve conditions for all people around the world.

Discussion

'All charity should be given anonymously.' Do you agree with this statement? Consider different view points in your discussion.

Activity

1 Explain Biblical teaching about concern for the poor.

2 Find out more about the work of a Jewish aid agency.

Take care lest you forget HASHEM, your G-d, by not observing His commandments, His ordinances, and His decrees, which I command you today lest you eat and be satisfied, and you build good houses and settle, and your cattle and sheep and goats increase, and you increase silver and gold for yourselves, and everything that you have will increase – and your heart will become haughty and you will forget HASHEM, your G-d, Who took you out of the land of Egypt from the house of slavery.

(Deuteronomy 8:11–14)

Jewish teaching about moral and immoral occupations

Work is an essential part of Jewish life and everyone is expected to work:

> By the sweat of your brow shall you eat bread until you return to the ground, from which you were taken; For you are dust, and to dust shall you return.
>
> *(Genesis 3:19)*

> Great is work. God's presence only rested upon the Jewish people when they began occupying themselves with useful work.
>
> *(Maimonides)*

Jewish teaching, however, stresses that work should also allow time for Torah study.

> Gather together the people – the men, the women, and the small children, and your stranger who is in your cities – so that they will hear and so that they will learn … this Torah.
>
> *(Deuteronomy 21:12)*

The importance of Torah study was stressed from the time of Ezra, when a programme of mass education developed into new centres for study.

> In the third year of his reign [Jehoshaphat] sent his officers Benhail, Obadiah, Zechariah, Nethanel, and Micaiah to give instruction in the cities of Judah … They gave instruction … taking with them the Book of the Torah of HASHEM.
>
> *(II Chronicles 17:7–9)*

Jewish law requires that all business transactions are honest.

> You shall not commit a perversion in justice, in measures of length, weight, or volume. You shall have correct scales, correct weights, correct dry measures, and correct liquid measures – I am HASHEM, your G-d, Who brought you forth from the land of Egypt.
>
> *(Leviticus 19:35–36)*

Jewish law also makes the person selling responsible for the quality of the goods they sell rather than the British practice of *caveat emptor* (let the buyer beware).

One of the most important aspects of Jewish working life is Shabbat, the Sabbath on which no work is done.

> Remember the Sabbath day to sanctify it. Six days shall you work and accomplish all your work; but the seventh day is Sabbath to HASHEM, your G-d; you shall not do any work – you, your son, your daughter, your slave, your maidservant, your animal, and your convert within your gates – for in six days HASHEM made the heavens and the earth, the seas and all that is in them, and He rested on the seventh day. Therefore, HASHEM blessed the Sabbath day and sanctified it.
>
> *(Exodus 20:8–11)*

The rabbis laid down 39 different types of forbidden activities for the Sabbath which include all work, writing, cooking and travelling except on foot.

Growing and preparing food
Ploughing
Stacking sheaves
Selecting out
Kneading
Sowing
Threshing
Sifting
Cooking
Reaping
Winnowing
Grinding

Making clothing
Sheep shearing
Dyeing
Weaving
Separating threads
Sewing
Washing
Spinning
Removing a finished article
Tying knots
Combining raw materials

Threading a loom
Untying knots
Tearing

Leatherwork and writing
Trapping
Tanning
Cutting
Slaughtering
Scraping
Writing
Flaying skins
Marking out
Erasing

Providing shelter
Building
Demolishing

Creating fire
Kindling a fire
Extinguishing a fire

Work completion
Completing an object or making it useable

Transporting goods
Carrying in a public place

- **Muktzeh** – objects which are not useable on the Sabbath, such as work tools and money, should not be handled.
- **Sh'vut** – you should not ask someone else to do something on the Sabbath which you cannot do yourself unless you ask them in advance.
- **Uvdin d'chol** – weekday things. You should not read business papers, etc.

Pikuakh nefesh means that the Sabbath laws can be broken in order to save life.

The only time on which these laws can be broken is in the case of **pikuakh nefesh**. This mitzvah means that almost any law can be broken in order to save life:

> Whoever destroys a single life is considered as if he had destroyed the whole world, and whoever saves a single life as if he had saved the whole world.
>
> *(Mishnah)*

The sanctity of the Sabbath cannot be broken by asking someone to do a task for you on that day which you cannot do yourself, but non-Jews, who are not bound by the Sabbath rules can work for Jews on the Sabbath if it is for the benefit of health, for example lighting a fire in a cold climate, provided that the arrangement is made beforehand.

Even activities like milking cows are now controlled by electrical time switches. All Jewish businesses must close on the Sabbath and in Jewish hotels lifts stop automatically at every floor so that people do not have to push buttons. In Israel there is generally no public transport on the Sabbath.

Discussion

'Having strict religious laws about what can and cannot be done is a disadvantage to religious believers.' Consider this statement.

Activity

1 What does Judaism teach about money and greed?

2 Do you think that Jews should ever break the Sabbath laws? Give reasons for your answer.

Practice GCSE questions

Christianity

(a) Describe Christian teaching about poverty.
(8 marks)

(b) Explain why a Christian might regularly give money to charity. (7 marks)

(c) 'People should look after their own families first rather than giving money to others.' Do you agree? Give reasons to support your answer and show that you have thought about different points of view. You must refer to Christianity in your answer. (5 marks)

Hinduism

(a) Describe Hindu teaching about poverty. (8 marks)

(b) Explain why a Hindu might regularly give money to charity. (7 marks)

(c) 'People should look after their own families first rather than giving money to others.' Do you agree? Give reasons to support your answer and show that you have thought about different points of view. You must refer to Hinduism in your answer. (5 marks)

Islam

(a) Describe Muslim teaching about poverty. (8 marks)

(b) Explain why a Muslim might regularly give money to charity. (7 marks)

(c) 'People should look after their own families first rather than giving money to others.' Do you agree? Give reasons to support your answer and show that you have thought about different points of view. You must refer to Islam in your answer. (5 marks)

Judaism

(a) Describe Jewish teaching about poverty. (8 marks)

(b) Explain why a Jew might regularly give money to charity. (7 marks)

(c) 'People should look after their own families first rather than giving money to others.' Do you agree? Give reasons to support your answer and show that you have thought about different points of view. You must refer to Judaism in your answer. (5 marks)

Tips

For all four questions

In part (a), you need to concentrate on describing the teachings of the religion you are studying, rather than giving your own opinion. What might a religious believer say about the causes of poverty? Would they blame it on God, or the Devil, or on humanity itself? What specific teachings about poverty does the religion have? For high marks, you should try and express religious ideas as clearly as you can, and perhaps give some examples.

In part (b) you should demonstrate your understanding of giving money to charity. Try to think of several different ideas. You might write about the teachings of the holy books and traditions of the religion you are studying, or the ways in which religious leaders in a community might help people with decisions.

For part (c), you need to show that you realise people might have different views about this. How might a religious believer respond – what might they say about why people should care for others apart from their own family? What might a non-believer, or someone from a different religion, say in response to this question? Would they support the statement or might they feel that they should be humanitarian in their approach to others. Remember as well to give your own view. It might be the same as one of the ideas you have already expressed, or it might be another, different point of view.

UNIT 10

Religion, Peace and Justice

Christianity

Christians attitudes towards war

Christians believe that war is wrong and that God wants everyone to live in peace. However, most Christians also believe that war is sometimes necessary in order to overcome evil; it is still wrong in itself, but it is not as bad as whatever might happen if the enemy were allowed to win. The teaching of the Bible contains different views about whether or not war is right, and Christians have to try to decide which view they think is the right one in their own situation. Sometimes it can seem that all kinds of fighting are wrong, but at other times it seems necessary to defend the weak and resist evil.

In the 13th century, a Christian monk called Thomas Aquinas decided that there should be guidelines for people to follow, so that they could tell whether or not going to war was the Christian thing to do. The guidelines he made have become known as the **Just War Theory**.

The Just War

According to Thomas Aquinas, a war is only 'just' or 'fair' if it meets the following conditions:

1 The war must be started by the proper authority, such as the government or the ruler, not by other independent groups.
2 The reason for going to war must be just. It should not be for greed or for revenge, but as a sincere attempt to make the world a better place in the end.
3 Everything should be done to make sure that good, rather than evil, results from the war. At the end of the war the nations should restore peace.

Later on, other people added to Thomas Aquinas' conditions:

4 The war must be a last resort, when every other way of solving the conflict has been tried first.
5 The force used during the war should be enough to win, but no more than that. It is wrong to attack people who do not present a threat (such as old people or children), and wrong to use unnecessary cruelty during wars.

Christians today still use these guidelines when they are trying to decide whether it is right to support their country in times of international conflict. Some Christians think that, as long as the conditions for a Just War are met, then it is acceptable to go to war.

People who are firmly opposed to any form of warfare in any circumstances are called, in times of war, **conscientious objectors** – their consciences tell them to object to war. During a war, they refuse to fight as soldiers or work in the production of arms, but instead aim to promote peace in other ways such as nursing. The Religious Society of Friends, commonly known as the Quaker movement, holds this view. Quakers believe that war is never right, under any conditions.

Some Christians believe that war can be necessary to overcome evil, and to defend the weak.

Violence and pacifism

There are different views in the Bible about whether violence is ever acceptable. In the Old Testament, people are often told by God to go to war. In the books of Judges and Deuteronomy, for example, God commands his chosen people to fight and destroy foreign tribes in order to gain possession of the Promised Land. Later, too, the prophets sometimes tell the people that God wants them to go and fight. For example, in the book of Joel, the prophet gave this message from God to the people:

> Proclaim this among the nations:
> Prepare for war!
> Rouse the warriors!
> Let all the fighting men draw near and attack.
> Beat your ploughshares into swords and your pruning hooks into spears.
> *(Joel 3:9)*

Although one of the Ten Commandments is 'Do not kill', this literally translates as 'Do not murder', and a lot of people would say that killing in a war is not the same as murder.

But the Old Testament also looks forward to a time of peace, as the ideal. The prophet Micah spoke of a time in the future when God would rule the world and people could live in peace, without being afraid or worrying about defending their property:

> Nation will not take up sword against nation, nor will they train for war any more.
> Every man will sit under his own vine and under his own fig-tree,
> and no-one will make them afraid.
> *(Micah 4:3–4)*

The New Testament, too, teaches about the need for peace and forgiveness. In the Sermon on the Mount, Jesus said that the peacemakers would be called 'children of God'. He taught that people should not treat each other with hatred, but with love, even if they were enemies:

> Love your enemies and pray for those who persecute you, that you may be sons of your Father in heaven.
> *(Matthew 5:44–45)*

Some Christians therefore believe that it is never right to retaliate with the use of violence, even when other people are aggressive. These people (whether Christian or not) are called **pacifists**. Pacifists do not think that other people should be able to get away with any kind of unjust or aggressive behaviour, but they believe that the way to deal with conflict must always be non-violent. When countries are in disagreement, non-violent methods of dealing with this might include trade sanctions and peaceful negotiation, to try to reach agreement without losing any lives. Some Christians are pacifists because they believe that the Christian principle of love can never allow fighting and killing, even during war.

Non-violent protest is also used at other times, as well as during wars, if people have objections to the laws of their own governments for example. Non-violent protest can include demonstrations and marches, speeches, and advertising campaigns, or sit-ins and boycotts. People can use their votes carefully as a way of making a non-violent protest, although in some countries not everyone has the right to vote at all.

Discussion

Would you be prepared to fight in a war to defend your country? Explain why, or why not.

Activity

1 Explain what is meant by a 'Just War'.

2 Do you think that the rules for a Just War are practical for use in wartime? Give reasons for your answer.

3 Explain what pacifism is, and why some Christians hold pacifist views.

Christian beliefs about the treatment of criminals

Christianity teaches a message of forgiveness, and of love for enemies. This might seem to mean that Christians should not punish criminals, but should forgive them instead. In a story which is traditionally placed in John's Gospel, a woman was about to be stoned to death because she had been caught committing adultery; but Jesus said to the people who were waiting to kill her:

> If any one of you is without sin, let him be the first to throw a stone at her.
>
> *(John 8:7)*

One by one, everyone went away, because they all knew that they had done wrong themselves and therefore were not in a position to condemn someone else. In the Sermon on the Mount, Jesus taught people to think about their own faults, rather than always being quick to find fault with other people:

> Why do you look at the speck of sawdust in your brother's eye and pay no attention to the plank in your own eye?
>
> *(Matthew 7:3)*

However, Christians do believe that it is important to have a system of punishments for those who break the law. They believe this because although they should forgive one another, they also have a duty to protect the weak, and if people were forgiven every time they committed a crime, then innocent people would be at risk.

Some Christians believe in capital punishment (the death penalty), because the Bible recommends it in parts of the Old Testament for serious crimes. But other Christians believe that it is wrong, because in their view human life is sacred, and the criminal should be offered the opportunity to change his or her behaviour.

Christians believe that punishment has four main aims:

1 Deterrence – it should act as a warning, so that everyone in society knows what will happen to them if they break the law.
2 Protection – it should protect innocent people from those who might wish to harm them.
3 Retribution – it should be a way for the victims of the crime to see that the person has been paid back for what they have done.
4 Reformation – it should give the criminal the opportunity to think about his or her mistakes, and become a better person.

Some Christians have been appalled at the treatment of prisoners, and have worked to provide better, more humane conditions for them. Elizabeth Fry, who was a Quaker, was one of the first people to stress the need for prisoners to be given basic human rights. She lived from 1780 to 1845, and worked to improve conditions for prisoners in Newgate, especially women. Newgate was a prison which was renowned for its cruelty and terrible neglect of prisoners. She also campaigned for better conditions for those whose punishment was to be shipped overseas to places such as Australia. The prisons and the prison ships kept people together in dirty, overcrowded quarters, and many died; their crimes were often as small as the theft of a loaf of bread, and some of the prisoners were only seven or eight years old. Because of her Christian beliefs, Elizabeth Fry thought that this was unacceptable. She introduced ideas such as privacy for prisoners and the need to teach them a trade, and these ideas are still being used today.

Christian responses to social injustice

'Social injustice' is a term used to refer to occasions when some members of society are given fewer rights and privileges than others. Christians believe that all people are equally valuable to God, and therefore they believe that any form of injustice is always wrong. Christians have not always lived up to the standards set for them, but at least in principle, they do everything

Elizabeth Fry put her Christian faith into action by campaigning for prisoners to be treated as human beings.

they can to try and make the world a fairer place for those who live in it.

The Bible teaches that it is wrong to mistreat the poor and the weak. In the Old Testament, the prophets often spoke out against social injustice, telling the people that God saw what they were doing and would punish them unless they changed their ways.

In the New Testament, Christians are warned against having favourites and against being more respectful to those who have money, while ignoring the poor:

> Suppose a man comes into your meeting wearing a gold ring and fine clothes, and a poor man in shabby clothes also comes in. If you show special attention to the man wearing fine clothes and say, 'Here's a good seat for you,' but say to the poor man, 'You stand there' or 'Sit on the floor by my feet,' have you not discriminated among yourselves and become judges with evil thoughts?
>
> *(James 2:2–4)*

The Bible teaches that people from ethnic minorities and immigrants (often called 'aliens' in the Bible) should be treated just the same as relatives; they should be welcomed and given fair chances at employment:

> When an alien lives with you in your land, do not ill-treat him. The alien living with you must be treated as one of your native-born. Love him as yourself.
>
> *(Leviticus 19:33–34)*

Because of this belief, some Christians join organisations which aim to promote racial equality. Some have devoted their lives to campaigning against racism (see pages 138–9)

Amnesty International is an organisation that helps people who have been unjustly imprisoned, and many of its members are Christians. Some Christians visit their local prisons on a regular basis, or join movement such as the Howard League for Penal Reform which tries to improve conditions for prisoners in the UK.

Sometimes, people are treated unjustly because they have learning difficulties or are physically disabled. It is harder for them to find employment, and often difficult for them to get appropriate housing. Because Christians believe that everyone has equal value, they sometimes become involved in local groups and national organisations that work for equal rights for people with disabilities, such as MENCAP.

Liberation theology is the name of a Christian movement which tries to put beliefs about justice into action. In countries where people are oppressed and where the police kidnap, torture and execute those who disagree with the government, some Christians have spoken out against injustice and have risked their lives.

Discussion

Do you think that prisoners today are treated properly, or do you think that conditions in prisons are too harsh or too lenient? Give reasons for your answer.

Activity

1 Look up Luke 4:18–19. What did Jesus say he had come to do, when he began his ministry?

2 Find out more, and write about the work of Elizabeth Fry.

Hindu attitudes towards war

The concept of ahimsa

Ahimsa is one of the most important principles in Hindu morality. It is often translated as 'harmlessness', but it means more than that. It involves trying to overcome injustice and fight against evil, although not by the use of any physical force. Many Hindus believe that violence in any form is always wrong, whether it is fighting in a war, defending someone against attack, or even harming another living creature by hunting or eating meat. Harming other people or animals gives rise to bad karma, and the person who behaves aggressively or violently will one day be the victim of violence, either in this life or in the next.

But this does not mean that war is forbidden in Hinduism. The gods of the ancient Hindu texts, the Vedas, are sometimes sent prayers for help in battle, and the gods are asked to take the soldiers who are killed in battle straight into the after-life. In this verse from the Rig Veda, prayers are said for the success of an arrow shot in a battle:

> Once shot, fly far away, arrow, sharpened with prayer. Go straight to our foes, and do not leave a single one of them there.
>
> *(Rig Veda)*

Hindus are divided into different social groups, and one of these is known as the Kshatriya, or warrior, class. It is the duty, or dharma, of Kshatriyas to fight in battles when necessary, to defend the people and to use their fighting skills. In the Bhagavad Gita, which is one of the most famous pieces of Hindu literature, the god Krishna has a discussion with Arjuna, a Kshatriya, in a chariot on the battlefield. Arjuna did not want to take part in the battle, even though it was his duty as a member of the warrior class. The enemies were not strangers, but members of his family, and Arjuna felt that it would be wrong to kill them in battle. He asked Krishna what he should do:

> Shall I kill with my arrows my grandfather's brother, great Bhisma? Shall my arrows in battle slay Drona, my teacher?
>
> *(Bhagavad Gita 2:4)*

The god Krishna told Arjuna that he should fight in the battle, whatever his feelings might be. It was his duty as a Kshatriya:

> Think thou also of thy duty and do not waver. There is no greater good for a warrior than to fight in a righteous war.
>
> *(Bhagavad Gita 2:31)*

Within Hinduism, then, there are different opinions about violence and fighting in wars. Some Hindus believe that war is always wrong, and that violence must never be used, because it goes against the principle of ahimsa. But others believe that war can be necessary, and that fighting in battle is part of the religious duty of Kshatriya Hindus.

The **Laws of Manu** is a very old piece of Hindu writing, said to date back to the very first human being. It gives Hindus guidelines about the right ways to behave during war time. The book says that Kshatriyas should fight, because it is their duty, but they should behave at all times with honour, mercy and dignity. They should only fight other soldiers, and not hurt the elderly, women or children. They should fight fairly, never attacking people while they are sleeping or after they have surrendered. Many Hindus believe that these rules apply for all times, and in all circumstances, because right and wrong never change; but others argue that the guidelines are not appropriate for modern wars. They are for a time when people fought face to face with the enemy in small battles. Now that the world has weapons of mass destruction, and missiles can be sent by computers from far away, it is impossible to avoid harming innocent civilians.

Violence and pacifism

One of the world's most well-known Hindus, Mohandas (known as Mahatma) Gandhi, believed that violence is always wrong. He was a pacifist, someone who believed that all violence is wrong, no matter what the circumstances. According to Gandhi, it was better to risk being killed than to use violence.

Gandhi put the principle of ahimsa into practice by refusing to use violence in the struggle for Indian independence.

Gandhi was born in India, but lived for some time in South Africa, and then later in India, at a time when white people had many more rights than either Africans or Indians. He knew from experience about prejudice and discrimination, and he became involved in the struggle for equality and for Indian independence. But although there were important battles to be won, Gandhi believed that the way to fight the battles could never be violent. Instead, he set an example of peaceful, non-violent protest. His followers were encouraged not to co-operate with injustice, but to use methods such as sit-ins and demonstrations to make their point. However badly he was treated, Gandhi never used violence, and his example embarrassed his opponents because it made their own behaviour look brutal and immature.

Gandhi was greatly admired for his achievements. The British left India in 1947, and the people were free to form their own government. Many believed that Gandhi's peaceful protests had played a large part in the struggle for independence, because he had shown that the ancient Hindu ways of ahimsa and truth were brave and dignified ways of making a point. Strength could be found even without the use of weapons.

Discussion

Do you think that there are times when it is right to use violence? Explain your answer.

Activity

1 Do you think the Hindu rules for honourable warfare can be applied in the modern world? If not, how do you think they should be changed? Give reasons for your answer.

2 Explain why people still admire the example set by Mahatma Gandhi.

Hindu beliefs about the treatment of criminals

The ancient Hindu texts suggest that in the past, crimes were punished by the local leaders and rulers. The person who had committed the crime would be brought before the king, and the king would decide what should happen as a punishment. This was done to stop the criminal from doing the same thing again, and also to discourage other people from committing similar crimes. It was believed that the society would be peaceful and the king would be stronger, because everyone would appreciate living with well-established rules. Today, of course, it is not possible for this to happen, because people no longer live in such small societies, and there have to be national laws which apply to everyone and which form the basis of the justice system.

The Laws of Manu (see page 180) gives lists of actions that are considered to be crimes and also the punishments which are suited to them. For example, a shopkeeper who was found guilty of cheating the customers would be given a fine. Murder is seen as the most serious offence, particularly murder of a Brahmin (someone from the highest social group). Hinduism allows punishment by death for the most serious crimes. It also recognises that people who are never caught for crimes they have committed will still be punished, because their bad deeds will bring them bad karma, and this will work itself out, either in this life or a future life. So someone who has stolen will at some stage be the victim of a robbery, and someone who has been violent will be the victim of violence. Those who are punished in this life will have already paid their penalty.

According to Hindu teaching, crimes need to be punished for three reasons:

1 Restraint – the criminal is prevented from committing further crimes, which protects the rest of the society.
2 Retribution (revenge) – society has revenge on the criminal for the wrong that was done.
3 Reformation – the punishment should make the criminal realise that he or she has done wrong, and it should change their behaviour for the better. Of course, if the death penalty is carried out, then the criminal cannot behave well in this life, but it should make him or her a better person in the next life.

Hindu responses to social injustice

Hinduism teaches that people belong to different social groups, or varnas. According to Hinduism, these different groups have existed since the world began, and each different group has its own responsibilities according to the eternal law of dharma. A person cannot change the group to which he or she belongs, except by being reborn, and therefore Hindus will try hard to lead a good life so that next time they are born into a group that has more wealth and more respect.

Hindus believe that past lives affect the present. If someone is poor, or disabled, or disadvantaged in another way, this is as a result of past behaviour. For many Hindus, then, life does not seem unfair, even if one person has many more privileges than another, because everyone deserves the life that they get.

In India, the varna system is not as strong as it used to be, and in the cities many Hindus no longer care about whether their friends come from one group or another. However, in the villages, the old traditions are still important, and this can mean that some people are treated in a way that people in the West might regard as very unfair. Some people are still regarded as 'untouchable', and live in housing just outside the village, where people from higher castes will not have to come into contact with them, in case they cause ritual pollution. This is because these people have to do jobs which other Hindus regard as unclean, such as disposing of dead animals, refuse collection and clearing drains. It is thought that they will make everyone else impure if they are allowed to use the same wells, temples or public transport.

Dalits are regarded by some Hindus as impure, because they have to do dirty jobs.

However, some Hindus, such as Mahatma Gandhi (see page 185) have taken the view that this sort of treatment is completely unacceptable. They have worked to make everyone aware of how unfair this treatment is, and have campaigned for improved status for the lowest social groups. In 1950, it became illegal to regard anyone as 'untouchable', or even to give them that name. Today, they are known as 'dalits', or 'the oppressed', because of the treatment that they have been given. It is against the law in India to discriminate against dalits, and they have to be allowed the same rights to housing, health care and schooling as everyone else. But although the law does not allow discrimination, it cannot always change people's feelings, and there are still many who are prejudiced against dalits even though they are not allowed to treat them unjustly.

Many Hindus have worked to try and make the world a fairer place for everyone. Hindus have founded schools and colleges for women, to try and provide equal opportunities for both sexes. Some of the schools are designed to be 'mixed-caste' centres, to encourage people from all of the different Hindu social groups to work together and respect each other. Some Hindus have worked to help the poor and the disabled, by giving money for hospitals and clinics. There are projects to promote health education, where people travel around the rural parts of India encouraging breastfeeding, immunisation and family planning.

Discussion

Although there are many attempts to change the ways that people think so that there is justice for everyone, some people do not want to change. What reasons might they give for keeping society the way it has always been?

Activity

1 Hindus give three reasons for punishing criminals. Explain what they are, and say which you think is the most important. Try to support your choice with reasons.

2 How might a Hindu explain why dalits are so often badly treated? (Think about karma and rebirth, and about the kinds of jobs that dalits do.)

Islam

Muslim attitudes towards war

The concept of jihad

The Arabic word **jihad** is often wrongly translated in the West as 'Holy War'. Jihad actually means 'to struggle in the way of Allah'. It is the personal effort made by every Muslim to devote his or her life to carrying out Allah's will and also means the fight against evil. A person who performs jihad is called **Mujahid**.

> The most excellent jihad is the uttering of truth in the presence of an unjust ruler.
>
> *(Hadith)*

Although jihad does not mean war, many Muslims believe that the fight against evil and the preservation of Islam may justify going into battle. This is then described as **Harb al-Muqadis,** which is technically a Holy War.

> The Prophet was asked about people fighting because they are brave, or in honour of a certain loyalty, or to show off: which of them fights for the cause of Allah? He replied, 'The person who struggles so that Allah's word is supreme is the one serving Allah's cause.'
>
> *(Hadith)*

Muhammad ﷺ himself led his followers into battle at the Battle of Badr in 624 CE, this was to defend the safety of the Muslims in al-Madinah. This was the first example of jihad being put into action on the battlefield.

Islam sees self-defence as a just cause for war, but Muslims are forbidden from being the first to attack.

> Fight in the cause of Allah those who fight you, but do not transgress limits; for Allah loveth not transgressors.
>
> *(Surah 2:190)*

A war cannot be described as jihad if:
- the war is started by a political leader rather than a religious leader
- an individual person declares war without the backing of the Muslim community
- the war is aggressive not defensive
- peaceful ways of solving the problem have not been tried first
- the purpose of the war is to force people to convert to Islam
- the purpose of the war is to gain land or power
- innocent women and children are put at physical risk
- trees, crops and animals have not been protected.
- the war involves the destruction of homes or places of worship.

The medieval Crusades were seen by Christians as a Holy War to recapture Jerusalem from the Muslims for Christianity, but did the Muslims see their defence of their way of life as a Holy War?

Muslims see jihad as a way to peace. The aim is to create a society where Muslims can worship Allah in peace, without other beliefs or politics being forced upon them. According to the Qur'an and the sayings of the Prophet (contained in the Hadith), Muslims are forbidden from starting a war. If the enemy offer peace, then Muslims too must put down their weapons.

In countries where Islam governs politics as well as religion, living in a Muslim state is seen as something that people should fight for if necessary.

Violence and pacifism

As well as 'submission' the word 'Islam' can also mean 'peace'. Peace in Islam does not mean accepting a situation if it is unjust, but enemies and oppressors must be fought without hatred or vengeance, and once the battle is over, peace must be restored and differences reconciled.

> Hate your enemy mildly; he may become your friend one day.
>
> *(Hadith)*

The Qur'an teaches that all people are created by Allah and are therefore equal:

> Of His Signs is the creation of the heavens and the earth, and the diversity of your tongues and colours.
>
> *(Surah 30:22)*

> O mankind, We have created you from male and female; and We have divided you into tribes and sub-tribes for greater facility of intercourse. Verily, the most honoured among you in the sight of Allah is he who is the most righteous among you. Surely, Allah is All-Knowing, All-Aware.
>
> *(Surah 49:14)*

Muslims must take these teachings about equality from the Qur'an and try to implement them in the world.

Islam is a peace-loving religion and aims to see an international order in the world which would enable people to live without the threat of attack or unjust rulers and without prejudice or discrimination on religious, cultural, social or economic grounds. Muslims view this as the only way forward for humanity. The struggle to reach this world order is jihad. By working towards peaceful co-existence Muslims are living in obedience and submission to Allah and helping to save humanity from destruction.

Muslims are openly critical of any struggle or fighting between Muslim countries, as this goes against the whole concept of jihad.

Discussion

Do you consider that there are occasions when pacifism is not the correct response to a situation?

Activity

1 Explain what is meant by a Harb al-Muqadis.

2 Explain the importance of the concept of jihad.

Muslim beliefs about the treatment of criminals

Islamic law, shari'ah, is the basis for judgement and the treatment of criminals. Shari'ah means the 'way to water', or the source of life. Living according to shari'ah is the way in which Muslims can reach Allah.

Islam recognises three types of sin: the first is shirk, associating someone or something with God; the second, zalim, consists of crimes such as murder, theft, suicide and illegal sexual relations; the third type covers lying, cursing and envy.

Punishment in Islam has nothing to do with the removal of sin, as only God can forgive and this only happens when someone is really repentant and asks God for forgiveness. Punishment is seen as a means of protecting and strengthening society.

In Islam there is no attempt to 'fit the punishment to the crime'. It is believed that only God can know all the circumstances surrounding a particular person and their actions.

Penalties are known as **hudu** – 'boundaries' rather than punishments as they enforce boundaries between right and wrong that have been crossed.

Hudu applies to crimes which are dealt with in the Qur'an or Hadith. For example in a case of murder:

> ...if anyone slew a person – unless it be for murder or for spreading mischief in the land – it would be as if he slew the whole people
>
> *(Surah 5:32)*

This means that the only justification for murder is if the victim has committed a murder or if they are guilty of speaking against Allah and corrupting his teachings.

However, it is still not permitted to kill anyone except through legal means.

Adultery or fornication (sex outside of marriage):

> The woman and the man guilty of adultery or fornication – flog each of them with a hundred stripes: let not compassion move you in their case, in a matter prescribed by Allah, if ye believe in Allah and the Last Day: and let a party of the Believers witness their punishment.
>
> *(Surah 24:2)*

Defamation – destroying someone's character:

> And those who launch a charge against chaste women, and produce not four witnesses (to support their allegations) – flog them with eighty stripes; and reject their evidence ever after: for such men are wicked transgressors.
>
> *(Surah 24:4)*

Theft:

> As to the thief, male or female, cut off his or her hands: a punishment by way of example, from Allah, for their crime.
>
> *(Surah 5:38)*

Islam also allows for the person who has suffered from the crime to have recompense:

> O ye who believe! The law of equality is prescribed to you in cases of murder: the free for the free, the slave for the slave, the woman for the woman. But if any remission is made by the brother of the slain, then grant any reasonable demand, and compensate him with handsome gratitude. This is a concession and a Mercy from your Lord. After this, whoever exceeds the limits shall be in grave penalty.
>
> *(Surah 2:178)*

It is important to remember that once a person has been punished, repented and asked God for forgiveness, they must be treated normally – there is no further guilt and they must not be punished further in any way.

These punishments are those laid down by Shari'ah but are not necessarily imposed, and much depends on the country in which the crimes are committed. The underlying principle here is that the laws are to protect society, not just to seek punishment of the criminal. Individual courts and countries may therefore interpret Hudu in different ways. It has always to be remembered that Allah is seen as forgiving and merciful and people are therefore urged to do likewise.

Muslim responses to social injustice

Islam sees three groups of people as being in need and requiring special care and attention: orphans, the needy and travellers.

> What Allah has bestowed on His Messenger (and taken away) from the people of the townships – belongs to Allah – to his Messenger and to kindred and orphans, the needy and the wayfarer; in order that it may not (merely) make a circuit between the wealthy among you.
> *(Surah 59:7)*

Islam hopes that orphans can be brought up by relatives or family rather than in an institution. Orphans are entitled to know their family's history and background and to receive any inheritance that comes from their parents.

> To orphans restore their property (when they reach their age), nor substitute (your) worthless things for (their) good ones; and devour not their substance (by mixing it up) with your own. For this is indeed a great sin.'
> *(Surah 4:2)*

The needy are the poor, disadvantaged or handicapped.

> It is not fault in the blind, nor in one born lame, nor in one afflicted with illness.
> *(Surah 24:61).*

Travellers are beggars or people who have lost all hope and Islam says they should be helped and encouraged to return to a stable and secure life.

Elderly people may be devalued in some societies, but in Muslim society they are shown great respect.

Finally, there are the elderly. Elderly people are seen as the wealth of Islam because of all the work they have done in their lives and Muslims must show great respect to them:

> Thy Lord hath decreed that ye worship none but Him, and that ye be kind to parents. Whether one or both of them attain old age in thy life, say not to them a word of contempt, nor repel them, but address them in terms of honour. And, out of kindness, lower to them the wing of humility, and say: 'My Lord! Bestow on them thy Mercy even as they cherished me in childhood.
> *(Surah 17:23–24)*

Discussion

Consider different ideas about the purposes of punishment, e.g. revenge, retribution, protection, and consider which of these might be the most important and why.

Activity

1 Islam has strict rules for dealing with criminals. Explain what they are why they are important.

2 How might a Muslim ensure that they protect and look after people who are weaker than themselves?

Judaism

Jewish attitudes towards war

The concept of Holy War

In the Jewish Scriptures there are examples of wars. Some of these were Holy Wars where the Jews were trying to maintain their religion when other people wanted to make them worship false gods. Others were perhaps 'Just Wars', but it could be argued that some of them were wrong and unjustified.

Judaism says that there are three kinds of wars which must be fought:

1 **milchemet mitzvah** (war commanded by) G-d – this is similar to a Holy War. Two such wars are described in the Hebrew Bible: the campaign against Amalek, and Joshua and the Israelites fighting for the Promised Land:

> Moses My servant has died. Now, arise, cross this Jordan, you and this entire people, to the land that I give to them, to the Children of Israel. Every place upon which the sole of your foot will tread I have given to you, as I spoke to Moses.
>
> *(Joshua 1:2–3)*

The conditions for this war are that the enemy has attacked first or that there is a need to pre-empt an attack.

2 **milchemet reshut** (optional war) – this is what would be described as a Just War. However:
   ● the war should be a last resort
   ● non-violent approaches should have been tried first
   ● civilians should not be targeted
   ● damage should be limited.

No war such as this has been called since the fall of the Temple in 70 CE.

3 **a pre-emptive war** – this may only be fought when an attack upon Israel is imminent. This happened in 1967, when Israel attacked the airfields of Egypt and Syria in the Six Day War to try to prevent a long and bloody siege.

Jews are obliged to protect themselves and other Jews, as well as going to the aid of other countries to prevent the spread of war.

Self-defence is also permissible:

> If a person intends to kill you, be first to kill him.
>
> *(Talmud)*

Some of the rules about war are found in the Torah (see Deuteronomy 20:10–13, 19–20).

Judaism teaches that wars must be fought properly and humanely:

> If your foe is hungry, feed him bread; and if he is thirsty, give him water to drink.
>
> *(Proverbs 25:21)*

Violence and pacifism

The struggle for peace and justice lies at the centre of Judaism:

> The world endures on three things – justice, truth and peace.
>
> *(Ethics of the Fathers 1:18)*

A rabbi said that only G-d could forgive the Nazis for the Holocaust.

HASHEM will give might to His nation,
HASHEM will bless His nation with peace.
(Psalm 29:11)

In G-d's eyes the man stands high who
makes peace between men – between
husband and wife, between parents
and children, between management
and labour, between neighbour and
neighbour. But he stands highest who
establishes peace among the nations.
(Talmud)

Indeed, 'shalom' – peace – is a word used in
Hebrew to mean both 'hello' and 'goodbye'.

There is a phrase in the Torah which has
led some people think that Judaism is
based on revenge:

But if there shall be a fatality, then you
shall award a life for a life; an eye for an
eye, a tooth for a tooth, a hand for a
hand, a foot for a foot.
(Exodus 21:23–24)

This is called **Lex Talionis** (the law of
retaliation). It does not mean that if
someone cuts off your hand then you
should cut off theirs. It was written to limit
revenge and says that if someone cuts off
your hand then you must *not cut off any
more* than their hand and in fact is
interpreted as a financial payment to make
good the wrong committed.

Jews believe that they should forgive other
people but that they cannot forgive on
behalf of others. When he was asked if he
could forgive the Nazis for the Holocaust,
in which six million Jews were murdered,
Rabbi Hugo Gryn said that only G-d could
forgive their crimes.

Judaism still thinks of most wars as wrong,
and believes that peace must always be
sought before fighting.

Turn from evil and do good, seek peace
and pursue it.
(Psalm 34:15)

This passage from Isaiah shows the hope
for peace:

It will happen in the end of days: The
mountain of the Temple of Hashem will
be firmly established as the head of the
mountains, and it will be exalted above
the hills, and all the nations will stream
to it. Many peoples will go and say,
'Come, let us go up to the Mountain of
HASHEM, to the Temple of the G-d of
Jacob, and He will teach us of His ways
and we will walk in His paths.' For from
Zion will the Torah come forth, and the
word of HASHEM from Jerusalem. He will
judge among the nations, and will
settle the arguments of many peoples.
They shall beat their swords into
plowshares and their spears into
pruning hooks; nation will not lift
sword against nation and they will no
longer study warfare.
(Isaiah 2:2–4)

So, although Judaism is not a pacifist
religion, it does believe that peace is the
highest good.

This teaching is found in a letter from a
Jewish philosopher Martin Buber which
was sent to Gandhi:

For I cannot help withstanding evil
when I see that it is about to destroy
the good. I am forced to withstand the
evil in the world as the evil within
myself. I can only strive not to have to
do so by force. I do not want force. But
if there is no other way of preventing
the evil destroying the good, I trust I
shall use force and give myself up into
G-d's hands.

Discussion

Do you consider that there are occasions
when pacifism is not the correct
response to a situation?

Activity

1 Explain what is meant by milchemet
mitzvah and milchemet reshut.

2 Do you think that Jews should now
forgive those responsible for the
Holocaust? Give reasons to support your
answer.

Jewish beliefs about the treatment of criminals

Judaism has always believed that criminals must be treated fairly. They are entitled to a fair trial by a court before sentence is passed.

According to Jewish law each of the 36 most serious crimes (which included adultery, sodomy, idolatry, witchcraft, or murder) carried one of four different types of death penalty: stoning, burning, beheading, or strangling. However, the rabbis tried to limit the possibility of capital punishment. There was very strict and thorough cross-examination of witnesses and a potential criminal had to be warned of the possible punishment before committing the crime. If all the judges agreed on a verdict it was felt likely that they were prejudiced and that the verdict was wrong. Therefore it was almost impossible to reach a death verdict.

If a death verdict was finally reached, every effort had to be made to have it reversed. Execution had to be carried out in the most humane way and the accused person was drugged before they were executed. The death penalty was abolished in 30 CE.

For 207 other crimes which included perjury, incest, and eating of forbidden foods, criminals were whipped with a maximum of 39 strokes. Even here, however, the criminal had to be forewarned and was given a very strict trial in an attempt to prove their innocence. Once the sentence had been passed, the guilty person was examined by a doctor to ensure that they could bear the lashes.

A final, less severe penalty was **makkat mardut,** or disciplinary lashes.

So, in all instances, Jewish law tries to limit the punishment and safeguard the criminal so that violence and suffering is kept to a minimum. Although Israel is a Jewish state, the laws of the country today have far more in common with those of most Western democracies than with the instructions of the Torah and Talmud.

Jewish responses to social injustice

Jewish teaching about how other people should be treated is very clear:

> When a proselyte dwells among you in your land, do not taunt him. The proselyte who dwells with you shall be like a native among you, and you shall love him like yourself, for you were aliens in the land of Egypt – I am HASHEM your G-d.
>
> *(Leviticus 19:33–34)*
>
> Note – a proselyte is a convert

Many of the prophets of the Jewish Scriptures wrote about social injustice:

> Remove from before Me the multitude of your songs, and the music of your lutes I will not hear. Rather, let justice be revealed like water, and righteousness like a mighty stream.
>
> *(Amos 5:23–24)*

> Woe to you who spurn the day of evil, while you convene sessions of injustice; who lie on ivory couches, stretched out on their beds, eating the fattened sheep of the flock and calves from inside the stall; who sing along to the tune of the lute … who drink wine out of bowls, anoint themselves with choicest oils, and are not pained by the destruction of Joseph.
>
> *(Amos 6:3–6)*

Jews believe that it is their responsibility to try to help any one or any country in terms of money and development. As well as helping fight injustice in whatever way they can, they should also contribute financially to help people.

Jews are expected to give a tenth of their wealth as **tzedaka** (righteousness). This money is owing to the poor and so not to give it is to rob them. Even the very poorest people should try to give something as tzedaka.

The worst way to give tzedaka is to hand someone the money; the best way is to lend it to them indefinitely and without interest.

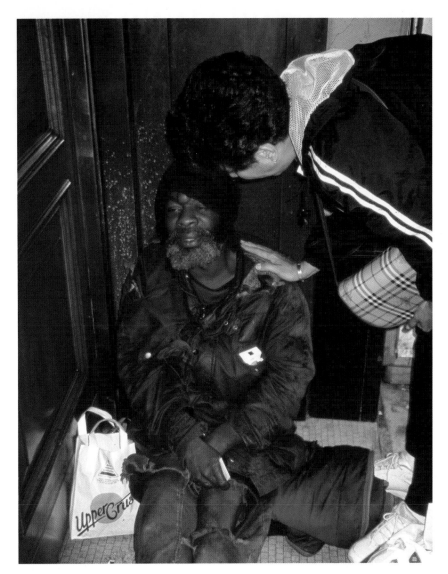

Judaism teaches that by doing this you are saving people the embarrassment of taking a gift. The hope is that this money will help a poor person to become self-supporting so that they no longer need help.

The obligation to give tzedaka applies even if the person receiving it is not grateful or gracious.

Discussion

Consider different ideas about the purposes of punishment, e.g. revenge, retribution, protection, and consider which of these might be the most important and why.

Activity

1 Judaism has strict rules for dealing with criminals. Explain what they are and why they are important.

2 How might a Jew ensure that they protect and look after people who are weaker than themselves?

Practice GCSE questions

Christianity

(a) Describe Christian beliefs about crime and punishment. (8 marks)

(b) Explain how a Christian might work to make the world a fairer place. (7 marks)

(c) 'It can never be right to fight in a war.' Do you agree? Give reasons to support your answer, and show that you have thought about different points of view. You must refer to Christianity in your answer. (5 marks)

Hinduism

(a) Describe Hindu beliefs about crime and punishment. (8 marks)

(b) Explain how a Hindu might work to make the world a fairer place. (7 marks)

(c) 'It can never be right to fight in a war.' Do you agree? Give reasons to support your answer, and show that you have thought about different points of view. You must refer to Hinduism in your answer. (5 marks)

Islam

(a) Describe Muslim beliefs about crime and punishment. (8 marks)

(b) Explain how a Muslim might work to make the world a fairer place. (7 marks)

(c) 'It can never be right to fight in a war.' Do you agree? Give reasons to support your answer, and show that you have thought about different points of view. You must refer to Islam in your answer. (5 marks)

Judaism

(a) Describe Jewish beliefs about crime and punishment. (8 marks)

(b) Explain how a Jew might work to make the world a fairer place. (7 marks)

(c) 'It can never be right to fight in a war.' Do you agree? Give reasons to support your answer, and show that you have thought about different points of view. You must refer to Judaism in your answer. (5 marks)

Tips

For all four questions

In part (a), you need to show your knowledge of religious beliefs about crime and punishment. You are being tested on your knowledge here, so you do not need to give your own opinions, but should concentrate on demonstrating that you know what followers of the religion you are studying believe. Try to explain the reasons behind their beliefs if you can.

In part (b), you need to think of different ways in which followers of the religion you are studying might help to make the world fairer. Perhaps they have started organisations, or there are some which they might join, and you could say what these organisations do and why they might appeal to religious believers. You might be able to refer to particular individuals who have campaigned for justice in some way.

Part (c) asks you to give your own opinion, and to think about different points of view. You should try to include the ways in which religious believers would answer this question. Perhaps they would agree, or disagree, and you need to say why. Maybe they would have different opinions about war, even if they all belong to the same religion, and you could explain what these different viewpoints might be.

Christianity

abortion *when a pregnancy ends before a baby is born, either by accident (miscarriage) or deliberately (procured abortion)*

active euthanasia *when steps are taken to bring death more quickly*

agape *a Greek word for unconditional love*

altar *a table used for sacrifice; in Christianity, it is the table where the Eucharist is celebrated*

annulled *dissolved – when a marriage is annulled, it means that it is not considered to have been a real marriage from the beginning*

apartheid *a system of government in which people of different races are kept apart*

Apostles' creed *a statement of Christian beliefs*

Ascension *when Jesus went into heaven after his resurrection*

Big Bang *a massive explosion which many scientists believe marked the beginning of the universe*

Church of England *the Anglican Church, founded by Henry VIII*

conscientious objectors *people whose consciences lead them to object to fighting wars*

cosmology *the science which includes study of the origins of the universe*

Desmond Tutu *a black South African Christian who has campaigned against racism*

Devil *a supernatural power of evil*

doctrine of the Trinity *the belief that God has 'three persons', the Father, Son and Holy Spirit*

double effect *the argument that actions such as euthanasia can be allowed if they are a side-effect of a good action such as pain relief*

ecumenical movement *the work done by some Christians who try to promote unity between different denominations*

ensoulment *the time at which a person is believed to receive a soul from God*

ethical monotheists *people who believe that there is one God who gives them moral rules*

Eucharist *another name for Holy Communion; the sacrament of the sacrifice of Jesus and the unity of Christians*

euthanasia *a 'good death'; mercy-killing; the deliberate ending of a life*

evangelical *a kind of believer who emphasises the need to share the Christian faith, and who often takes a more literal view of the Bible*

evolution *the process by which living things change through natural selection*

font *a basin used for holding water for baptisms*

Gospels *the four books which tell the story of the life, death, and resurrection of Jesus*

Holy Communion *see Eucharist*

hospice *a place where terminally ill people can go for nursing and respite care*

hymns *prayers set to music, for use in worship*

in vitro fertilisation *a form of fertility treatment where an egg is fertilised outside the womb*

involuntary euthanasia *a form of euthanasia where the patient cannot or does not give consent*

Just War theory *a theory which outlines the conditions necessary for it to be right to go to war or continue to fight a war*

Kingdom of God/Kingdom of heaven *a time when humanity is ruled by God and behaves according to agape (unconditional love)*

lectern *a raised desk on which the Bible is rested when it is being read in church*

liberation theology *a way of thinking which says that Christians should fight against injustice on behalf of the weak*

Lord's Supper *another name for Holy Communion (see Eucharist)*

Martin Luther King *a black Christian civil rights activist*

Mass *the name given to the Eucharist by Roman Catholics (see Eucharist)*

medical ethics *questions of morality which are raised by medical situations*

monogamy *remaining faithful to only one sexual partner for life*

monotheists *people who believe that there is only one God*

moral evil *the kind of evil and suffering that is caused by people doing wrong*

natural evil *the kind of evil and suffering that is caused by natural events such as earthquakes and floods*

natural selection *the process by which the fittest creatures best suited to their environment survive and the weaker ones die out*

New Testament *the part of the Bible which contains stories of the life of Jesus and teachings about Christian living*

Old Testament *the part of the Christian Bible which also forms the Jewish scriptures, and was written before Jesus was born*

omnipotent *all-powerful; able to do anything*

omniscient *all-knowing; able to know everything that can be known*

pacifists *people who believe that violence is never justified*

palliative care *medical care which involves pain control*

parables *stories told by Jesus and by others, which illustrate a moral or religious message*

passive euthanasia *a form of euthanasia where no action is taken to postpone death*

prayer *communication between God and humanity*

pulpit *a raised platform on which a speaker stands in church to be more easily seen and heard*

resurrection *being raised from the dead to new life*

Roman Catholic Church *the Christian Church which accepts the authority of the Pope as a successor of Peter*

sacrament *a symbolic way of acknowledging the grace of God*

sermon *a speech in which religious and moral ideas are explained, usually in church*

Sermon on the Mount *a collection of Jesus' teachings about the right way to live, found in Matthew 5-7*

stoup *a container for holy water, placed near the entrance of some churches*

Taizé *a Christian ecumenical centre*

Ten Commandments *ten rules about right conduct, which form the basis of Christian and Jewish morality*

Trevor Huddleston *a white priest who campaigned against apartheid in South Africa*

voluntary euthanasia *a form of euthanasia known as 'assisted suicide', where someone asks for help to bring death more quickly*

Hinduism

ahimsa *non-violence, harmlessness; doing no injury to any living creature*

amrit *holy water, the drink of immortality*

artha *goal of life; wealth, achievement and success*

arti *the offering of light to God during worship*

ashramas *four stages of life, each with its own code of conduct*

Atman *the eternal Self*

AUM *a sacred and eternal sound used in meditation and worship*

avatars *appearances of the god Vishnu on the earth, at times of trouble*

Bhagavad Gita *'the song of the Lord'; part of the Mahabharata, one of the best-known and most popular pieces of Hindu literature*

bhajan *a sacred song used during worship*

bhakti *loving devotion to God*

brahmacarya *one of the four ashramas, or stages of life. Brahmacarya is the 'student' stage*

Brahman *God; the essence of all reality; the one truth of which all the different deities are aspects*

brahmins *members of the highest, priestly caste*

dalits *the oppressed; members of the lowest, 'untouchable' group*

dana *charitable giving*

deities *gods and goddesses*

dharma *truth, virtue, the right code of conduct appropriate for someone's social status and stage of life*

Ganesha *a popular Hindu deity, with an elephant's head; the god of wisdom and the remover of obstacles*

garba-griha *the inner sanctuary of the Hindu mandir*

Gayatri mantra *the name of a verse in the Vedas addressing the sun, which is recited at the beginning and end of every day when puja is performed*

grihasta *the second of the traditional stages of life – the householder*

guru *a teacher or spiritual guide*

harijans *a term invented by Gandhi for the people who had been known as 'untouchables'; it means 'children of God'*

kama *desire, pleasure, sexual love*

karma *action, deed; also the natural law which brings about good results for good deeds and suffering for bad deeds*

kshatriyas *members of the second, warrior caste*

Lakshmi *the goddess of beauty, good luck and prosperity, often shown with a lotus in her hand*

Laws of Manu *a code of conduct, traditionally written by Manu, the first man; it is also known as Manusmriti*

Mahabharata *an epic work of Hindu literature, telling the story of two warring families, and dealing with topics such as dharma, morality and salvation*

mandapa *the main hall of a Hindu temple, often with a dome over it*

mandir *Hindu temple, a 'dwelling-place' of God*

mantras *ways of communicating with God using words, often words from the Vedas repeated as chants and in meditation*

Manusmriti *see Laws of Manu*

mehndi *traditional patterns painted on the body with henna, for decoration*

moksha *salvation or liberation; freedom from the endless chain of death and rebirth*

murti *a statue or picture of a deity, used as a focus for worship and mediation*

Om *see AUM*

puja *an act of worship, a ritual*

Purusha Sukta *a piece of Hindu literature which tells the story of the creation of the world through the sacrifice of primeval man*

purushartas *the four traditional goals of life: dharma, arta, karma and moksha*

Rama *a favourite deity of Hinduism; an avatar of the god Vishnu and the hero of the epic tale, the Ramayana*

Ramakrishna Mission *a movement seeking to promote the equality of Hinduism with other world religions, and working for religious tolerance*

Ramayana *an epic tale of Rama and his wife Sita, their exile and adventures and eventual return to the throne*

rangoli patterns *drawn to welcome guests and friendly deities, particularly on special occasions*

rebirth (reincarnation) *the movement of Atman, the essential Self, from one life at the point of death to the next life at birth*

Rig Veda *the oldest religious book known to humanity, a collection of sacred hymns*

rishis *'seers', sometimes used for the inspired composers of the Vedas, sometimes used in a wider sense for other people who have taught Hindu wisdom*

samsara *the endless cycle of birth, death and rebirth; the continual flow of change and rebecoming*

sannyasin *someone who has reached the fourth stage of life and renounced worldly possessions to become a homeless wanderer*

Sanskrit *the holy language of Hinduism*

sati *a practice, now illegal, in which widows threw themselves onto their husband's funeral pyres, sometimes spelt suttee*

Shiva *one of the most important deities of Hinduism, the 'lord of the dance', creator and destroyer (see Trimurti)*

Sita *a goddess, the wife of Rama, a Hindu model of faithfulness and ideal womanhood*

smriti *'that which is remembered'; traditional Hindu writings which are often very popular but do not have the authority of sruti*

sruti *'that which is heard'; Hindu texts with great authority, believed to have been heard as eternal sounds and recorded in the Vedas*

sudras *members of the fourth, servant caste of Hinduism*

Supreme Reality *a Hindu way of expressing belief about God*

suttee *see sati*

swastika *a Hindu symbol of good luck*

trimurti *the three Hindu gods Brahma the creator, Vishnu the preserver and Shiva the destroyer, who together represent the whole of reality*

Upanishads *sacred Hindu texts which come after the Vedas and deal with matters of morality and philosophy*

vaishyas *members of the third, professional caste of Hinduism*

vanaprastha *a forest-dweller, someone who has passed the householder stage of life and is ready to renounce the world*

Vedas *the oldest and most sacred texts of Hinduism*

vimana *the inner shrine of a mandir, where the images of the deities are kept*

Islam

'al-Janna *paradise*

Adhan *call to prayer. From the same root, Mu'adhin (one who makes the call to prayer)*

Akhirah *everlasting life after death–the hereafter*

al-Fatihah *the Opener. Surah 1 of the Qur'an. Recited at least 17 times daily during the five times of salah. Also known as 'The Essence' of the Qur'an*

Al-Mi'ra j *the ascent through the heavens of the Prophet Muhammad* ﷺ

Laylat-ul-Qadr *the Night of Power, when the first revelation of the Qur'an was made to Prophet Muhammad ﷺ. It is believed to be one of the last ten nights of Ramadan*

Din-ul-Fitrah *a description of Islam as the natural way of life*

Hadith *saying; report; account. The sayings of the Prophet Muhammad ﷺ, as recounted by his household, progeny and companions. These are a major source of Islamic law. Some Hadith are referred to as Hadith Qudsi (sacred Hadith) having been divinely communicated to the Prophet Muhammad* ﷺ

Hajj *annual pilgrimage to Makkah, which each Muslim must undertake at least once in a lifetime if he or she has the health and wealth. A Muslim male who has completed Hajj is called Hajji, and a female, Hajjah*

Harb al-Muqadis *Holy War*

Hudu *boundaries or penalties*

Ibadah *all acts of worship. Any permissible action performed with the intention to obey Allah*

'Iblis *the Jinn who defied Allah by refusing to bow to Adam (peace be upon him), and later became the tempter of all human beings*

'Iddah *a three month period of reconciliation before a divorce may take place*

Islam *peace attained through willing obedience to Allah's divine guidance*

Jahannam *the fires of Hell*

Jihad *personal individual struggle against evil in the way of Allah. It can also be collective defence of the Muslim community*

Jinn *being created by Allah from fire*

Ka'bah *a cube-shaped structure in the centre of the grand mosque in Makkah. The first house built for the worship of the One True God*

Khalifah *successor; inheritor; custodian; vice-regent*

Khutbah *speech. Talk delivered on special occasions such as the Jum'uah and Id prayers*

Makkah *city where the Prophet Muhammad ﷺ was born, and where the Ka'bah is located*

mala'ikah *angels*

mihrab *niche or alcove in a mosque wall, indicating the Qiblah – the direction of Makkah, towards which all Muslims face to perform salah*

minaret *a tower on a mosque from which the Adhan or call to prayer is made*

minbar *rostrum; platform; dais. The stand from which the Imam delivers the khutbah or speech in the mosque or praying ground*

monotheists *believers in one God*

Mujahid *the name give to a person who completes jihad*

Qur'an *that which is read or recited. The Divine Book revealed to the Prophet Muhammad ﷺ. Allah's final revelation to humankind*

Ramadan *the ninth month of the Islamic calendar, during which fasting is required from just before dawn until sunset, as ordered by Allah in the Qur'an*

riba *interest made on money*

Risalah *Prophets*

Sabians *an ancient race of people referred to in the Qur'an*

Sadaqah *additional voluntary charity which can be given when someone is in need*

Salah *prescribed communication with, and worship of Allah, performed under specific conditions, in the manner taught by the Prophet Muhammad ﷺ, and recited in the Arabic language. The five daily times of salah are fixed by Allah*

Salat-ul-Jumu'ah *friday prayers at the mosque*

Shahadah *declaration of faith, which consists of the statement, 'There is no god except Allah, Muhammad is the Messenger of Allah'*

Shaytan *rebellious; proud. The devil*

shirk *association. Regarding anything as being equal or partner to Allah. Shirk is forbidden in Islam*

Surah *Division of the Qur'an (114 in all)*

Ummah *community. World-wide community of Muslims; the nation of Islam*

Yawmuddin *The Day of Judgement*

Zalim *wrongdoing against Allah, other people, or yourself*

Aron Hakodesh *Holy Ark. The focal point of the synagogue, containing Torah scrolls*

Adonai *Lord*

apocryphal books *holy books which were not placed in the canon of Jewish scripture*

Beth Din *Jewish religious court*

Challah *enriched bread used particularly on Shabbat and during festivals*

Chazzan *leader of reading, singing and chanting in the Cantor services of some synagogues*

Chevra Kadisha *the Sacred Burial Society which prepares dead bodies for burial*

Covenant *an agreement made between God and the Israelites*

decke *a cloth placed over the challot*

Final Solution *the name given by the Nazis to Hitler's attempt to completely wipe out the Jews during the Second World War (1939-45)*

Gan Eden *Paradise*

Gehenna (Gehinnom) *Hell, where the wicked will be punished*

Gemilut Hasadim *'Kind actions' – a form of Jewish charity*

ghettos *areas of towns or villages where Jews have been forced to live apart from non-Jews*

Hagaddah *telling. A book used at Seder*

Hanukkah *dedication. An eight-day festival of lights to celebrate the re-dedication of the temple following the Maccabean victory over the Greeks*

hanukiah *nine-branched Hanukkah lamp used at the Menorah festival of Hanukkah*

Hashem *Lord*

Havdalah *distinction. Ceremony marking the conclusion of Shabbat*

Holocaust *originally a burnt offering – a sacrifice. Now used to describe the massacre of the Jews during the Second World War (1939-45)*

huppah *canopy used for a wedding ceremony, under which the bride and groom stand*

K'tiv *that which is written in the Torah – used of words or phrases which are difficult to interpret or understand*

Kaddish *prayer publicly recited by mourners.*

Keri *that which is read from the Torah when a passage is K'tiv (see K'tiv)*

Keriah *a tear which people make in their clothes when they hear of a death*

Ketubah *document that defines rights and obligations within Jewish marriage*

Ketuvim Writings *third section of the Tenakh*

Kiddushin *wedding ceremony*

kosher *fit; proper. Foods permitted by Jewish dietary laws*

Lex Talionis *The Law of Retaliation - Exodus 21:23-24. This limits the amount of revenge which can be taken*

Lucifer *the archangel who fell from grace and became the Devil*

Magen David *Shield of David, popularly called Star of David*

makkat mardut *disciplinary lashes used as punishment*

Master Race *the name given by Hitler to his German people whom he intended to rule the world*

menorah *seven-branched candelabrum which was lit daily in the Temple*

mezuzah *a scroll placed on doorposts of Jewish homes, containing a section from the Torah and often enclosed in a decorative case*

Midrash *collections of various Rabbinic commentaries on the Tenakh*

milchemet reshut *an optional war – in effect a Just War*

Mishnah *first writing down of the Oral Tradition. An authoritative document forming part of the Talmud, codified about 200 CE*

mitzvah *mitzvot (pl.) commandment. The Torah contains 613 Mitzvot. Commonly used to describe good deeds*

monotheists *people who believe in one God.*

Nevi'im *Prophets. Second section of the Tenakh*

Noachide Code *seven laws given to Noah after the flood, which humankind should follow. These laws form the foundation for a just society*

pikuakh nefesh *Save a soul. The setting aside of certain laws in order to save a life*

pogrom *organised attack on Jews, especially frequent in 19th and early 20th century Eastern Europe*

Schechitah *the manner in which animals are slaughtered for food according to Jewish law*

Scrolls *the rolls on which the Torah is written*

Shabbat *day of spiritual renewal and rest commencing at sunset on Friday, terminating at nightfall on Saturday*

Shadchan *a matchmaker – someone who arranges marriages*

Shanah *the eleven months of mourning for a relative*

Shema *major Jewish prayer affirming belief in one G-d. The Shema is found in the Torah*

Sheol *a dark place where people go after death and where they stay for eternity*

Sheva Berachos *the seven blessings said at a marriage ceremony.*

Shoah *desolation. The suffering experienced by European Jews at the hands of the Nazis, including the systematic murder of six million Jews between 1933 and 1945*

Talmud *Mishnah and Gemara, collected together*

Tenakh *the collected 24 books of the Jewish Bible, comprising three sections: Torah, Nevi'im, and Ketuvim (Te;Na;Kh)*

Terefah *forbidden – the opposite of kosher*

Tetragrammaton *the four consonants YHWH which are used in the Jewish scriptures for G-d's name*

Torah *law; teaching. The Five Books of Moses*

Tu B'Shevat *New Year for Trees, this festival takes place on day 15 of the Jewish month of Shevat*

tzedaka *righteousness. An act of charity*

yahrzeit *year-time. Anniversary of a death*

Yom Kippur *Day of Atonement. Fast day occurring on the tenth day after Rosh Hashanah; a solemn day of Tefillah and Teshuva*

The publishers are grateful to the following for permission to reproduce photographs or other illustrative material:

Ann and Bury Peerless: pp. 14, 32, 34, 69, 91 (with kind permission Baroda Museum);

Art Directors and Trip Photo Library: pp. 20, 57, 62, 110; *I. Genut*: pp. 80, 117, 138, 174; *F. Good*: p. 133; *J. Highet*: p. 17; *E. James*: pp. 42, 154; *H. Rogers*: pp. 16, 18, 31 (middle left, middle right, bottom), 35 (top and bottom), 36 (right), 41, 54, 67, 72, 74, 76 (right), 86, 97, 106, 108, 148, 151, 167, 168, 172, 175, 195; *S. Shapiro*: p. 114 (bottom); *J. Soester*: p. 43; *A. Tovy*: pp. 13, 24, 114 (top); *B. Turner*: pp. 59, 107;

The Associated Press Ltd: p. 139; *Kamran Jebreili*: pp. 93, 152; *Yoav Lemmer*: p. 84;

Corbis Images: *David Bartruff*: 145; *Bojan Brecelj*: p. 156; *Philip Gould*: p. 127; *Annie Griffiths Belt*: pp. 81, 125; *Lindsay Hebberd*: pp. 70, 170; *Historical Picture Archive*: p. 136; *Earl and Nazima Kowall*: p. 88; *Danny Lehman*: p. 164; *Francis G. Mayer*: p. 48; *Francoise de Mulder*: p. 77; *Chris Rainier*: p. 55; *Steve Raymer*: p. 94; *David and Peter Turnley*: pp. 76 (left), 143; *David H. Wells*: pp. 60, 173;

Corel (NT): pp. 28, 30, 38 (right), 98, 102, 121, 162, 180;

Digital Stock (NT): pp. 25, 31 (top), 36 (left), 38 (left), 130;

Digital Vision (NT): pp. 46, 50, 52;

C.M. Dixon: p.10;

Illustrated London News (NT): p. 185;

Image100 (NT): p. 128;

Mary Evans Picture Library: pp. 47, 165, 183, 188, 192;

Panos Pictures: *Piers Benatari*: p. 135; *Nancy Durrell McKenna*: p. 79; *Jeremy Horner*: p. 191; *Roderick Johnson*: p. 111; *Paul Smith*: p. 187; *Chris Stowers*: pp. 147, 177;

Stockpix (NT): p. 105, *Martin Soukias*: p. 22.